125 Gluten-Free Vegetarian Recipes

125 Gluten-Free Vegetarian Recipes

Quick and Delicious Mouthwatering Dishes for the Healthy Cook

CAROL FENSTER, PH.D.

AVERY

a member of Penguin Group (USA) Inc.,

New York

Published by the Penguin Group

Penguin Group (USA) Inc., 375 Hudson Street, New York, New York 10014, USA •
Penguin Group (Canada), 90 Eglinton Avenue East, Suite 700, Toronto, Ontario M4P 2Y3, Canada
(a division of Pearson Penguin Canada Inc.) • Penguin Books Ltd, 80 Strand, London WC2R 0RL, England •
Penguin Ireland, 25 St Stephen's Green, Dublin 2, Ireland (a division of Penguin Books Ltd) •
Penguin Group (Australia), 250 Camberwell Road, Camberwell, Victoria 3124, Australia (a division of
Pearson Australia Group Pty Ltd) • Penguin Books India Pvt Ltd, 11 Community Centre, Panchsheel Park,
New Delhi–110 017, India • Penguin Group (NZ), 67 Apollo Drive, Rosedale, North Shore 0632,
New Zealand (a division of Pearson New Zealand Ltd) • Penguin Books (South Africa) (Pty) Ltd,
24 Sturdee Avenue, Rosebank, Johannesburg 2196, South Africa

Penguin Books Ltd, Registered Offices: 80 Strand, London WC2R 0RL, England

Most Avery books are available at special quantity discounts for bulk purchase for sales promotions, premiums,
fund-raising, and educational needs. Special books or book excerpts also can be created to fit specific needs.
For details, write Penguin Group (USA) Inc. Special Markets, 375 Hudson Street, New York, NY 10014.

Library of Congress Cataloging-in-Publication Data

Fenster, Carol Lee.
125 gluten-free vegetarian recipes : quick and delicious mouthwatering dishes for the healthy cook / Carol Fenster.
p.   cm.
Includes bibliographical references and index.
ISBN 978-1-58333-425-6
1. Gluten-free diet—Recipes.   2. Vegetarian cooking.   3. Quick and easy cooking.   4. Cookbooks.
I. Title.   II. Title: One hundred twenty-five gluten-free vegetarian recipes.
RM237.86F4525   2011   2011006907
641.5'638—dc22

Printed in the United States of America
1   3   5   7   9   10   8   6   4   2

Book design by Jennifer Daddio/Bookmark Design & Media Inc.

To my wonderful family—

Larry, Brett, Helke, Keene, Romi, and Cole.

I love you.

Acknowledgments

I am especially grateful to my husband, Larry, who is always the first person to taste each recipe. If he says, "This needs more work, doesn't it?" then it's back to the kitchen. Thanks also to the family, friends, neighbors, professional colleagues, attendees at my cooking school classes and speaking engagements, and total strangers who visited my trade show booths and book signings: All of you provided extremely useful feedback on these dishes. I am also grateful to the early experts in plant-based diets whose work inspired me to write this gluten-free cookbook for those who want more plant-based options.

The people who volunteered their kitchens, time, and patience, and the venturesome palates of their friends and family members to give me constructive feedback on the recipes or help me in other ways include: Janet L. Armil; Desiree Castillo; Susan Cox-Gilbertson, Bob's Red Mill; Sally Ekus; Sherrie Glogosh; Lesley Jacobs, Regional Sales Manager, Bob's Red Mill; Melissa McLean Jory, MNT, Nutrition Therapy & Exercise Science, glutenfreeforgood.com; Cindy Koller-Kass, President, Greater Cleveland Celiac Association, CSAI USA; Andrea Levario and Pablo Douros; Susan M. Piergeorge, M.S., R.D.; Genevieve Potts; Tracy Roberts; Lori Sobelson, Program Director, Bob's Red Mill; Virginia Schmuck; Cecile Weed, founder of Orange County, California, CSA/USA; and Margie Winter. Thanks to all for your very helpful input.

Several companies provided products for me to use as I wrote this cookbook; thanks to my wonderfully supportive colleagues at Bob's Red Mill and Pamela's, as well as Cream Hill Estates, Gifts of Nature, Mary's Gone Crackers, and Udi's Gluten-Free Foods.

Special thanks to my marvelously inspirational agent, Lisa Ekus, who is so generous with her guidance and support. Lisa, I am so lucky to have you and your superb staff on my team.

And finally, to my great team at Avery—editor Miriam Rich; Megan Newman, who suggested this book; and cover designer Andrea Ho. I truly appreciate your support with the book and your belief in the importance of a plant-based diet for the gluten-free community.

Contents

Main Dishes

• PASTA •

Vegetables

Soups and Stews

Little Meals or Appetizers

Quick Breads and Yeast Breads

Breakfast

Desserts

Basics: Homemade Ingredients

125 Gluten-Free Vegetarian Recipes

Introduction

Many of us can remember when "gluten-free" and "vegetarian" were two terms seldom seen in print, much less used in the same sentence. Today, gluten-free and vegetarian diets are two of the fastest-growing food movements in the nation. We need more options for those who combine both diets into their lifestyles, and that's why I wrote this book. I believe we all deserve delicious, nutritious choices when we eat, and this book provides that mouth-watering variety for the gluten-free vegetarian.

Statistics on Vegetarianism and Gluten-Free Diets

Vegetarianism is on the rise. Three percent of Americans follow a plant-based diet. About a million of them are vegan, meaning they consume no animal products at all, according to a 2008 Harris poll commissioned by *Vegetarian Times* magazine. Another ten percent of adult Americans, nearly 23 million, say they "largely follow a vegetarian-inclined diet." This same poll indicates that of the meat eaters surveyed, five percent, or nearly 12 million people, are "definitely interested" in pursuing a vegetarian diet.

Kids are getting into the act, too. About one in two hundred American kids is vegetarian, according to a 2009 study by the Centers for Disease Control and Prevention. And sales of vegetarian food are expected to grow to $1.7 billion in 2012, up half a billion from 2005.

The media are also paying more attention to plant-based diets. We hear about the Great

American Meatout on the first day of spring, the White House vegetable garden, Michael Pollan's books, the Meatless Mondays movement, vegetarian restaurants springing up around the country, and the movie stars who write cookbooks about their plant-based lifestyles.

Gluten-free diets are no small potatoes either (pardon the vegetarian pun). Avoiding gluten was once rare and thought to be unnecessary, and little mainstream food (or compassion) was available. Today, experts estimate that eight percent, or about 24.5 million people, shop for gluten-free food. Sales of gluten-free food increased seventy-four percent from 2004 to 2009, and the market is expected to reach $2.6 billion in 2012. Since there are no cures for the conditions that require a gluten-free diet, experts expect this growth to continue.

Why Follow a Plant-Based Diet?

America is showing greater interest in plant-based diets for health considerations but also for environmental reasons. There are many benefits—certain of them more important to some people than to others—and they are likely to include the following:

1. Maintain a healthy body weight
2. Reduce the risk of cardiovascular disease
3. Increase energy and overall well-being
4. Improve digestion with the higher fiber of plants and grains
5. Lessen the risk of food-borne illnesses from undercooked or contaminated dairy, fish, or meat
6. Reduce environmental pollution of chemical and animal waste from farms
7. Spare animals from perceived inhumane treatment in factories and on farms

Why Follow a Gluten-Free Diet?

In case you're not familiar with the various medical conditions addressed by the gluten-free diet, here is a quick summary. You will find more information about these conditions in the Appendix under Resources.

People with wheat allergies must avoid all forms of wheat (including spelt) because they can suffer severe and sudden reactions, such as anaphylaxis, which requires immediate medical attention. Wheat allergies affect only a small percentage of people, but reactions are serious and can be fatal. Allergies are diagnosed by a food allergist.

Persons with celiac disease, an autoimmune condition, must avoid wheat and other gluten-containing grains such as spelt, barley, rye, kamut, and triticale because the protein in gluten damages the lining of their small intestines, inhibiting proper absorption of nutrients from food. This condition affects one percent, or about 3 million, Americans and is diagnosed by a gastroenterologist.

Another form of gluten intolerance is known as non-celiac gluten intolerance (or gluten sensitivity; the terms are often used interchangeably), which experts such as Dr. Alessio Fasano of the University of Maryland Center for Celiac Research believe may be six to seven times more prevalent than celiac disease. Gluten sickens these patients with symptoms ranging from migraines, nausea, rashes, and stomachaches to a host of other symptoms varying in intensity. I am in this category: gluten gives me brain fog, fatigue, and nasal congestion, often leading to sinus infections. An allergist typically diagnoses this condition.

Other conditions may be treated with a gluten-free diet, although it is important to note that the diet is only part of the overall treatment in these cases, not the cure in and of itself. One of the better known of these conditions is autism, which affects about one in 110 children. The gluten-free diet remains controversial for autism, and there is little research to support its effectiveness, yet many parents of autistic children praise the diet anecdotally.

Combining Gluten-Free and Vegetarian Diets

Unlike avoiding gluten, choosing vegetarianism is often just that—a choice. And unlike a gluten-free person, who can become violently ill by ingesting just a little gluten, a vegetarian doesn't usually have to follow the diet one hundred percent of the time to stay healthy. In fact, in a recent survey in *Food & Wine* magazine, only fifty-nine percent of respondents said that they avoid meat and fish at all times. Some forty percent of those who call themselves vegetarians fall into the group known as "flexitarians" or "almost-meatless" and occasionally eat meat or fish.

Yet another statistic from *Food & Wine*'s survey—and one that shapes the philosophy of this book—states that half of surveyed vegetarians say they prepare meat for someone else in the household. So these households are composed of some vegetarians and some meat-eaters.

Likewise, in my twenty-three years of gluten-free life, I have found that—in the majority of households with a gluten-free member—some gluten-containing food is consumed by other family members. This means that the cook in this household often prepares multiple versions of the same meal so that everyone is satisfied.

Dinners and dinner parties get even more complicated when some individuals are both gluten-free and vegetarian. For these households, it may require even more kitchen time to get appropriate meals on the table. This book addresses how to serve delicious food that meets everyone's needs. In line with the politically correct policy of complying with guests' requirements, this book provides many delicious options to serve to your gluten-free, vegetarian diners.

How is that possible? Every meal in this book is gluten-free and vegetarian (and most are also vegan, except for four recipes in the Breakfast chapter and one in the Main Dishes chapter). They are so delicious, satisfying, and nutritious that everyone can enjoy them, regardless of dietary preferences or requirements. But I also planned for those households where meat, poultry, or fish is still consumed. Many of the recipes are written so that cooks can prepare the dish up to a certain stage and then add animal protein in the right amount for that dish if desired. You will find a corresponding chart in "Adding Animal Protein to Recipes" in the Appendix.

• My Position •

It's only fair that you know my position on eating. I think it's a good thing. In fact, I barely finish one meal before contemplating the next. I love to cook, but I also enjoy dining out. In other words, I just enjoy good food.

I have lived the gluten-free lifestyle for more than two decades, but the transition from a gluten-based world was not a smooth one. I was raised on a wheat-growing farm, and I later married into a wheat-farming family. Suffice it to say, giving up gluten caused major ripples throughout the family network. Yet today, my family is supportive of my efforts to educate others about the gluten-free lifestyle.

And I eat meat—the Nebraska farm where I grew up boasted a freezer full of home-grown Angus beef, chicken, and pork for those infamous midwestern meat-and-potatoes meals. We ate local long before it became popular. But I am mindful of good nutrition, so now I eat a wide variety of fruits, vegetables, and whole grains because I like them and know they are important for my overall health (especially whole grains since I can't eat the wheat-based foods such as fortified bread, cereals, and pasta that provide everyone else with important nutrients).

Occasionally, I eat meatless meals. But more often I use meat as a side dish rather than the focal point of the meal. In fact, my rule of thumb is that vegetables and grains cover three-quarters of my plate, with meat taking up the remaining quarter. That puts increased importance on the plant-based portion of my plate, and that is why I took such joy in writing this book. I think you'll enjoy the recipes whether you are a gluten-free vegetarian or not.

Semantics

Given the wide variety of terms that apply to someone who follows a plant-based diet (see "Vegetarian Versus Vegan" below), I'm going to use the term "vegetarian" throughout this book, even though all but five of the recipes are appropriate for vegans as well.

Vegetarian Versus Vegan

It is easy to be confused by differing definitions of the word *vegetarian*. Here is a quick breakdown:

OVO-VEGETARIAN: eats eggs, but no fish, meat, or poultry

LACTO-VEGETARIAN: eats dairy products, but no eggs, fish, meat, or poultry

LACTO-OVO VEGETARIAN: eats dairy and egg products, but no fish, meat, or poultry (most vegetarians)

PESCO-VEGETARIAN: allows fish in diet, but no meat or poultry

POLLO-VEGETARIAN: avoids red meat, but eats poultry

VEGETARIAN: eats no dairy, fish, meat, or poultry and consumes no meat by-products, such as gelatin

FLEXITARIAN OR SEMI-VEGETARIAN: usually avoids meat, fish, or poultry, but occasionally makes exceptions

VEGAN: doesn't consume, use, or wear any animal products or by-products: no dairy, eggs, honey, meat, fish, or poultry

• About the Recipes •

I don't believe in criticizing other people's eating styles. Instead, setting a good example and having healthy, nutritious choices available are the best ways to influence others. You won't find any political messages in this book, except that I think eating is the most profound thing we do to our bodies every day. Americans would be healthier if they ate more wisely, and this means more fruits, vegetables, whole grains, beans, and legumes. There, I'm done with political statements.

Instead, I focus on the joy of eating well. Is there anything more enjoyable than a good meal, one that tantalizes our taste buds, shared with people we love (or at least like)? I want this book to meet the needs of the most people, so each vegetarian recipe is, of course, gluten-free—most are also dairy-free and egg-free. I think it is important to include a few classic egg-based dishes (for example, Quiche), though, for those vegetarians who rely on egg protein in their diets.

I wanted this book to be as useful as possible to the gluten-free vegetarian household, so it includes a wide variety of recipes in several categories: appetizers, breads, breakfast foods, desserts, entrées, casseroles, sides, soups, and stews. Here are the principles that guided me as I wrote this book:

- Feature beans, fruits, legumes, vegetables, and whole grains so inviting, wholesome, and appealing that you *can't* resist eating them.

- Include dishes hearty enough for center-of-the-plate status, or light enough for sides or snacks.
- Maintain recipe flexibility so both vegetarians and vegans can use the same recipe by choosing appropriate ingredients (e.g., hemp milk, not cow's milk; agave nectar, not honey). Many dishes can also be made soy-free by using soy-free Earth Balance buttery spread.
- Provide versatile meals that households with both vegetarians and non-vegetarians can easily use. See the Appendix for tips on how to incorporate animal protein into the dish, if desired.
- Include gluten-free versions of basic baked items, such as breads and desserts, made without dairy and eggs so everyone can enjoy them, regardless of allergies, intolerances, chronic conditions, or the like.
- Include hard-to-find (or better-when-homemade) vegan ingredients such as broth, bread crumbs, cheese, yogurt, and so on.
- Include suggestions for making a dish go from everyday to elegant with easy modifications.

· Flavor Boosters ·

When we remove familiar flavors from our diet—such as wheat, milk, and eggs—we can toss in other ingredients to compensate. Most of these flavor boosters contain the fifth taste, called umami (a Japanese word meaning "deliciousness"), and add depth and character to our food. In case you're wondering, the other tastes are sweet, salty, sour, and bitter. Anything that is aged, fermented, concentrated, or distilled tends to add loads of flavor.

Throughout the recipes, you will find several of these ingredients. Most are listed below, but look in the Appendix for the chart "Brand-Name Ingredients Used in This Book" to see what I used to round out the included recipes.

- Broths
- Capers
- Cheese, especially aged cheese such as Parmesan or blue cheese
- Chiles (powder or whole): ancho, chipotle, green, poblano

- Citrus zest: from grapefruit, lemon, lime, and orange—their oils lend loads of flavor
- Garlic
- Herbs
- Horseradish (grated or sauce)
- Ketchup
- Mayonnaise (vegan)
- Miso: but not made with wheat or barley
- Mushrooms (fresh or dried)
- Mustard (both Dijon and good ol' ballpark yellow)
- Nuts and nut oils
- Oil: corn (experts say cold-pressed corn oil resembles melted butter in color and flavor); grapeseed; olive; truffle; white truffle (tastes garlicky and really punches up flavor)
- Onions, especially caramelized or onion powder
- Picante sauce
- Pickle relish (dill or sweet)
- *Pico de gallo*
- Roasted red peppers (homemade or jarred)
- Salt, especially smoked
- Soy sauce (gluten-free)
- Smoked ingredients such as paprika and salt
- Tahini (sesame seed paste)
- Tomatillo sauce
- Tomatoes (especially fire-roasted, for fuller flavor)
- Tomato paste
- Wine and other gluten-free alcohols such as distilled liquor, liqueurs, and gluten-free beer
- Worcestershire sauce (gluten-free)
- Yogurt (coconut or soy-based versions if you're dairy-free; see also "Basics: Home-made Ingredients")

Taste and Season As You Go

Seasoning can make the difference between a delicious dish and one that seems inadequate and unfulfilling. Sometimes food has insufficient herbs and spices; other times it simply needs more salt and pepper. In many dishes, the seasoning must be added in stages, perhaps in the salted water in which pasta is cooked and then again in the sauce used on the pasta. If you wait to add salt and pepper to the finished dish, it can't penetrate the ingredients properly. So it is key to season when the recipe suggests it. Finally, taste your food just before serving and feel free to make any final adjustments.

How Nutrients Are Calculated

Nutrient content for each recipe is calculated with software by MasterCook Version 9.0.00.2 (2005). When more than one set of options for a dairy-related ingredient appears in a list (such as butter or buttery spread), the analysis is for the more traditional ingredient—in this case, butter. Salted butter is used in the calculations for comparability to buttery spreads, which contain salt and are the most likely replacement for butter. Other examples include cow's milk rather than non-dairy milk; Parmesan cheese instead of soy Parmesan; cow's milk cream cheese instead of non-dairy cream cheese, and so on. Or, when options are given for an ingredient, the analysis is conducted with the first ingredient in the list. For example, rice bran is analyzed when the ingredient list reads "rice bran or Montina Pure Baking Supplement."

Staples for the Gluten-Free Vegetarian Pantry

A well-stocked pantry means a well-prepared cook; and a well-prepared cook is more likely to serve safe, nutritious, tasty foods. In this chapter you'll get an idea of items to keep on hand so you're always ready to prepare the recipes in this book as well as your own favorites.

Gluten-Free Flours as the Foundation for Baked Goods

Gluten-free baking usually requires a blend of flours, rather than just one flour type, as in wheat baking. Many recipes in this book use Carol's Sorghum Flour Blend, an extremely versatile blend of gluten-free flours that can be used as the basis for many dishes. If you keep the following blend in your pantry, you'll always be prepared to bake whenever the need arises.

> ## CAROL'S SORGHUM FLOUR BLEND (MAKES 4 CUPS)
>
> 1½ cups sorghum flour   1 cup tapioca flour
> 1½ cups potato starch or cornstarch
>
> Whisk the ingredients together until well blended. Store, tightly covered, in a dark, dry place. You may refrigerate or freeze the blend, but bring it to room temperature before using. You can also double or triple the recipe.

Measure Carefully

Whenever the topic of baking comes up, it's time to talk about proper measuring.

All of the recipes in this book measure dry ingredients by whisking the flour a few times to aerate, or fluff, it and then lightly spooning it into a measuring cup before leveling it off with a knife. Don't use the measuring cup as a scoop and don't pack the flour down into the cup; you'll add up to twenty percent more flour that way, which can affect the composition of the batter. Avoid using glass, spouted measuring cups to measure dry ingredients like flour or sugar, because (1) they're for liquids and (2) it's hard to determine an accurate amount of flour in them—you may measure more flour than necessary, which will make your baked goods dry.

I use Bob's Red Mill flours, purchased in natural food stores or supermarkets. I don't use superfine flours, such as those from Asian markets, because they absorb liquids differently than the standard brands and can be inconsistent from store to store or brand to brand.

Read the Labels

Food labels are there for your protection, so read them carefully. The Food Allergen Labeling and Consumer Protection Act of 2004 (FALCPA) makes shopping easier, because at the bottom of the ingredient list the word "Contains" must appear on food that contains the top eight food allergens: egg, fish, shellfish, milk, peanuts, tree nuts, soy, and wheat. Read labels before purchasing new and familiar foods, because manufacturers can change procedures or ingredients at any time. Also, the law requires a warning about wheat (which includes spelt), but not the other gluten-containing grains like barley, kamut, rye, triticale, and non-gluten-free oats. But rest assured, they will be identified in the ingredient list, so you will know if the food contains a gluten ingredient. The Food and Drug Administration has not yet issued its definition of what "gluten-free" really means in terms of parts per million.

Whenever I use an ingredient that is available in both gluten-containing and gluten-free brands (such as Worcestershire sauce), I specify gluten-free, as in "gluten-free Worcestershire sauce." I use the Celiac Food SmartList from www.ClanThompson.com to determine which brands are gluten-free, or I call the manufacturer. So, for example, if a recipe calls for gluten-free Worcestershire sauce, take a look at the chart "Brand-Name Ingredients Used in This Book" in the Appendix to find the gluten-free brand I use. Or use your own resources to find a gluten-free brand in your area.

In addition, these recipes can be made with dairy substitutes, thereby eliminating casein and lactose, so the chart also lists dairy-free brands. But, as noted above, you must continue to read labels. During your search you may find other brands that suit your needs.

The Pantry

Here's a peek inside a well-stocked pantry, organized in categories of baking and cooking ingredients, dairy substitutes, egg substitutes, fats and oils, flours, and sweeteners. You may not need all of them for the recipes in this book, but a gluten-free vegetarian lifestyle may require them at some point, so stock up and be ready.

Flours and Whole Grains

Flours and whole grains are the backbone of the gluten-free diet. Here are the ones I keep in my pantry (or fridge, for longer shelf life), and I indicate whether they are available in grain, flour (or meal), or both. See the Appendix for the brands I used in writing this book.

- Amaranth: Ancient grain once grown by the Aztecs; highly nutritious (grain and flour).
- Arrowroot: Fine white powder ground from the arrowroot plant (flour).
- Brown Rice: The whole rice kernel, including germ, endosperm, and bran (whole kernel and flour).
- Buckwheat: Usually roasted, which lends a stronger flavor. I grind unroasted Bob's Red Mill Creamy Buckwheat Cereal with a small coffee/spice grinder to make my own mild buckwheat flour, which can be used in mild-flavored baked goods (whole groats and flour).
- Chestnut: Ground from chestnuts (whole and flour).
- Chickpea (Garbanzo): Ground from whole chickpeas, also known as garbanzo beans (whole bean or flour).
- Corn Flour: The whole corn kernel ground into protein-rich, yellow flour (whole kernel or flour).
- Cornmeal: Ground corn, ranging from very fine to quite coarse in texture (flour or meal).
- Cornstarch: Fine powder from the starch of corn (flour).
- Flax: Ground from whole flaxseed, preferably golden for its lighter color (whole seed or meal).
- Garbanzo-Fava Flour: A combination of garbanzo (chickpea) flour and fava bean flour (whole bean and flour).
- Millet: Ground from whole grain millet; light yellow in color (grain and flour).
- Nut Meals: Grind your own in a food processor from whole almonds, hazelnuts, pecans, or walnuts, or use almond or hazelnut meal.
- Oats (gluten-free): Rolled, quick-cooking, steel-cut, or bran (grain and flour).
- Potato Starch: Fine white starch from potato; potato flour, which is ground from the whole potato, skin and all (flour).
- Quinoa: Ancient grain of Peru, called "mother" grain because of its high nutrient density (grain and flour).
- Rice Bran: Polished off from whole rice kernel.
- Sorghum: Ground from whole sorghum, an ancient grain originating in India and Africa (grain and flour).
- Soy: Ground from whole soy beans (whole beans and flour).
- Tapioca: Fine white powder ground from manioc or cassava plant. Not the same as Expandex, a modified tapioca starch (www.expandexglutenfree.com) that has been

altered to produce higher rise, better texture, and longer shelf life for baked goods (whole pearls or flour).

- Teff: Ground from whole teff, which means "tiny" in Ethiopia, where it originated (grain and flour).
- White Rice: For dusting dough or dredging before frying (grain and flour).

Sweeteners

Most baked goods require a certain amount of sweetening for flavor, texture, and appearance. Here are some choices for my pantry:

- Agave Nectar or Syrup: Natural sweetener from cactus plant grown in Mexico. Pours like corn syrup; a good alternative to honey but with a comparatively lower glycemic level.
- Brown Rice Syrup: Made from brown rice. (Choose gluten-free brands.)
- Brown Sugar: Granulated sugar with some molasses added; available as light and dark varieties.
- Corn Syrup: A highly processed sweetener best used in small quantities; has nice traits for certain foods.
- Evaporated Cane Juice: Made from dried cane crystals. Not as processed as white sugar; used throughout this book, but granulated sugar may be used instead.
- Maple Syrup: From maple tree sap; choose pure maple syrup with no fillers.
- Molasses: An unrefined thick liquid (not blackstrap) with a distinctive flavor.
- Powdered Sugar: Highly processed, but useful in some desserts where fine texture is required.

Fats and Oils

They get a bad rap these days, but good fats are essential for our bodies and for successful baking. Here are the ones in my pantry:

- Buttery Spread: Try buttery-flavored Earth Balance, my favorite; it comes in soy and soy-free versions.

- Canola Oil: A light, mild-flavored oil from the canola plant (originally called rape-seed); good for frying, sautéing, baking, and salad dressings. Note: If using canola, which contains no salt, to replace salted butter or buttery spread, which does, make sure to increase the salt in the recipe a little bit to compensate.
- Coconut Oil: Good in baking; use refined for less coconut flavor.
- Grapeseed Oil: From grapeseeds; it has a clean, light taste and color.
- Olive Oil: Use extra-virgin for salad dressings and drizzling; virgin works well for baking.
- Nut Oils: Though a bit more expensive, almond, hazelnut, and walnut oils are good to have on hand.
- Shortening: Choose non-hydrogenated versions made from soy or palm oil. For most baking, I prefer greasing pans with shortening rather than cooking spray because the spray often creates pools of moisture that can contribute to sogginess. I also prefer shortening to cooking spray for greasing pizza pans because shortening holds the dough in place as I press it onto the pan.

Baking and Cooking Ingredients

See also "Dairy Substitutions" and "Egg Substitutions" below.

- Baking Powder: An acidic leavening agent. Choose double-acting, which means it reacts twice: first to the liquid, then again from the oven heat.
- Baking Soda: An alkaline leavening agent; used alone or with baking powder.
- Bread Crumbs: Store-bought gluten-free varieties are available, but the best ones are homemade (see page 243).
- Broth (mushroom or vegetable): My favorite store-bought vegetable broth is Imagine No-Chicken Broth, because of its light color and great taste. Try making a savory Mushroom Broth of your own from the recipe on page 244.
- Cellophane Noodles: Good in Asian dishes.
- Chocolate Chips: Read labels carefully to verify that they're gluten-free.
- Cocoa: Natural cocoa has been untreated and is acidic; Dutch, European, and alkalized cocoa have been processed with alkali, which makes them more alkaline. Be sure to use the type of cocoa specified in a recipe to ensure that it reacts correctly with the leavening agent, usually baking powder or baking soda.

- Coconut flakes: Most recipes in this book use the large, natural, unsweetened flakes.
- Cream of Tartar: An acidic leavening agent from sediment produced in winemaking.
- Gelatin: In place of animal-based gelatin, use plant-derived agar. Follow package directions. I prefer the powder over the granular version because it dissolves more quickly and thoroughly in liquid.
- Guar Gum: From the guar plant; performs same binding function as xanthan gum. It may be used interchangeably or together with xanthan since their natural synergy produces better baked goods.
- Pasta: Use the brand your family will eat, but my favorite for sturdiness and appearance is Tinkyada gluten-free pasta.
- Sea Salt: Lighter and gentler than kosher salt without the additives found in table salt.
- Tofu: Use extra-firm for entrées where you want it to hold its shape while cooking and soft or silken for sauces, dips, and in baking, where it will be pureed with other ingredients.
- Vanilla: Despite years of misinformation, vanilla is gluten-free since it is distilled; gluten can't survive the distillation process even if it was present, which is unlikely in U.S.-made brands.
- Vinegar: Apple cider, balsamic, champagne, mirin, red and white wine, sherry, *umeboshi* (plum)—but not malt vinegar. Vinegar is a principal component in salad dressings; the acidity of apple cider vinegar transforms milk into buttermilk, and vinegar is a great finisher for soups and sauces.
- Xanthan Gum: Critical for baking, it performs the function of gluten by keeping baked goods from crumbling. Don't forget it or you'll be sorry. Or use one and a half times more guar gum instead.
- Yeast: It comes as active dry yeast and instant (or quick-rising) yeast. Use the type specified in the recipe.

Dairy Substitutions

The recipes in this book allow you to use dairy products if you wish, or replace them with a non-dairy choice such as the following:

- Cheese: Most vegan cheeses are available in cheddar and mozzarella flavors, in natural food stores. Daiya cheese melts and tastes closest to real cheese.

- Cream Cheese: Soy-based brands are good substitutes for the dairy-based version, although they have more fillers than cream cheese made from cow's milk.
- Creamer: Used for coffee; the plain flavor can also be used in soups and sauces instead of half-and-half or heavy cream. However, it doesn't whip into whipped cream like real cream does.
- Dry (Nonfat) Milk Powder: Fine powder usually found in natural food stores. It is not Carnation, which is coarse granules, and doesn't contain as much sugar and protein, which makes a big difference in baking. Or use the same amount of Better Than Milk soy-based milk powder; the rice-based version has a slight vanilla flavor, making it less suited for savory baking.
- Kefir: Similar to thin yogurt, So Delicious brand's fermented coconut milk–based drink comes in original, vanilla, and strawberry flavors. Use the original flavor in soups instead of heavy cream.
- Milk (Almond, Coconut, Cow, Hemp, Rice, and Soy): Each imparts its own color and flavor. Don't confuse canned Asian coconut milk with the So Delicious brand by Turtle Mountain, which is sold in milk cartons in the dairy section. Fat-free milks are thinner and may dilute the batter or dough slightly. Don't use unsweetened non-dairy milks for baking without adding more sugar to the recipe as compensation. This is because cow's milk has up to 12 grams of sugar in each cup (equivalent to about 3 teaspoons), which in turn does nice things for our baking. So make sure your milk substitutes contain sugar as well or the recipe will lack flavor, and baked goods will not brown as well.
- Parmesan Cheese: Soy-based grated Parmesan cheese is available in natural food stores. Note: Galaxy Nutritional Foods' rice-based version contains casein, a cow's milk protein.
- Sour Cream: Available in soy-based brands, they perform quite well in baking and cooking.
- Yogurt (Coconut, Cow, and Soy): Use plain yogurt for cooking and baking. I prefer plain Wildwood soy yogurt because it is unsweetened and better for savory dishes. Flavored varieties work well in smoothies. Make your own yogurt from nuts with the recipe on page 249 in " Basics: Homemade Ingredients."

- *Egg Substitutions*

If you are vegan or don't tolerate eggs because of allergies or other health conditions, you can use the following substitutes. Some of the baked goods in this book use these items and others are formulated without them. I list these substitutions here so you can adapt your own recipes to be egg-free if you wish. Egg-free baked goods are best eaten on the same day.

- Flaxseed Meal: Mix 1 to 3 teaspoons ground flax meal with 1 cup of boiling water until smooth and let stand 10 minutes to soften and become gelatinous. Use ¼ cup per large egg called for in baking. It works best when replacing one egg but not as well when replacing three or more eggs because it adds lots of fat. Refrigerate leftovers for a week, tightly covered. It can be used in cakes, cookies, breads, and muffins that mask or complement flax's nutty flavor and slightly darker color. I prefer golden flax-seed because of its lighter hue, but it tastes the same and has the same nutrients as brown flax. Refrigerate flaxseeds or flax meal to maintain freshness.
- Egg Replacer Powder: Fine white powder by Ener-G Foods or Bob's Red Mill. Follow package directions, but I use twice as much powder as water, then use ¼ cup of this mixture for each large egg. Use for baking that doesn't rise very much such as bars, cookies, and snack cakes.
- Soft-Silken Tofu: Puree ¼ cup soft-silken tofu in a blender, mash it with a fork, or beat it with an electric mixer along with the other liquid ingredients in the recipe.
- Modified Tapioca Starch: Although it isn't a true egg replacer, Expandex, a brand of modified tapioca starch, compensates for eggs' absence by increasing the rise, improving the texture, and extending the shelf life of baked goods—all without altering the flavor or color. I use it frequently in my personal baking. For more information, see "How to Use Modified Tapioca Starch in These Recipes" in the Appendix.

- *Nuts and Seeds*

Nuts and seeds play a very important role in the gluten-free vegetarian diet because they are an important source of fiber, protein, and other important nutrients (depending on the variety) and are filling as well. They are great as snacks, in baking, sprinkled on salads and cooked vegetables, and as garnishes. In my refrigerator or freezer, you'll always find almonds, cashews, hazelnuts, pecans, pine nuts (pignoli), pumpkin seeds, sesame seeds, sunflower seeds, and walnuts.

- *Beans and Lentils*

The types of beans and lentils known in the United States as legumes, and in other parts of the world as pulses, are a vital component of the gluten-free diet because they supply important fiber and protein. Keep a stash of these legumes in your pantry: canned beans such as black, cannellini (white kidney), kidney, and pinto. Canned lentils are also handy. Dry beans—such as red beans, black beans, and split peas—and lentils are much more economical than canned ones, and they belong in your pantry.

Main Dishes

As this chapter shows, a gluten-free vegetarian diet is full of abundance and variety. These dishes don't have to be "main" in the strict sense of the word, so feel free to mix and match them with other dishes (and in serving portions of your choice) in this book to round out your meals. You will find all of your favorites here—especially dishes that typically contain gluten—modified to be gluten-free. For other main dishes, see my other cookbooks: *Wheat-Free Recipes & Menus*, *Cooking Free*, and *Gluten-Free Quick & Easy*.

· PASTA ·

Lasagna

Spaghetti with Spaghetti Sauce

Parsley-Buttered Pasta

Soba Noodles with Peanut-Ginger Sauce

Stuffed Pasta Shells

Thai Noodle Bowl

Tofu au Vin

Tofu Stroganoff

BREAD

Panzanella (Bread Salad)
Stuffing with Pears and Pecans
Savory Leek-Onion Bread Pudding
Veggie Pizza

POLENTA

Peperonata on Soft Polenta
Polenta Triangles with Warm Cannellini and Capers Salad
Sherried Mushrooms on Crispy Polenta Rounds

STUFFED (WITH RICE)

Stuffed Bell Peppers with Picadillo Rice
Stuffed Cabbage Rolls
Stuffed Poblano Peppers
Stuffed Swiss Chard Bundles with Pomegranate Glaze

RICE ON THE BOTTOM

Creole Vegetables on Basmati Rice
Red Beans and Brown Rice
Vegetable Tikka Masala
Sweet-and-Sour Tofu Casserole
Wild Mushroom Risotto
Vegetable Paella

CASSEROLES

Chili Corn Bread Casserole

Enchiladas

Tortilla Torte

Eggplant Roll-Ups

Eggplant Parmesan Stacks

Moussaka

Old-Fashioned Vegetable Pot Pie with Savory Pastry Crust

Onion-Leek Tart

Summer's Bounty Vegetable Casserole

BEANS AND LENTILS

Southwestern Bean and Grain Casserole

Black-Eyed Peas in Barbecue Sauce

Smothered Bean Burritos with Green Chile Sauce

Soft Corn Tacos with Black Bean Burgers

Pinto Bean–Polenta Fajitas with Tomatillo Sauce

Falafel with Dill Yogurt Sauce

GRAINS

Amaranth Porridge (see the Breakfast chapter)

Quinoa Pilaf with Pine Nuts and Dried Fruit

Warm Millet Salad

Moroccan Millet-Stuffed Acorn Squash

Sorghum Salad

Wild Rice Salad

Whole Grains for Breakfast—or Any Time of Day—(see the Breakfast chapter)

Lasagna

Even though it is Italian, lasagna seems like an all-American dish . . . almost a birthright for most of us. Thank goodness for gluten-free lasagna noodles! I boost the nutrient content of this dish with pureed beans in the filling. You can assemble this lasagna the night before and bake it the next day if you'd like. And if time is short, feel free to use your favorite store-bought gluten-free marinara sauce instead. **SERVES 9**

MARINARA SAUCE (MAKES 3 CUPS)

2 teaspoons olive oil

1 small onion, diced

3 medium garlic cloves, minced

3 cups chopped fresh tomatoes (about 5 medium), or 1 large can (28 ounces) crushed or diced

1 tablespoon dried basil

1½ teaspoons dried rosemary, crushed in your palm

1 teaspoon dried oregano

1 teaspoon evaporated cane juice

½ teaspoon sea salt

¼ teaspoon cayenne pepper

FILLING

2 medium garlic cloves, minced

1 can (15 ounces) white kidney beans or navy beans, rinsed and drained

2 cups shredded low-fat mozzarella cheese or cheese alternative, divided

15 ounces low-fat ricotta cheese or 12 ounces (1 package) soft silken tofu

8 tablespoons grated Parmesan cheese or soy Parmesan, divided, plus more for garnish

1½ teaspoons Italian seasoning

½ teaspoon sea salt

¼ teaspoon freshly ground black pepper

9 GF uncooked lasagna noodles

1 tablespoon chopped fresh parsley, or 1 teaspoon dried

1. Place rack in the middle of the oven. Preheat the oven to 350°F. Coat a 7 x 11-inch glass baking dish with cooking spray.

2. Make the Sauce: In a small saucepan, heat the oil over medium heat. Add the onion and cook, covered, 3 minutes. Add the garlic and cook, stirring constantly, 1 minute. Add the tomatoes, basil, rosemary, oregano, evaporated cane juice, salt, and cayenne pepper and simmer, covered, 10 minutes. Remove from the heat. The sauce will be thin; that works well to soak into the uncooked lasagna noodles.

3. Make the Filling: In a food processor, combine the garlic and beans and process until the beans are smooth. Add 1 cup of the mozzarella, the ricotta cheese, 5 tablespoons of the Parmesan, the Italian seasoning, salt, and pepper and pulse until blended. You will have about 2 cups of filling.

4. Spread 1 cup of the marinara sauce on the bottom of the baking dish. Place 3 lasagna noodles on top. Spread 1 cup of the filling over the noodles, top with 1 cup of sauce, then add another layer of 3 lasagna noodles, and spread the remaining filling evenly on top with a spatula. Place 3 lasagna noodles on top, then cover the noodles completely with the remaining 1 cup of sauce. Sprinkle the top with the remaining cup of mozzarella cheese and then with the remaining 3 tablespoons of Parmesan cheese. Cover the dish tightly with foil, then place the dish on a 9 x 13-inch rimmed baking sheet to catch any spills.

5. Bake 45 minutes. Remove the foil and bake until the cheese is browned, about another 15 minutes. If using a cheese alternative, broil until the cheese melts and becomes shiny (leave the dish on the middle rack during broiling). Remove from the oven and serve immediately, garnished with the parsley and additional Parmesan, if desired.

Calories 690 · Fat 14g · Protein 37g · Carbohydrates 104g · Cholesterol 41mg · Sodium 603mg · Fiber 12g

Spaghetti with Spaghetti Sauce

This is one of the first whole foods my grandchildren ate as toddlers, and it has remained one of their favorite dishes as they grow. We adults are quite fond of it as well. You can certainly use store-bought spaghetti sauce, but making your own gives you the sensory pleasure of smelling this savory classic as it simmers on the stove. **SERVES 6**

16 ounces GF spaghetti

6 tablespoons Parmesan cheese or soy
    Parmesan, or more to taste

SPAGHETTI SAUCE (MAKES 3 CUPS)

1 teaspoon olive oil

3 medium garlic cloves, minced

1½ teaspoons dried oregano

½ teaspoon dried basil

½ teaspoon sea salt

3 cups chopped fresh tomatoes, or
    2 cans (15 ounces each) diced

¼ teaspoon crushed red pepper flakes

1. Make the Spaghetti Sauce: Heat the oil in a medium saucepan over medium heat. Add the garlic and cook, stirring constantly, for 1 minute. Add the oregano, basil, salt, tomatoes, and red pepper flakes and bring to a boil. Reduce heat to low and simmer, stirring occasionally, for 10 minutes. For a thicker sauce, simmer another 2 to 3 minutes, stirring constantly.

2. Cook the spaghetti according to package directions. Drain thoroughly. To serve, divide the spaghetti onto 6 plates and drizzle each with ½ cup sauce. Top each plate with a tablespoon of Parmesan and serve immediately.

Calories 345 · Fat 4g · Protein 13g · Carbohydrates 64g · Cholesterol 4mg · Sodium 268mg · Fiber 4g

Parsley-Buttered Pasta

Simple yet flavorful, this dish is lovely with the vibrant green of the parsley. Serve it alone or with other dishes to round out a meal. **SERVES 4**

8 ounces GF penne, or fusilli or other spiral pasta

2 tablespoons butter or buttery spread

1/4 cup chopped Italian flat-leaf parsley

Salt to taste

1. Cook the pasta according to package directions, stirring occasionally to prevent sticking, until done, about 10 minutes. Drain and return to the pot.
2. Stir in the butter and toss to coat, then add the parsley and toss to mix in thoroughly. Serve immediately.

Calories 265 · Fat 7g · Protein 7g · Carbohydrates 43g · Cholesterol 16mg · Sodium 7mg · Fiber 1g

Soba Noodles with Peanut-Ginger Sauce

Soba noodles are made from Japanese buckwheat, a fruit-derived grain that is actually gluten-free, but they can also be manufactured with wheat, so look for 100 percent buckwheat noodles by Eden in natural food stores. These noodles tend to stick together after cooking, so rinse them with hot water just before tossing with the sauce. **SERVES 4**

PEANUT-GINGER SAUCE

½ cup natural creamy peanut butter

5 tablespoons seasoned rice vinegar

1 tablespoon agave nectar or honey

1 tablespoon minced fresh ginger, or
   1½ teaspoons ground ginger

1 tablespoon gluten-free tamari soy sauce

1 teaspoon ground coriander

1 large garlic clove, minced

½ teaspoon crushed red pepper flakes

2 tablespoons hot water

SOBA NOODLES

6 ounces 100 percent buckwheat soba noodles

1 red bell pepper, seeded, cut in ⅛-inch
   vertical slices

1 large carrot, peeled, cut in ⅛-inch
   diagonal slices

1 English cucumber, unpeeled and
   chopped

½ cup chopped fresh cilantro, divided

¼ cup chopped peanuts, for garnish

1. In a blender, combine the peanut butter, rice vinegar, agave nectar, ginger, soy sauce, coriander, garlic, red pepper flakes, and hot water. Process the sauce until very smooth. Set aside.

2. Cook the noodles according to package directions, stirring occasionally to prevent sticking, until done, about 8 to 10 minutes. Drain the noodles, rinse with hot water, and place in a large serving bowl.

3. Toss the noodles with the sauce until well coated. Add the red bell pepper, carrot, cucumber, and half of the cilantro; toss again. Serve immediately, garnished with the peanuts and the remaining cilantro.

Calories 455 · Fat 21g · Protein 19g · Carbohydrates 52g · Cholesterol 0mg · Sodium 720mg · Fiber 6g

ASIAN DINNER

Miso Soup with Wakame (page 136)

Soba Noodles with Peanut-Ginger Sauce (page 28)

Bok Choy (page 110)

Vanilla Bean Pudding (page 230)

Stuffed Pasta Shells

A perfect dish for a cold winter's night, this will make your kitchen smell like an Italian trattoria. Serve it with a mixed green salad and a crunchy homemade French Baguette (page 181). **SERVES 8 (3 SHELLS EACH)**

8 ounces GF jumbo pasta shells, about 24 shells

16 ounces nonfat cream cheese or vegan cream cheese, about 2½ cups

½ cup nonfat sour cream or vegan sour cream

1 cup grated Parmesan cheese or soy Parmesan, divided

2 medium garlic cloves, minced

2 tablespoons chopped fresh parsley or 1 tablespoon dried, plus more for garnish

1 teaspoon dried oregano, or 1 tablespoon chopped fresh

3 cups homemade Spaghetti Sauce (page 26) or store-bought spaghetti sauce

1. Place a rack in the middle of the oven. Preheat the oven to 375°F. Grease a 9 x 13-inch glass baking dish.
2. Cook the pasta shells according to package directions, stirring occasionally to prevent sticking, until done, about 20 minutes. Drain thoroughly. Cool the shells in a single layer on a sheet of waxed paper and blot them dry with paper towels. Handle gently; they are easily torn.
3. While the pasta simmers, make the filling: In a medium bowl, beat the cream cheese, sour cream, ¾ cup of the Parmesan cheese and the garlic, parsley, and oregano with an electric mixer on low speed until well blended.
4. Spread a thin layer of sauce on the bottom of the dish. Gently fill each shell with 2 tablespoons filling and place in the dish, cheese side up. Cover with remaining spaghetti sauce and sprinkle with remaining Parmesan cheese. Cover with foil.
5. Bake 20 minutes. Uncover and bake 10 minutes more or until hot and bubbly. Serve immediately, garnished with chopped parsley.

Calories 285 · Fat 36g · Protein 20g · Carbohydrates 35g · Cholesterol 15mg · Sodium 972mg · Fiber 2g

Thai Noodle Bowl

Though we were both raised in the Midwest and never tasted Thai food until we were married, my husband and I now adore this ethnic food. Our favorite is the "noodle bowl," which translates into many variations, depending on the Thai restaurant you choose. But it is so simple to make at home, so give this version a try. If you can't find super-fresh bean sprouts, skip them and use more cucumber instead. **SERVES 6**

DRESSING

¼ cup unseasoned rice wine vinegar

2 tablespoons low-sodium gluten-free tamari soy sauce

2 tablespoons packed light brown sugar

1 teaspoon sesame oil

1 to 2 garlic cloves, minced

1 teaspoon grated fresh ginger

¼ to ½ teaspoon crushed red pepper flakes

¼ teaspoon freshly ground black pepper

NOODLES

12 ounces GF fettucine or Pad Thai noodles, cooked and drained

1 cup snow peas, halved diagonally

2 cups very fresh mung bean sprouts

1 large carrot, peeled and cut in ¼-inch diagonal slices

1 cup unpeeled English cucumber, diced

½ cup sliced red bell pepper, cut in ⅛-inch strips

½ cup chopped fresh cilantro

¼ cup peanuts, chopped, for garnish

1. Place all of the dressing ingredients in a blender and process until very smooth. Set aside.
2. Cook the noodles according to package directions, stirring occasionally to prevent sticking, until done, and dropping the snow peas into the boiling water during the last minute of cooking to blanch them. Drain the noodles and snow peas in a sieve, then place them in a large bowl. Add the bean sprouts, carrot, cucumber, bell pepper, and ¼ cup of the cilantro. Drizzle with enough of the dressing to coat thoroughly and toss well. Serve, garnished with the remaining ¼ cup cilantro and the peanuts.

Calories 305 · Fat 6g · Protein 12g · Carbohydrates 51g · Cholesterol 55mg · Sodium 358mg · Fiber 4g

Tofu au Vin

This is a vegetarian rendition of the classic French dish called Coq au Vin, traditionally made with stewed chicken (the coq) and red wine. The cumin adds depth and a slight smoky flavor to the tofu, so be sure to use it. Serve it with a mixed green salad and homemade French Baguettes (page 181). **SERVES 4**

1 package (15 ounces) extra-firm tofu, drained, pressed, and cut in ½-inch cubes

½ teaspoon ground cumin

4 teaspoons canola oil, divided

1 package (10 ounces) frozen pearl onions, thawed, or 2½ cups fresh

1 pound baby carrots

3 medium garlic cloves, minced

½ pound button mushrooms, cut in ¼-inch slices

2 cups dry red wine, such as Merlot or Beaujolais

1 tablespoon Dijon mustard

1 teaspoon dried thyme, or 1 tablespoon chopped fresh

1 teaspoon dried rosemary, or 1 tablespoon chopped fresh

1 tablespoon agave nectar or honey

½ teaspoon celery salt

½ teaspoon freshly ground black pepper

1 teaspoon paprika

1 large bay leaf

2 teaspoons cornstarch, whisked into 2 tablespoons water until smooth

4 cups hot cooked GF penne pasta

½ cup chopped fresh parsley, for garnish

1. Place the tofu on a plate and dust it with the cumin. Set aside.
2. In a Dutch oven, heat 3 teaspoons of the oil over medium heat and cook the pearl onions, carrots, garlic, and mushrooms, stirring occasionally, until the onions have golden brown marks on them, about 5 to 7 minutes.
3. While the vegetables cook, heat the remaining teaspoon of oil in a large nonstick skillet over medium heat. Add the tofu and cook until lightly browned on all sides, about 5 to 7 minutes. Set aside.
4. Add the wine to the Dutch oven, bring to a boil, and simmer 3 minutes to reduce the wine a bit. Add the mustard, thyme, rosemary, agave nectar, celery salt, black pepper,

paprika, and bay leaf. Bring to a boil, reduce the heat to low, and simmer, covered, for 10 minutes. Whisk in the cornstarch mixture and cook, stirring constantly, until slightly thickened. Stir in the tofu and heat to serving temperature. Serve immediately over the hot cooked pasta, garnished with the parsley.

Calories 535 · Fat 13g · Protein 21g · Carbohydrates 68g · Cholesterol 0mg · Sodium 387mg · Fiber 7g

Tofu Stroganoff

My first taste of stroganoff was at the home of my supervisor when I was a student teacher in college. I fell in love with it immediately and truly enjoy this vegetarian version as well. Serve it with a mixed green salad and homemade French Baguettes (page 181). The techniques used in Steps 2 and 3 lend depth to the dish by caramelizing the ingredients and intensifying their flavors, so don't skip them. **SERVES 4**

1 package (15 ounces) extra-firm tofu, drained, pressed, and cut in 1/2-inch cubes

1/2 teaspoon ground cumin

2 tablespoons canola oil, divided

1 medium onion, coarsely chopped

2 cups button mushrooms, cut in 1/4-inch slices

1 small garlic clove, minced

2 tablespoons tomato paste

2 teaspoons Dijon mustard

2 tablespoons gluten-free tamari soy sauce

1 tablespoon chopped fresh dill, or 2 teaspoons dried

1/2 teaspoon sea salt

1/4 teaspoon freshly ground black pepper

1 can (10.5 ounces) gluten-free vegetable broth, or homemade Mushroom Broth (page 244) or homemade Vegetable Broth (page 245)

2 tablespoons sweet rice flour

1 tablespoon dry sherry, white wine, or vermouth

1 cup nonfat sour cream or sour cream alternative

4 cups cooked GF penne pasta

2 tablespoons chopped fresh parsley

1. Place the tofu on a plate and dust it with the cumin. In a large heavy nonstick skillet, heat 1 tablespoon of the canola oil and cook the tofu until lightly browned, stirring occasionally, about 5 minutes. Transfer the tofu to a plate.

2. Add the remaining tablespoon of oil, and cook the onions and mushrooms over medium heat until the onion is lightly browned and the mushroom juices evaporate, about 5 minutes. Add the garlic and cook, stirring constantly, for 1 minute.

3. Add the tomato paste, mustard, soy sauce, dill, salt, and pepper and cook, stirring constantly, 2 minutes. Stir in all but 1/4 cup of the broth, bring to a boil, reduce the heat to low, and simmer, covered, 30 minutes.

4. Just before serving, whisk the sweet rice flour into the remaining broth until smooth, then mix into the stroganoff. Increase the heat to medium and cook, whisking constantly, until it thickens slightly, about 1 minute. Whisk the sherry into the sour cream and add to the stroganoff, continuing to whisk until thoroughly blended, but do not boil or the mixture will curdle. Serve immediately over the hot cooked pasta, garnished with the parsley.

Calories 615 · Fat 13g · Protein 27g · Carbohydrates 99g · Cholesterol 6mg · Sodium 896mg · Fiber 5g

Panzanella (Bread Salad)

It was a breakthrough day when I learned how to make this dish, which I had long coveted since traveling in Italy. It was originally created by the Italians as a way to use leftover or stale bread and is often served in the summer months with fresh vegetables such as tomatoes, but I see it as a way to get lovely crunch and color into my food (and enjoy gluten-free bread). I have given this dish some Greek notes by using oregano, but you can use basil instead if you wish. If you can find cocktail-size marinated artichoke hearts, they're the perfect size for this recipe. **SERVES 6 MAIN COURSES OF 1 CUP EACH, OR 10 APPETIZER COURSES OF ABOUT 1/2 CUP EACH**

1 cup red grape tomatoes, halved

1 small red onion, cut in 1/2-inch pieces

2 tablespoons capers, rinsed and drained

1 small unpeeled English cucumber, quartered, then cut in 1/2-inch pieces

1/2 cup Kalamata olives, halved, or other Greek olives, rinsed and drained

1 jar (6 ounces) marinated artichoke hearts, drained and coarsely chopped

1/2 cup chopped fresh parsley, plus more for garnish

1 tablespoon chopped fresh oregano, tightly packed, or 1 teaspoon dried (or more to taste)

DRESSING

3 tablespoons fresh lemon juice

2 teaspoons Dijon mustard

1/2 teaspoon sea salt

1/2 teaspoon freshly ground black pepper

2 medium garlic cloves, minced

1/2 teaspoon agave nectar or honey

3 tablespoons extra-virgin olive oil

6 slices GF white bread, Hearty Flax Bread (page 184), or your favorite GF bread

1. Place the tomatoes, onion, capers, cucumber, olives, artichoke hearts, parsley, and oregano in a medium serving bowl.

2. Make the Dressing: In a glass jar or measuring cup, whisk together the lemon juice, mustard, salt, pepper, garlic, and agave nectar until well blended. Gradually whisk in the olive oil until the dressing thickens. Or whirl the dressing ingredients in a blender until thickened. Pour over the vegetables and toss to coat thoroughly.

3. Just before serving, toast the bread in a toaster until lightly browned. Cut away any burned parts or tough crusts and cut into ¾-inch pieces. Add to the vegetables and toss gently with a spatula. Serve immediately, garnished with parsley.

Calories 215 · Fat 14g · Protein 3g · Carbohydrates 21g · Cholesterol 0mg · Sodium 674mg · Fiber 2g

SUMMER BUFFET PARTY ON THE PATIO

Gazpacho Shooters (page 150)

Apple-Fennel Slaw (page 105)

Panzanella (Bread Salad) (page 36)

Sorghum Salad (page 99)

Black-Eyed Peas in Barbecue Sauce (page 85)

Breadsticks (page 177)

Ice Cream Pie with Granola and Fresh Fruit Sauce (page 234)

Stuffing with Pears and Pecans

This hearty stuffing, studded with pears and pecans, is a meal all by itself. Or use it to stuff roasted vegetables such as butternut squash. A red (instead of yellow) pear lends a bit of interesting color. **SERVES 10**

8 cups 1-inch GF bread cubes, (made from about 12 to 16 slices GF bread, depending on slice size)

4 tablespoons butter or buttery spread, divided

1/2 cup chopped pecans

1 small onion, finely chopped

2 celery ribs, finely chopped

1 large unpeeled pear, cored, chopped, about 1 cup

1 small garlic clove, minced (optional)

1/4 cup dry white wine

1/4 cup chopped fresh parsley, or 2 tablespoons dried, plus more for garnish

2 tablespoons chopped fresh thyme, or 1 tablespoon dried

1 tablespoon chopped fresh sage, or 1 1/2 teaspoons rubbed sage

3/4 teaspoon celery salt

1/4 teaspoon freshly grated nutmeg (optional)

1/4 teaspoon freshly ground black pepper

1 1/2 cups GF vegetable broth, homemade Vegetable Broth (page 245), or homemade Mushroom Broth (page 244), or more if needed

1. Place a rack in the middle of the oven. Preheat the oven to 375°F. Generously grease a 2-quart glass baking dish.

2. Place the bread cubes on an ungreased 13 x 18-inch baking sheet. Bake until the cubes are lightly browned and dry, about 10 minutes. Cool the bread completely; transfer to a large bowl.

3. While the bread toasts, heat 1 tablespoon of the butter in a large skillet over medium heat. Toast the pecans, stirring constantly, until fragrant and lightly browned, about 3 minutes. Add the pecans to the bread cubes.

4. Heat 2 tablespoons of the butter in the same skillet over medium heat. Add the onion and celery and cook, stirring occasionally, until the vegetables are soft and tender, about 7 to 10 minutes. Add the pear and garlic and cook, stirring constantly, just until the pear begins to soften, about 3 minutes. Add the wine and cook until it is barely visible, about 1 minute.

5. Add the cooked vegetables to the toasted bread cubes, along with the parsley, thyme, sage, celery salt, nutmeg, and pepper, and toss to coat thoroughly. Add the broth and the remaining butter and toss until the bread cubes are completely moistened, adding more broth if necessary.

6. Transfer the stuffing to the baking dish. Bake, covered, for 30 minutes. Uncover, and bake until the top is crisp and golden brown, another 15 minutes. Garnish with the remaining parsley and serve immediately.

Calories 190 · Fat 10g · Protein 4g · Carbohydrates 22g · Cholesterol 0mg · Sodium 387mg · Fiber 2g

Savory Leek-Onion Bread Pudding

Bread puddings are a hearty foundation for a main dish; add your favorite roasted vegetable such as mushrooms, cauliflower, or artichokes for added interest. **SERVES 6**

3 tablespoons olive oil

1 large leek (white parts only), washed, rinsed, and sliced

1 small onion, diced

1 small garlic clove, minced

1/4 cup dry white wine

1 tablespoon chopped fresh thyme, or other favorite herb such as rosemary or basil, or more to taste

1 cup fat-free half-and-half or plain coffee creamer (soy or coconut)

3 large eggs

3/4 cup Parmesan cheese or soy Parmesan, divided

1/2 teaspoon sea salt

1/4 teaspoon freshly ground black pepper

3 1/2 cups 1-inch GF bread cubes (made from about 8 slices, depending on slice size)

1. Place a rack in the middle of the oven. Preheat the oven to 375°F. Generously grease an 8-inch square glass baking dish with 2-inch sides.
2. In a heavy 12-inch skillet, heat the oil over medium heat. Add the leek and onion and cook, stirring occasionally, until they are tender, about 5 minutes. Add the garlic and continue to cook another minute. Set aside.
3. In a medium bowl, whisk together the wine, thyme, half-and-half, eggs, 1/2 cup of the Parmesan cheese, and the salt and pepper. Add the leek-onion mixture and mix thoroughly.
4. Layer the cubed bread evenly in the baking dish and pour the leek-onion mixture on top, pressing down on the bread with a spatula to make sure it is immersed. Cover tightly with foil.
5. Bake 40 minutes, then remove the foil, sprinkle with the remaining Parmesan cheese, and continue to bake, uncovered, until the top is crusty and brown, about 10 to 12 minutes more. Serve hot.

Calories 280 · Fat 14g · Protein 11g · Carbohydrates 24g · Cholesterol 116mg · Sodium 584mg · Fiber 2g

Veggie Pizza

Pizza is my most requested dish, especially from newly diagnosed patients. They all say the same thing: "I want my pizza back." You can use your favorite store-bought pizza sauce for convenience, but this one is so thick it won't make the crust soggy. For even better texture and fuller flavor in the crust, make the dough the day before (using cold rather than warm milk), and refrigerate, tightly covered. The next day, bring the dough to room temperature, and begin with Step 5. You start the pizza baking in a cold oven, which produces a lovely crust (see Step 6), but you can also bake it in a preheated oven (see Step 1 for preheating instructions). You can also freeze the dough ball (tightly wrapped) for up to a week; thaw in the fridge for best results. **MAKES A 12-INCH PIZZA: 6 SLICES**

PIZZA SAUCE

1 teaspoon olive oil

3 medium garlic cloves, minced

1 small can (8 ounces) tomato sauce

2 teaspoons dried oregano

1 teaspoon dried basil

1/2 teaspoon sea salt

1/4 teaspoon crushed red pepper flakes

TOPPING

1 teaspoon olive oil

1/2 cup sliced black olives

1 small green bell pepper, seeded, cut in 1/8-inch slices

6 marinated artichoke hearts, drained, cut in 1/2-inch slices

1 small onion, cut in 1/8-inch slices

1 garlic clove, minced

6 button mushrooms, cut in 1/4-inch slices

1 cup grated low-fat mozzarella cheese or cheese alternative

PIZZA DOUGH

1 tablespoon active dry yeast

2 teaspoons evaporated cane juice,
   divided

²/₃ cup brown rice flour, plus more for
   dusting the dough while shaping

½ cup tapioca flour

2 teaspoons xanthan gum

¾ cup warm (110°F) milk of choice,
   unless making the day before, in
   which case use cold milk

1 teaspoon dried oregano

½ teaspoon sea salt

1 tablespoon olive oil, divided

2 teaspoons apple cider vinegar

1. Place racks in the lower and middle positions of the oven, but do not preheat the oven if using the cold-oven start (see Step 6). Otherwise, preheat the oven to 400°F.

2. Make the Pizza Sauce: Heat the oil in a medium saucepan over medium heat. Add the garlic and cook, stirring constantly, for 1 minute. Add the remaining ingredients, bring to a boil, reduce the heat to low, and simmer, stirring occasionally, for 10 minutes. For a thicker sauce, simmer another 3 to 5 minutes, stirring constantly. Set aside to cool.

3. Make the Topping: In a heavy medium skillet, heat the olive oil over medium heat. Cook the olives, bell pepper, artichoke hearts, onion, garlic, and mushrooms, stirring occasionally, until the vegetables have released their juices and the onion is slightly translucent, about 3 to 5 minutes. Set aside to cool slightly.

4. Make the Pizza Crust: In a small bowl, dissolve the yeast and ½ teaspoon of the cane juice in the milk. Set aside to foam 5 minutes. In a food processor, blend yeast mixture, rice and tapioca flours, xanthan gum, oregano, salt, 1 teaspoon of the oil, the vinegar, and the remaining cane juice until a ball forms. If it doesn't, add more milk a tablespoon at a time until it does. The dough will be very soft.

5. Generously grease a 12-inch nonstick (gray, not black) metal pizza pan with shortening (not cooking spray; it makes it harder to shape the dough). Place the dough on the pizza pan. Liberally dust the dough with rice flour; then press the dough onto the pan with your hands, continuing to dust with rice flour to prevent sticking, as needed. The smoother the dough, the smoother the baked crust will be. Make the edges very smooth and somewhat thicker to contain the toppings.

6. Place the formed crust on the bottom rack of the cold oven. Turn the oven to 400°F and bake the crust for 15 minutes. Remove the pizza crust from the oven and brush the crust edge with the remaining 2 teaspoons of olive oil. Spread with the Pizza Sauce and then arrange the topping over the sauce. Top with the cheese.

7. Bake the pizza on the middle rack until the cheese is lightly browned, about 15 to 20 minutes. Cool the pizza 5 minutes on a wire rack, then cut into 6 pieces. Serve hot.

Calories 295 · Fat 12g · Protein 11g · Carbohydrates 40g · Cholesterol 12mg · Sodium 845mg · Fiber 6g

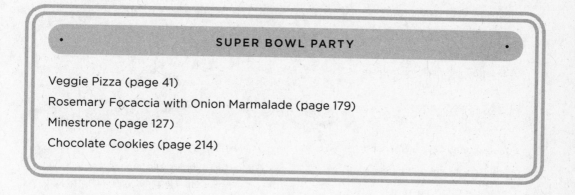

SUPER BOWL PARTY

Veggie Pizza (page 41)

Rosemary Focaccia with Onion Marmalade (page 179)

Minestrone (page 127)

Chocolate Cookies (page 214)

Peperonata on Soft Polenta

Peperonata, an Italian concoction of peppers, is amazingly versatile. If you prefer, you may serve it over large slices of toasted gluten-free bread or buttered gluten-free pasta, or use it as a topping for Crostini (page 158). But it is fantastic when served over soft polenta. Poblano or pasilla peppers are typically found in natural food stores or Mexican markets. **SERVES 4**

SOFT POLENTA

6 cups GF vegetable broth or homemade Vegetable Broth (page 245)

1½ cups GF polenta or corn grits

½ teaspoon sea salt, or to taste

1 tablespoon olive oil

¼ teaspoon freshly ground black pepper

PEPERONATA

5 tablespoons olive oil, divided

2 tablespoons sherry vinegar

1 teaspoon Dijon mustard

2 tablespoons chopped fresh oregano, or 2 teaspoons dried, divided

1 teaspoon ground coriander, divided

¼ teaspoon sea salt, or to taste

⅛ teaspoon freshly ground black pepper

3 large bell peppers (red, orange, and yellow), cored, seeded, and cut in ¼-inch strips

1 whole poblano pepper or pasilla pepper, cored, seeded, and cut in ¼-inch strips

1 small red onion, diced

½ cup chopped fresh cilantro, divided

1. In a heavy medium saucepan whisk together the broth, polenta, salt, oil, and pepper. Bring the mixture to a boil over medium-high heat, then reduce the heat to low and cook according to package directions, stirring occasionally, until all the liquid is absorbed. Cooking time can vary by polenta brand, and you may need more broth to keep it at a soft consistency. Set aside, keeping it warm and stirring occasionally.

2. In a small jar with a tight-fitting lid, shake together 4 tablespoons of the oil with the sherry vinegar, mustard, 1 tablespoon fresh or 1 teaspoon dried oregano, ½ teaspoon coriander, and the salt and pepper until smooth and slightly thickened. This will be the dressing; set aside.

3. Heat the remaining 1 tablespoon of the oil in a skillet over medium heat. Cook the bell peppers, poblano pepper, red onion, the remaining 1 tablespoon fresh or 1 teaspoon dried oregano, and the remaining ½ teaspoon coriander, stirring constantly, until the peppers are just tender, about 5 to 8 minutes. Cover and cook another 2 minutes. Pour half of the dressing over the peppers, add half of the cilantro, and toss to coat thoroughly.

4. Divide the polenta among 4 pasta bowls or individual serving bowls, top each with the pepper mixture, and serve, drizzled with the remaining dressing and garnished with the remaining cilantro.

Calories 305 · Fat 14g · Protein 5g · Carbohydrates 40g · Cholesterol 0mg · Sodium 250mg · Fiber 3g

Polenta Triangles with Warm Cannellini and Capers Salad

Down South, it's called grits. In Italy, the same thing is called polenta. In my mind, polenta has a much lovelier ring to it. Be sure to make it ahead of time to allow it to firm up. I love when the polenta is extra crispy. **SERVES 6**

POLENTA TRIANGLES

6 cups GF vegetable broth or homemade Vegetable Broth (page 245)

1½ cups GF polenta or corn grits

1½ teaspoons sea salt

1 tablespoon olive oil

¼ cup cornstarch, divided

¼ cup olive oil for frying

WARM CANNELLINI AND CAPERS SALAD

3 tablespoons extra-virgin olive oil

½ cup fresh shallots or 2 tablespoons jarred shallots, minced

2 medium garlic cloves, minced

2 tablespoons chopped fresh rosemary, or 1 tablespoon dried

2 tablespoons balsamic vinegar or sherry vinegar

2 tablespoons capers, rinsed and drained

2 tablespoons lemon juice

2 teaspoons lemon zest

1 can (15 ounces) cannellini (white kidney beans), rinsed and drained

1 cup baby spinach leaves

½ cup grape tomatoes, halved, or roasted red pepper strips, for garnish

1. Make the Polenta: Grease a 9 x 13-inch glass baking dish, or for easier removal of the polenta, line with plastic wrap and set aside.
2. Bring the broth to a boil in a medium saucepan. Slowly pour in a continuous stream of polenta, stirring constantly. Add the salt. Reduce the heat to low, add the oil, and cook uncovered, stirring occasionally, until the polenta begins to pull away from the sides of

the pan, about 20 minutes. Cooking time can vary by the brand and coarseness of the polenta. Pour into the baking dish and refrigerate until firm, about 2 hours.

3. Dust the top of the polenta with half of the cornstarch, then invert the polenta onto a large cutting board and dust with the remaining cornstarch. Cut two vertical lines crosswise through the polenta to make three rectangles. Make diagonal cuts from corner to corner of each rectangle to make an X, creating 4 triangles within each of the 3 rectangles. You will have 12 triangles.

4. Heat 2 tablespoons of the oil in a large nonstick skillet over medium heat. Working in batches, cook the polenta triangles until crispy and lightly browned, about 8 minutes per side. Transfer the triangles to a baking sheet or ovenproof platter and place in a 200°F oven to keep them warm while frying the remaining polenta triangles, using the remaining oil if needed.

5. Make the Warm Cannellini and Capers Salad: In a large skillet, heat the oil over medium-low heat. Add the shallots, garlic, and rosemary and cook, stirring constantly, for 1 minute. Add the vinegar, capers, and lemon juice and zest, and stir to combine. Add the beans and spinach and toss to coat thoroughly. Remove from the heat, cover, and let stand (the spinach will wilt during this time) while arranging the polenta on plates.

6. To serve, stack 2 polenta triangles attractively on each plate. Top with the salad and its juices and garnish with the tomatoes or roasted red pepper strips. Serve immediately.

Calories 685 · Fat 19g · Protein 23g · Carbohydrates 106g · Cholesterol 0mg · Sodium 522mg · Fiber 18g

Sherried Mushrooms on Crispy Polenta Rounds

Mushrooms are chock-full of flavor and hearty enough to be quite filling. When combined with the full-bodied sherry, they're irresistible. This versatile dish can be served on polenta, as shown here, or on mashed potatoes, GF toast, or grilled tofu. **SERVES 4**

4 tablespoons olive oil, divided

1 pound mushrooms (button, cremini, shiitake, or a mixture), cut in ¼-inch-thick slices

1 small onion, chopped

3 teaspoons chopped fresh rosemary

⅛ teaspoon crushed red pepper flakes

½ teaspoon sea salt

¼ teaspoon freshly ground black pepper

2 garlic cloves, minced

½ cup dry sherry or dry white wine

¼ cup chopped fresh parsley, plus extra for garnish

1 tablespoon fresh lemon juice

1 package (18 ounces) GF ready-made polenta, cut in ½-inch rounds

1. Heat 2 tablespoons of the oil in a large skillet or Dutch oven over medium heat. Add the mushrooms, onion, rosemary, red pepper flakes, salt, and pepper. Cook, stirring occasionally, until the onion is softened and the mushroom juices have evaporated, about 10 minutes.

2. Stir in the garlic and sherry and continue to cook, stirring constantly, until most of the liquid has evaporated, about another 10 to 15 minutes. Stir in the ¼ cup of parsley and the lemon juice. Set aside.

3. Preheat the oven to 300°F. In a 10-inch nonstick skillet, heat the remaining 2 tablespoons of oil over medium heat. Working in batches, cook the polenta rounds until crisp and lightly browned, about 8 minutes per side. Transfer to a baking sheet and place in the oven to stay warm and get crispier, while frying the remaining polenta rounds. To serve, arrange the polenta rounds in a single layer on a large serving platter. Spoon the mushrooms on top and serve immediately, garnished with the remaining parsley.

Calories 280 · Fat 14g · Protein 5g · Carbohydrates 27g · Cholesterol 0mg · Sodium 641mg · Fiber 3g

Stuffed Bell Peppers with Picadillo Rice

For the most colorful presentation, use three colors of peppers—red, yellow, and orange. Nestled on a bed of spinach, they are especially colorful and inviting. Or drape the peppers across a bed of pristine white basmati rice for an equally attractive presentation.

SERVES 4

4 medium bell peppers (2 red, 1 yellow, 1 orange), stemmed, seeded, and diced; divided

1/4 cup grated Parmesan cheese or soy Parmesan

4 cups baby spinach, washed and dried

PICADILLO RICE

1 tablespoon canola oil

1/2 cup yellow onion, chopped

1 1/2 teaspoons dried oregano, or
    1 tablespoon chopped fresh

1/4 teaspoon ground cumin

1/4 teaspoon ground cinnamon

1/8 teaspoon ground cloves

2 medium garlic cloves, minced

2 tablespoons golden or dark raisins

1/4 cup pimento-stuffed green olives, sliced

1 1/2 cups diced fresh tomatoes, or 1 can
    (15 ounces), undrained

1/4 teaspoon crushed red pepper flakes

1/4 teaspoon sea salt, or to taste

1 cup cooked brown rice

1 1/2 teaspoons red wine vinegar

1. Place a rack in the middle of the oven. Preheat the oven to 375°F. Coat a 9 x 13-inch glass baking dish with cooking spray; set aside.

2. Cut the peppers in half, lengthwise, through the stem end. Remove the seeds and membranes. Place all but one red bell pepper on a microwave-safe plate and cook in the microwave oven on high power, covered with waxed paper, 5 minutes. Remove and let cool 10 minutes.

3. Dice the remaining red bell pepper. In a medium saucepan, heat the oil over medium-low heat. Add the diced pepper and onion and cook, covered, until the vegetables are

soft, stirring occasionally, about 5 minutes. Add the oregano, cumin, cinnamon, cloves, and garlic, and continue to cook, stirring constantly, another minute.

4. Add the raisins, olives, tomatoes, crushed red pepper flakes, salt, and rice, and bring to a boil. Reduce the heat to low and simmer, covered, 20 minutes. Remove from the heat and stir in the vinegar.

5. Spoon the Picadillo Rice into the peppers and arrange in the baking dish. Spoon any leftover rice around the peppers. (You may prepare this dish up to this point the night before; cover and refrigerate to bake the next day.) To bake, pour ½ cup hot water around the peppers and cover tightly with foil.

6. Bake 25 minutes. Discard the foil and sprinkle with Parmesan cheese. Bake another 10 minutes or until the filling is bubbling. Serve immediately over the baby spinach.

Calories 215 · Fat 7g · Protein 7g · Carbohydrates 36g · Cholesterol 4mg · Sodium 338mg · Fiber 7g

COMFORT FOOD MEAL

Stuffed Bell Peppers with Picadillo Rice (page 49)

Roasted Fennel with Garlic and Thyme (page 120)

Mixed green salad

Oatmeal Chocolate-Chip Cookies (page 218)

Stuffed Cabbage Rolls

This dish may look complicated and impossible—how can you possibly roll cabbage? The secret is gently simmering the crisp leaves until they are buttery soft and pliable; then you can fold them quite easily. If you can't find Savoy cabbage, the regular green kind also works quite well. **SERVES 6 (12 ROLLS TOTAL)**

12 large cabbage leaves, preferably Savoy, but regular cabbage works

3 cups cooked brown rice or millet

1 tablespoon dried onion flakes or ¼ cup diced fresh onion

¼ cup pine nuts (toasted, if you wish)

2 tablespoons raisins, optional

2 teaspoons Beau Monde seasoning salt, divided, or your favorite seasoning blend

1 teaspoon Italian seasoning, divided

¼ teaspoon freshly ground black pepper

2 garlic cloves, minced

⅛ teaspoon freshly ground nutmeg

1 large can (28 ounces) diced tomatoes

1 small can (8 ounces) tomato sauce

1 tablespoon apple cider vinegar, divided

½ cup nonfat sour cream or vegan sour cream, for garnish

2 tablespoons chopped Italian flat-leaf parsley, for garnish

Toothpicks

1. Place a rack in the middle of the oven. Preheat the oven to 325°F. Grease a lidded 7 x 11-inch glass baking dish or a 12-inch ovenproof skillet.
2. In a large pot of gently boiling water, simmer the cabbage leaves until soft and pliable, about 8 to 10 minutes. Remove from the water, drain, and cool.
3. In a large bowl, combine the rice, onion, nuts, raisins, seasoning salt, ½ teaspoon of the Italian seasoning, and the black pepper, garlic, and nutmeg. Stir until thoroughly mixed.
4. Place a cabbage leaf, rib side up, on a large cutting board. Cut along either side of the rib and discard the rib. Overlap the two sections of each leaf to make a solid surface.
5. Place ¼ cup of the rice mixture about two inches up from the bottom of the leaf. Fold the bottom of the leaf up over the filling, then tuck in each side of the leaf, and keep rolling away from you until you have a roll. Secure with a toothpick, if necessary, and place, seam side down, in the baking dish. Repeat with remaining leaves.

6. In a medium bowl, combine the tomatoes, tomato sauce, 1½ teaspoons vinegar, and remaining Italian seasoning. Pour over cabbage rolls.

7. Bake, covered, 1 hour. Stir the remaining vinegar into the sour cream. Serve the cabbage rolls hot, drizzled with the sauce from the pan and garnished with a dollop of the sour cream mixture and a sprinkle of the parsley.

Calories 220 · Fat 4g · Protein 8g · Carbohydrates 40g · Cholesterol 2mg · Sodium 901mg · Fiber 5g

Stuffed Poblano Peppers

Poblano peppers are a lovely mild chile; when dried they're called ancho chiles. They are flavorful (but not too hot) and strong, so they stand up to stuffing quite nicely. Some people roast them and then peel the skins, but I prefer to leave the skins on. **SERVES 4**

1 tablespoon olive oil

1 small yellow onion, chopped

3 medium garlic cloves, minced

½ cup dried apricots, diced

2 tablespoons dried cranberries

2 tablespoons pumpkin seeds, roasted and chopped

¼ cup chopped fresh cilantro

1 to 1½ teaspoons ground cumin, or to taste

¼ teaspoon ground cloves

¼ teaspoon ground cinnamon

½ teaspoon sea salt

½ teaspoon freshly ground black pepper

1 cup cooked brown rice

4 large poblano peppers

1. Place a rack in the middle of the oven. Preheat the oven to 350°F. Lightly grease a 9 x 13-inch glass baking dish.

2. Heat the oil in a large skillet over medium heat. Cook the onion and garlic, stirring occasionally, until soft, about 3 minutes. Stir in the apricots, cranberries, pumpkin seeds, cilantro, cumin, cloves, cinnamon, salt, and pepper. Stir in the rice until thoroughly blended.

3. Wash the peppers and pat them dry with paper towels. Leave the stems intact and rest each poblano on a cutting board. Cut a T-shape from the top side of each poblano and pull out the seeds and ribs with gloved hands (pepper oils can be harsh on your fingers). Stuff the peppers evenly with the rice mixture and place in the baking dish, slit side up.

4. Bake, covered, for 20 minutes. Uncover and bake 10 more minutes, or until the mixture is bubbling and the peppers are tender. Serve immediately.

Calories 175 · Fat 5g · Protein 4g · Carbohydrates 32g · Cholesterol 0mg · Sodium 246mg · Fiber 4g

Stuffed Swiss Chard Bundles with Pomegranate Glaze

Like cabbage, these leaves look too difficult to roll. Yet a little steaming turns them into lovely, soft sheets that bend whichever way you please. They are beautifully green, and taste delightful, especially when drizzled with the unexpectedly piquant Pomegranate Glaze. **SERVES 8**

STUFFED SWISS CHARD BUNDLES

8 large Swiss chard leaves, rinsed, with long stems cut off

1 tablespoon olive oil

1 small onion, finely chopped

1 cup cooked brown rice or quinoa

¼ cup golden raisins

¼ cup pine nuts, toasted

1 small bunch fresh parsley, finely chopped

1 tablespoon chopped fresh oregano, or 1 teaspoon dried

1 garlic clove, minced

2 teaspoons red wine vinegar

1 teaspoon ground turmeric

½ cup olive tapenade, Basil Pesto (see page 252), or Kalamata olives, finely chopped

Olive oil for brushing on bundles

POMEGRANATE GLAZE (MAKES ⅓ CUP)

1 cup pomegranate juice

2 teaspoons packed light brown sugar

1 tablespoon balsamic vinegar

Salt and freshly ground black pepper, to taste

1. Bring a large, deep pot of water to boil, then add some salt, reduce the heat to a simmer, and keep it simmering. Line a 13 x 18-inch baking sheet with paper towels.
2. Using tongs, dip a Swiss chard leaf into the simmering water until it becomes limp, about 30 seconds. Transfer the leaf to the paper towels to drain. Repeat with the remaining leaves.

3. While the leaves cool, heat the oil in a small skillet over medium heat and cook the onion, stirring occasionally, until it is tender, about 5 minutes.
4. In a medium bowl, combine the onion, brown rice, raisins, pine nuts, parsley, oregano, garlic, vinegar, and turmeric, and toss to combine thoroughly. Set aside.
5. Place a leaf, rib side up, on a large cutting board. Cut along either side of the rib and discard the rib. Overlap the two sections of each leaf to make a solid surface. If the leaves are extra large, halve them along the center rib to make two leaves.
6. Place ¼ cup of the rice mixture about two inches up from the bottom of the leaf. Top with a tablespoon of tapenade. Fold the bottom of the leaf up over the filling, then tuck in each side of the leaf, and keep rolling away from you until you have a 2-inch bundle. Brush both sides generously with olive oil and place, seam side down, on a large platter. Repeat with remaining leaves.
7. Make the Pomegranate Glaze: In a small saucepan over medium-high heat add the pomegranate juice, brown sugar, and balsamic vinegar. Bring to a boil, reduce the heat to low, and simmer, uncovered, until reduced to about ⅓ cup, stirring occasionally, about 5 minutes. Season to taste with salt and pepper.
8. While the glaze simmers, heat a grill pan over medium heat. Arrange the bundles, seam side down, and cook until they are hot, about 4 minutes per side. Transfer to the serving platter and serve hot with a drizzle of Pomegranate Glaze.

Calories 150 · Fat 7g · Protein 3g · Carbohydrates 20g · Cholesterol 0mg · Sodium 291mg · Fiber 2g

Creole Vegetables
on Basmati Rice

Creole food, which originated in French Louisiana, is usually associated with spice, vibrant flavors, and a little heat. This dish is no exception. You control the heat by how much hot sauce you use, so taste it first and add more as you please. **SERVES 4**

1 tablespoon olive oil

1 small onion, diced

2 celery ribs, trimmed and cut in ½-inch pieces

1 small green zucchini, trimmed and cut in ¼-inch slices

1 small yellow zucchini, trimmed and cut in ¼-inch slices

1 cup button mushrooms, chopped

½ cup green bell pepper, seeded and diced

2 garlic cloves, minced

1 can (15 ounces) diced petite tomatoes, preferably fire-roasted

1 can (8 ounces) tomato sauce

1 tablespoon GF Worcestershire sauce

1 teaspoon agave nectar or honey

½ teaspoon chili powder

½ teaspoon celery salt, or to taste

2 dashes hot sauce, or to taste

2 teaspoons cornstarch, whisked into 2 tablespoons cold water until smooth

4 cups hot cooked basmati rice

½ cup chopped fresh parsley, for garnish

1. In a large heavy Dutch oven, heat the oil over medium heat. Add the onion and celery and cook until tender, stirring constantly, about 5 minutes. Add the zucchini, mushrooms, bell pepper, and garlic, and cook, stirring constantly, 5 minutes.

2. Add the tomatoes, tomato sauce, Worcestershire sauce, agave nectar, chili powder, celery salt, and hot sauce. Bring the mixture to a boil, then reduce the heat to low and simmer, covered, 20 minutes.

3. Whisk the cornstarch mixture into the sauce and cook over medium heat, stirring constantly, until slightly thickened. Serve over hot rice, garnished with the parsley.

Calories 365 · Fat 5g · Protein 9g · Carbohydrates 73g · Cholesterol 0mg · Sodium 629mg · Fiber 6g

Red Beans and Brown Rice

Red beans and rice is a New Orleans–style dish commonly found in restaurants, and it is a staple in my kitchen because we like spicy foods. Red beans are not the same as kidney beans, so be sure to get the right kind. Preparing the beans in a slow cooker is ideal. Assemble the ingredients in the morning and they cook all day on their own. **SERVES 4**

½ pound dried red beans (not kidney beans)

1 tablespoon olive oil

1 small yellow onion, chopped

2 medium garlic cloves, minced

1 celery rib, chopped

1 small green bell pepper, chopped

1 teaspoon dried thyme, or 1 tablespoon chopped fresh

1 teaspoon onion powder

½ teaspoon hot pepper sauce, or to taste

1 teaspoon sea salt

½ teaspoon freshly ground black pepper

1 tablespoon packed brown sugar

1 whole bay leaf

1 dash liquid smoke, or to taste, optional

Water to cover beans

1 cup uncooked brown rice (or use 3½ cups cooked brown rice)

3 cups water

2 tablespoons parsley, for garnish

1. Pick over and rinse the beans to remove stones or debris. Soak beans overnight in water. Drain before using.

2. In a large heavy saucepan heat the oil over medium-low heat. Cook the onion, garlic, celery, and bell pepper, covered, until onion softens, about 5 minutes.

3. Add the red beans, thyme, onion powder, hot pepper sauce, salt, black pepper, brown sugar, bay leaf, and liquid smoke. Add water to two inches above beans and simmer, covered, over medium heat 3 hours (stirring occasionally and adding more water to cover as necessary). Taste, and add more salt and pepper, if desired.

4. While the beans simmer, make the rice: Bring the 3 cups of water to a boil over high heat. Add the salt and rice and bring to a boil again. Reduce the heat to low and simmer, covered, until the rice is done, about 40 to 45 minutes. Drain any excess water. Serve the beans over the rice, garnished with the parsley.

Calories 425 · Fat 5g · Protein 18g · Carbohydrates 79g · Cholesterol 0mg · Sodium 519mg · Fiber 16g

Vegetable Tikka Masala

In India, tikka refers to meat cooked on a skewer. This dish incorporates tikka's vibrant flavors, minus the meat, and marries them in this dish served over your choice of brown or white rice. **SERVES 4 (MAKES 4 CUPS)**

2 tablespoons canola oil or other neutral oil

1 large onion, diced

1 tablespoon garam masala

2 teaspoons ground turmeric

1/2 teaspoon ground coriander

1/2 teaspoon ground cumin

1/2 teaspoon crushed red pepper flakes

4 medium garlic cloves, crushed

A 2-inch slice ginger root, peeled and chopped

1/2 teaspoon sea salt, or to taste

1/2 pound carrots, peeled, cut in 1/2-inch slices

1/2 pound red potatoes, unpeeled, cut in 1/2-inch slices

1 can (15 ounces) diced petite tomatoes

1 cup plain yogurt (coconut, cow, or soy) or homemade Yogurt (see page 249)

3/4 cup water

1 tablespoon fresh lime juice or distilled vinegar

4 cups hot cooked brown or white rice (jasmine or basmati)

1/2 cup chopped fresh cilantro

1. In a large saucepan, heat the oil over medium-low heat. Add the onion and cook, covered, until soft, about 5 minutes. Add the garam masala, turmeric, coriander, cumin, red pepper flakes, garlic, ginger, and salt, and cook, stirring constantly, for 1 minute.

2. Add the carrots, potatoes, tomatoes, yogurt, and water. Bring the mixture to a boil, then reduce the heat to low and simmer, covered, until the vegetables are tender, about 20 to 25 minutes. Remove from the heat and stir in the lime juice.

3. Serve over the hot rice, garnished with the cilantro.

Calories 440 · Fat 11g · Protein 10g · Carbohydrates 77g · Cholesterol 8mg · Sodium 444mg · Fiber 8g

Sweet-and-Sour Tofu Casserole

This dish is a casserole version of the popular sweet-and-sour Chinese dishes that many of us grew up with. To keep the vegetables bright, don't overcook them. If they're a little al dente, that's okay. **SERVES 4**

2 tablespoons peanut oil or canola oil, divided

1 package (15 ounces) extra-firm tofu, drained, pressed, and patted dry

1 small onion, coarsely chopped

2 carrots, peeled, cut in diagonal $1/2$-inch slices

1 cup long-grain white rice

2 cups GF vegetable broth or homemade Vegetable Broth (page 245)

1 tablespoon fresh ginger, chopped

1 teaspoon onion powder

$1/4$ teaspoon crushed red pepper flakes

$1/8$ teaspoon ground cloves

1 medium garlic clove, minced

$1/4$ teaspoon sea salt

1 red bell pepper, stemmed, seeded, cut in $1/2$-inch pieces

$1/2$ pound broccoli florets, cut in half

1 large can (14 ounces) pineapple chunks in juice, drained (reserve juice)

$1/2$ cup roasted cashews

$1/4$ cup chopped cilantro, for garnish

SAUCE

1 tablespoon cornstarch

$1/4$ cup packed brown sugar

$1/4$ cup apple cider vinegar

$1/4$ cup gluten-free tamari soy sauce

1. In a 12-inch or larger deep lidded nonstick skillet, heat 1 tablespoon of the oil over medium heat. Add the tofu and cook, stirring occasionally, until lightly browned on one side, about 2 minutes. Turn and brown on another side. (If time permits, brown on all sides for best flavor.) Transfer to a plate; set aside.

2. Heat the remaining tablespoon of oil over medium heat. Add the onion and carrots and cook, stirring occasionally, until tender, about 5 minutes.

3. Add the rice, broth, ginger, onion powder, red pepper flakes, cloves, garlic, and salt, and stir to evenly distribute the rice. Bring to a boil, reduce the heat to low, and cook, covered, until the rice is almost done, about 15 minutes.

4. Arrange the red bell pepper, broccoli, pineapple, cashews, and the browned tofu evenly over the rice and cook, covered, until the broccoli is tender and the rice is done, about another 10 minutes. Remove from the heat, and stir to blend the vegetables, tofu, and rice; let stand, covered.

5. While the rice cooks, make the Sauce: In a small saucepan, whisk the cornstarch into the brown sugar until thoroughly blended and then whisk in the vinegar and soy sauce. Add enough water to the reserved pineapple juice to equal 1 cup and add to the saucepan. Cook over medium heat, stirring constantly, until the sauce thickens, about 2 to 3 minutes.

6. Serve the casserole in the skillet or transfer to a serving platter. Drizzle with the sauce and serve hot, garnished with the cilantro.

Calories 590 · Fat 21g · Protein 19g · Carbohydrates 88g · Cholesterol 0mg · Sodium 769mg · Fiber 7g

Wild Mushroom Risotto

Risotto is one of those dishes that requires your complete attention, so treat it as a way to mindfully connect with your food. If you are lucky enough to have dried morels, use them along with the button mushrooms. If you are even luckier and find fresh morels, they will be absolutely terrific in this dish. I grew up eating fresh morels growing in the 400 acres of timberland that surrounded my family's Nebraska farm, so I've experienced firsthand how wonderful they can be in dishes like this one. **SERVES 4**

½ cup dried porcini mushrooms

2½ cups GF vegetable broth, homemade Mushroom Broth (page 244), or homemade Vegetable Broth (page 245), heated

1 tablespoon olive oil

2 tablespoons butter or buttery spread

4 to 8 ounces button mushrooms, or chanterelles, oyster, shiitake, or morels, divided

½ cup chopped shallots or white onion

1 cup Arborio rice

2 medium garlic cloves, minced

1 tablespoon chopped fresh thyme, or 1 teaspoon dried

1 tablespoon chopped fresh oregano, or 1 teaspoon dried

¼ cup Madeira or dry white wine

½ cup Parmesan cheese or soy Parmesan, divided

Salt and freshly ground black pepper, to taste

¼ cup chopped fresh parsley, for garnish

1. Place the porcini mushrooms in 1 cup of hot water to soak for 30 minutes. Remove the mushrooms from the water, strain them through cheesecloth or a paper coffee filter, and reserve the soaking liquid. Coarsely chop the mushrooms and set aside.

2. Bring the broth and reserved soaking liquid to a simmer in a large saucepan; remove from the heat, and cover to keep hot.

3. Heat the oil and butter in a large nonstick skillet over medium heat. Add the porcini mushrooms, half the button mushrooms, and the shallots, and sauté until tender, about 10 minutes. Add the rice, garlic, thyme, and oregano, and cook, stirring constantly, until the rice is well coated, about 1 minute. Add the Madeira; boil until almost absorbed, about 1 minute.

4. Ladle 1 cup of the hot broth over the rice and simmer until almost absorbed, stirring constantly, about 3 minutes. Continue to cook until the rice is just tender and the mixture is creamy, adding more broth by cupfuls, stirring constantly, and allowing most of

the broth to be absorbed before adding more, about 25 to 30 minutes. (If there is any additional broth left over, use it to moisten the risotto just before serving.) Stir in half of the Parmesan cheese. Add salt and pepper to taste, if necessary.

5. Serve the risotto in 4 pasta bowls or large soup bowls, each garnished with the remaining chopped mushrooms (reheated if necessary), a tablespoon of the Parmesan, and a tablespoon of the parsley.

Calories 370 · Fat 10g · Protein 12g · Carbohydrates 51g · Cholesterol 23mg · Sodium 262mg · Fiber 2g

Vegetable Paella

Paella is often my standby dish for guests, especially when they have food sensitivities. It is easily varied to meet a variety of dietary needs, and it never fails to impress guests when you carry that huge platter to the table. Serve it with a mixed green salad and crusty, homemade French Baguettes (page 181) and you have a meal that everybody will enjoy.

SERVES 6

4 tablespoons olive oil, divided

1 small onion, chopped

1 small red bell pepper, seeded, cut in ½-inch strips

1 small yellow bell pepper, seeded, cut in ½-inch strips

4 ounces button mushrooms (about ½ package), sliced

2 small green zucchini, sliced in ½-inch pieces

3 medium garlic cloves, minced

1 cup marinated artichoke hearts, drained and coarsely chopped

1 cup sun-dried (or oven-dried) tomato halves in oil, undrained

2 teaspoons capers, rinsed and drained

½ cup dry white wine

½ teaspoon saffron threads, crushed

2 cups GF vegetable broth or homemade Vegetable Broth (page 245)

1 teaspoon smoked paprika

1 teaspoon Beau Monde seasoning

½ teaspoon crushed red pepper flakes

1 cup long-grain white rice

1 roasted red pepper, cut in ¼-inch strips

½ cup pimiento-stuffed green olives, halved horizontally

¼ cup chopped fresh parsley

1 whole lemon, quartered, for garnish

1. Preheat the oven to 400°F.
2. Heat 2 tablespoons of the oil over medium heat in a 12-inch ovenproof skillet or paella pan. Cook the onion until tender, about 5 minutes. Add the bell peppers, mushrooms, zucchini, and garlic, and cook another 2 minutes, stirring constantly. Add the artichoke hearts, tomatoes, capers, and wine, and continue cooking, stirring constantly, until the wine is reduced by half.
3. Stir the saffron into the broth and add to the pan, along with the paprika, Beau Monde seasoning, and red pepper flakes, stirring to blend. Add the rice and remaining oil and

stir again to thoroughly blend. Bring the mixture to a boil, then transfer to the oven and bake, covered, until the rice is done, about 20 to 25 minutes. Remove from the oven and arrange the red pepper strips and green olives decoratively on top. Cover and let stand 10 minutes. Serve from the pan, garnished with the parsley and wedges of lemon.

Calories 395 · Fat 14g · Protein 11g · Carbohydrates 60g · Cholesterol 0mg · Sodium 1297mg · Fiber 9g

Chili Corn Bread Casserole

Serve this Mexican classic with a side of guacamole, some Mexican salsa for drizzling on top, and a dollop of sour cream. It is also a great way to use leftover chili. This is a one-pot dish; you can cook and serve it in the same skillet, making for easy cleanup. **SERVES 4**

CHILI

1 tablespoon olive oil

1 large onion, chopped

1 large garlic clove, minced

1 small red bell pepper or green bell pepper, seeded and diced

1 can (15 ounces) diced tomatoes, preferably fire-roasted

1 cup GF vegetable broth or homemade Vegetable Broth (page 245)

1 can (15 ounces) pinto beans, rinsed and drained

1 tablespoon chili powder

1 teaspoon ground cumin

1 teaspoon dried oregano

1 teaspoon sea salt, or to taste

½ cup chopped fresh cilantro, divided

CORN BREAD CRUST

⅔ cup GF Flour Blend (page 12)

½ cup GF yellow cornmeal

1 teaspoon baking powder

½ teaspoon baking soda

½ teaspoon xanthan gum

½ teaspoon sea salt

1 cup milk of choice

3 tablespoons agave nectar or honey

3 tablespoons canola oil

½ teaspoon apple cider vinegar

¼ cup grated low-fat cheddar cheese or cheese alternative

Guacamole, Mexican salsa, and low-fat sour cream or vegan sour cream, for garnish

1. Make the Chili: Place a rack in the middle of the oven. Preheat the oven to 375°F.
2. Coat the sides and bottom of a 10-inch cast-iron skillet (preferably a deep one with straight sides) with cooking spray. Heat the oil in the skillet over medium heat. Add the

onion and cook, stirring occasionally, until tender, about 4 minutes. Add the garlic and bell pepper and cook another minute, stirring constantly.

3. Add the tomatoes, broth, beans, chili powder, cumin, oregano, salt, and half of the cilantro. Bring to a boil, reduce the heat to low, and simmer, covered, 5 minutes. Turn off the heat but leave the skillet on the stove.

4. Make the Corn Bread Crust: In a medium bowl, whisk together the flour blend, cornmeal, baking powder, baking soda, xanthan gum, and salt until well blended. Add the milk, agave nectar, oil, and vinegar, and whisk just until well blended, then stir in the cheese. Spread evenly over the chili and up to the edges of the skillet with a wet spatula.

5. Bake until a toothpick inserted into the center of the corn bread comes out clean, about 20 to 25 minutes. Serve hot, garnished with the remaining cilantro, with the guacamole, Mexican salsa, and sour cream on the side.

Calories 515 · Fat 20g · Protein 14g · Carbohydrates 76g · Cholesterol 16mg · Sodium 1602mg · Fiber 12g

---

BUSY SOCCER NIGHT SUPPER

Chili Corn Bread Casserole (page 65)
Mixed green salad
Chocolate Cookies (page 214)

Enchiladas

I live in the Southwest, and enchiladas are a way of life here. I probably eat them once a week, in a variety of ways, but this bean-based version is one of my favorites. If time is short, use your favorite store-bought GF enchilada sauce. I heat the tortillas in a dry skillet to reduce the fat content of this dish, but if you're accustomed to warming them in a little hot oil, you may do that instead. **SERVES 6**

ENCHILADA SAUCE (MAKES 3 CUPS)

2 tablespoons canola oil

2 medium garlic cloves, minced

1 tablespoon chili powder

1 teaspoon dried oregano, or 1 tablespoon chopped fresh

½ teaspoon chipotle chile powder

½ teaspoon ground coriander

2 cans (15 ounces each) diced tomatoes, undrained (about 3½ cups)

½ teaspoon sea salt

¼ teaspoon freshly ground black pepper

¼ cup chopped fresh cilantro, plus 2 tablespoons for garnish

1 tablespoon evaporated cane juice or agave nectar

FILLING

1 tablespoon canola oil

1 large onion, peeled and cut in ¼-inch slices

2 large garlic cloves, minced

1 can (15 ounces) pinto beans, rinsed and drained

½ teaspoon chili powder

½ cup Enchilada Sauce, see above

¼ cup chopped fresh cilantro

12 GF white corn tortillas, plus more in case some break

1½ cups shredded Monterey Jack cheese or vegan cheese, divided

½ cup white onion, finely chopped, for garnish

¼ cup nonfat sour cream or vegan sour cream, for garnish

1. Make the Sauce: In a heavy medium saucepan heat the canola oil over medium-low heat. Add the garlic, chili powder, oregano, chipotle chile powder, and coriander, and cook for 1 minute, stirring occasionally. Add the tomatoes and their juices, and the

salt and pepper, ¼ cup of the cilantro, and the cane juice, and bring to a boil. Reduce the heat, cover, and simmer until the sauce thickens, about 15 to 20 minutes. Puree in batches in a blender or with an immersion blender until smooth. Keep warm while preparing the enchiladas.

2. Place a rack in the lower-middle position of the oven. Preheat the oven to 350°F. Generously grease a 9 x 13-inch glass baking dish. Spread ½ cup of the sauce over the bottom of the dish.

3. Make the Filling: In a heavy medium skillet heat the oil over medium-low heat. Add the onion and cook, stirring occasionally, until tender, about 5 minutes. Add the garlic and pinto beans and mash with a fork until about half of the beans are mashed. Add the chili powder, enchilada sauce, and cilantro, and stir until thoroughly blended, then cook until heated through. Remove from the heat. (The filling makes about 1 ¾ cups or about 24 tablespoons, just right for a generous 2 tablespoons per tortilla.)

4. Heat a large skillet over medium heat until hot. Warm the tortillas one at a time, turning with tongs until softened and pliable, about 30 seconds (about 15 seconds for each side).

5. After warming each tortilla, immediately spread a generous 2 tablespoons of the filling and 1 tablespoon of the cheese down the center of each tortilla, roll tightly, and place close together in the baking dish, seam side down. Cover the enchiladas evenly with the remaining sauce. Cover the dish with foil and bake until the sauce is bubbly, about 25 minutes. Remove the foil, sprinkle with the remaining cheese, and bake until the cheese melts, about 5 minutes. Serve hot, garnished with the chopped onion, the remaining 2 tablespoons cilantro, and a dollop of the sour cream.

Calories 580 · Fat 20g · Protein 26g · Carbohydrates 79g · Cholesterol 31mg · Sodium 501mg · Fiber 22g

Tortilla Torte

The gluten-free community was delighted when gluten-free flour tortillas hit the market a few years ago. Since then, we've been able to enjoy dishes like this one. Feel free to vary the fillings as you wish. If you don't have black beans, use pinto beans; kale can substitute for spinach. I'm a huge fan of cilantro, so I use lots here, but you can use as much as you wish. **SERVES 6**

3 cups store-bought enchilada sauce or homemade Enchilada Sauce (page 67), divided

1 cup store-bought Mexican tomato salsa

½ cup chopped cilantro, or more to taste, plus more for garnish

4 large tomatillos, husks removed and finely chopped

2 cups shredded low-fat cheddar cheese or cheese alternative, plus ¼ cup for garnish

1 can (14 ounces) black beans, rinsed and drained

1 box (10 ounces) frozen spinach, drained and squeezed dry to equal ½ cup, or 12 ounces fresh baby spinach, cooked, drained, and squeezed dry

1 cup thinly sliced green onions, plus 2 tablespoons for garnish

6 GF 8-inch brown rice flour tortillas

2 tablespoons sliced black olives, for garnish

Guacamole and low-fat sour cream or vegan sour cream for additional garnish

1. Place a rack in the middle of the oven. Preheat the oven to 350 °F. Coat a 9-inch spring-form pan (one with removable sides) with cooking spray. Wrap the bottom in aluminum foil and place on a baking sheet.

2. In a medium bowl or 4-cup measuring cup, stir together 2 cups of the enchilada sauce, and the salsa. In another medium bowl, stir together the cilantro, tomatillos, and 2 cups of the cheese. In a third bowl, stir together the beans, spinach, and 1 cup of the green onions.

3. Place 1 tortilla on the bottom of the pan. Spread ½ cup of the enchilada sauce–salsa mixture evenly on top and out to the sides. Top with ⅓ cup of the cilantro-tomatillo mixture and ⅓ cup of the bean-spinach mixture. Repeat layers, ending with a tortilla. Pour ½ cup enchilada sauce–salsa mixture on top, spreading it out to the edges of the pan. Sprinkle with the remaining ¼ cup cheese.

4. Cover and bake until bubbly and hot, about 25 to 30 minutes. Remove from the oven and let stand 10 minutes. Heat the remaining cup of enchilada sauce to boiling. Remove the sides of the pan, cut the torte into 6 slices, and serve, garnished with the black olives, a drizzle of the enchilada sauce, and the remaining cilantro and green onions. Top with guacamole and sour cream, if desired.

Calories 615 · Fat 22g · Protein 26g · Carbohydrates 82g · Cholesterol 45mg · Sodium 959mg · Fiber 14g

Eggplant Roll-Ups

I have gained a much greater appreciation for eggplants since writing this book; in fact, I grew them in my garden pots this summer. It is an extremely versatile vegetable. I also love its shape and that deep aubergine color. These roll-ups are healthier and prettier if you don't peel the eggplants. Use the discarded parts of the eggplants in Caponata (page 155).

SERVES 4 (MAKES 12 ROLL-UPS)

2 small eggplants, cut lengthwise into ¼-inch slices (total of 12 slices)

1 cup nonfat cream cheese or vegan cream cheese, softened

½ cup grated low-fat mozzarella cheese or vegan cheese, divided

¾ cup chopped fresh basil, divided

¼ cup chopped fresh oregano, or 2 tablespoons dried

¼ cup chopped fresh parsley, or 2 tablespoons dried

¼ cup toasted pine nuts

½ cup Parmesan cheese or soy Parmesan, divided

2 large garlic cloves, minced

Salt and pepper to taste

3 cups homemade Marinara Sauce (page 24) or store-bought marinara sauce

1. Preheat the broiler. Line a 10 x 15-inch baking sheet with parchment paper and coat it with cooking spray. Coat a 9 x 13-inch baking dish with cooking spray.
2. Arrange the eggplant slices in a single layer on the baking sheet. Broil them until they are lightly browned on one side only and tender, about 5 minutes. Remove from the oven and let cool while making the filling. Preheat the oven to 375°F.
3. In a small bowl, stir together the cream cheese, ¼ cup of the mozzarella cheese, ½ cup of the basil, the oregano, parsley, pine nuts, ¼ cup of the Parmesan cheese, the garlic, and the salt and pepper until well blended.
4. Spread half of the marinara sauce in the bottom of the baking dish.
5. Place the eggplant slices, browned side down, on a smooth surface. With a spatula, spread 2 tablespoons of the filling lengthwise down the center of each slice. Roll up, starting at the short ends.
6. Place the eggplant roll-ups, seam side down, on the sauce. Pour the remaining marinara sauce over the roll-ups and use a pastry brush to make sure the tops of each are coated with sauce.

7. Bake, covered, until the sauce is bubbling, about 30 minutes. Sprinkle the remaining mozzarella and Parmesan over the roll-ups and bake, uncovered, until the cheese is melted, about 10 minutes. If using non-dairy cheese, broil the dish about 6 to 8 inches from the heat source until the cheese melts. Serve immediately, garnished with the remaining ¼ cup chopped basil.

Calories 360 · Fat 15g · Protein 24g · Carbohydrates 36g · Cholesterol 20mg · Sodium 1348mg · Fiber 10g

Eggplant Parmesan Stacks

Before I went gluten-free, I ate this dish at least once a week at a local Italian restaurant near my home and was deeply saddened when I learned that it contained lots of wheat! So now I make my own with gluten-free bread crumbs, and it tastes wonderful. I have learned that smaller eggplants are easier to work with, so search them out. **SERVES 4 (2 STACKS PER PERSON)**

2 small eggplants, about ¾ pound each

½ teaspoon sea salt

¼ teaspoon freshly ground black pepper

2 tablespoons water

½ cup Dijon-style mustard

1 teaspoon dried oregano, or
    1 tablespoon chopped fresh

1 cup GF Bread Crumbs (page 243) or
    store-bought bread crumbs

2 tablespoons olive oil, for frying

2 cups homemade Marinara Sauce
    (page 24) or GF store-bought
    marinara sauce

¼ pound shredded low-fat mozzarella
    cheese or vegan cheese, about
    1 cup

½ cup grated Parmesan cheese or soy
    Parmesan, divided

¼ cup chopped fresh basil, for garnish

1. Place a rack in the middle of the oven and another one in the broiler position (about 6 inches from the heat). Preheat the oven to 350°F. Lightly grease a 9 x 13-inch glass baking dish.

2. Peel the eggplants and cut them into sixteen ½-inch slices. Sprinkle on both sides with the salt and pepper.

3. In a small bowl, whisk together the water, mustard, and oregano until smooth. Spread the mixture evenly on a plate. Place the bread crumbs on another plate.

4. Dip the eggplant slices into the mustard-oregano mixture and then into the bread crumbs.

5. Heat 1 tablespoon of the oil in a large nonstick (gray, not black) skillet over medium heat. Working in batches, cook the eggplant slices until tender and lightly browned, about 2 to 3 minutes per side, adding more oil as needed. Between batches, wipe out any remaining bread crumbs.

6. Place 8 slices of eggplant in a single layer in the baking dish. Drizzle each slice with 2 tablespoons of the marinara sauce. Sprinkle each slice with 2 tablespoons of the mozzarella cheese and a tablespoon of the Parmesan cheese. Place the remaining 8 slices of

eggplant on top of the first layer to make 8 stacks of two slices each. Top each stack with 2 tablespoons of the marinara sauce and 1 tablespoon of the Parmesan cheese.

7. Bake 20 to 25 minutes. Transfer the baking dish to the broiler position and broil until the cheese is browned and slightly melted, watching carefully to make sure it doesn't burn. Serve in stacks, garnished with the fresh basil.

Calories 450 · Fat 22g · Protein 23g · Carbohydrates 42g · Cholesterol 28mg · Sodium 1751mg · Fiber 7g

Tip: Vegan cheeses are easier to grate when frozen. Some brands, such as Daiya, come in shredded form.

Moussaka

This Greek-inspired moussaka is hearty and tantalizing with its aromatic spices. It is usually made of layers of eggplant, pasta, cheese, and sauce, and is a great choice for dinner on a winter evening. **SERVES 4**

1 small eggplant, about ¾ pound

1 teaspoon sea salt, divided

½ teaspoon freshly ground black pepper, divided

1 small Russet potato

2 tablespoons olive oil, or more if needed

½ cup chopped onion

2 large garlic cloves, minced

½ teaspoon cayenne pepper

½ teaspoon dried oregano, or 2 teaspoons chopped fresh

½ teaspoon ground cinnamon

¼ teaspoon ground allspice

1 cup coarsely chopped fresh tomatoes

¼ cup dried currants

½ cup dry red wine

1 cup grated Parmesan cheese or soy Parmesan, divided

¼ cup sweet rice flour

2 cups milk of choice, divided

2 tablespoons butter or buttery spread

⅛ teaspoon freshly grated nutmeg

Salt and pepper

1. Cut off the stem of the eggplant and remove the skin with a vegetable peeler. Cut the eggplant in half lengthwise; cut each half into ½-inch-thick slices. Season the slices on both sides with ½ teaspoon of the salt and ¼ teaspoon of the pepper.
2. Peel the potato and cut it crosswise into ¼-inch slices. Sprinkle with the remaining salt and pepper.
3. In a large skillet, heat the oil over medium heat. Working in batches, fry the eggplant slices in a single layer, turning once, until browned on both sides, adding more oil if necessary. Drain the eggplant slices on paper towels. In the same skillet, adding more oil if necessary, fry the potato slices until tender, about 5 minutes. Set aside to drain on paper towels.
4. To the same skillet, add the onion, garlic, cayenne, oregano, cinnamon, and allspice. Cook over medium heat, stirring occasionally, until the onion is soft and fragrant, about 3 minutes. Add the tomatoes, currants, and wine, and simmer until the liquid has evaporated, stirring occasionally. Remove the sauce from the heat.
5. Place a rack in the middle of the oven. Preheat the oven to 350°F. Generously grease an 8-inch square baking dish. Layer the bottom of the dish with half of the eggplant, leaving

no gaps between slices. Spread half of the sauce over the eggplant, leveling it with a spatula, then layer half of the potatoes, sprinkling with ¼ cup of the Parmesan cheese. Repeat with another layer of eggplant and the remaining half of the sauce, ending with a final layer of potatoes.

6. Whisk the sweet rice flour into ½ cup of the milk until smooth and then add to a 2-quart saucepan, along with the remaining milk, the butter, and the nutmeg. Heat over medium heat, whisking constantly, until the mixture thickens. Remove from the heat and stir in ½ cup of the Parmesan cheese and additional salt and pepper to taste. Pour this sauce over the eggplant/potato mixture, spreading evenly with a spatula. Sprinkle with the remaining Parmesan cheese.

7. Bake until browned and bubbly, about 30 to 40 minutes. Let cool 10 minutes before serving. Serve hot.

Calories 410 · Fat 20g · Protein 16g · Carbohydrates 39g · Cholesterol 36mg · Sodium 932mg · Fiber 5g

Old-Fashioned Vegetable Pot Pie with Savory Pastry Crust

This is the time-honored dish we all grew up with. It never fails to please, whether it's Sunday night supper with the family or comfort food for your guests. To save time, instead of cooking the vegetables from scratch, use leftover cooked vegetables. You can also vary the herbs you use in the crust. **SERVES 4**

FILLING

2 medium russet potatoes, peeled and cut in 1/4-inch slices

2 medium carrots, peeled and cut in 1/4-inch slices

1 small onion, chopped

1 teaspoon sea salt

Water

3 tablespoons olive oil

2 cups button mushrooms, cleaned and sliced

1 cup broccoli florets, chopped

2 medium garlic cloves, minced

1/2 cup corn kernels, fresh or frozen

1/2 cup green peas, fresh or frozen

1/4 cup chopped red bell pepper

1 teaspoon onion powder

1 tablespoon chopped fresh thyme, or 1 teaspoon dried

1 tablespoon chopped fresh sage, or 1 teaspoon dried

1/4 cup dry white wine

1/4 cup sweet rice flour, or 2 tablespoons cornstarch

2 cups homemade Vegetable Broth (page 245) or GF store-bought vegetable broth, divided

1 tablespoon GF Worcestershire sauce

1 tablespoon Dijon mustard

SAVORY PASTRY CRUST

1/2 cup GF Flour Blend (page 12)

1/4 cup almond meal or flour (see Almond Meal Flour, page 240)

1/4 cup sweet rice flour

1 tablespoon evaporated cane juice

1 tablespoon grated Parmesan cheese or soy Parmesan

½ teaspoon dried thyme (or sage, tarragon, or summer savory)

¼ teaspoon xanthan gum

¼ teaspoon guar gum

¼ teaspoon celery salt

4 tablespoons non-hydrogenated shortening (palm oil or soy)

2 tablespoons butter or buttery spread

2 tablespoons milk of choice, plus more for brushing the crust

¼ teaspoon sea salt, for sprinkling on crust

1. Grease a 2-quart ovenproof glass casserole dish. Make the Filling: In a large pot, cover and cook the potatoes, carrots, onion, and salt in just enough water to cover the vegetables until tender, about 10 minutes. Drain and set aside.

2. In a large pot or Dutch oven, heat the oil over medium heat. Add the mushrooms and cook, stirring occasionally, for 2 minutes. Then add the broccoli and cook, stirring occasionally, another 5 minutes. Add the garlic, corn, peas, red bell pepper, onion powder, thyme, sage, and wine and cook until the wine is no longer visible. Whisk the sweet rice flour into ½ cup of the broth until smooth, then add it to the vegetables, along with the remaining broth, Worcestershire sauce, and mustard. Stir to combine, then continue to cook, stirring constantly, until the filling thickens, about 3 to 5 minutes. Add the cooked potatoes, carrots, and onions, and simmer, covered, for 10 minutes, then transfer the filling to the casserole dish and keep it warm while preparing the crust.

3. Make the Savory Pastry Crust: Place a rack in the middle of the oven. Preheat the oven to 375°F. In a food processor, place the flour blend, almond meal, sweet rice flour, powdered sugar, Parmesan cheese, thyme, xanthan gum, guar gum, celery salt, shortening, and butter, and process until crumbly. With the motor running, gradually add 2 tablespoons of the milk through the feed tube and process until the dough forms a ball. If it doesn't form a ball, use a spatula to break the dough into pieces, add another tablespoon of milk, and process again, scraping down the sides of the bowl if necessary. Remove the dough from the food processor and shape into a ball.

4. Massage the dough between your hands until it is warm and pliable, which makes the crust easier to handle. With a rolling pin, roll the dough to the diameter of the casserole dish between two pieces of heavy-duty plastic wrap. (Use a damp paper towel between the countertop and bottom plastic wrap to prevent slipping.) Move the rolling pin from

the center of the dough to the outer edge, moving around the circle in clockwise fashion to assure a uniform thickness.

5. Remove the top plastic wrap and invert the crust, centering it over the hot filling. Remove the remaining plastic wrap and gently press the crust into place around the edges of the dish. Brush milk all over the crust. Sprinkle with the sea salt.

6. Bake until the crust is golden brown and the filling bubbles around the edges of the dish, about 30 to 35 minutes. Let stand 10 minutes before serving. Serve hot.

Calories 590 · Fat 31g · Protein 8g · Carbohydrates 72g · Cholesterol 17mg · Sodium 881mg · Fiber 6g

Onion-Leek Tart

The French are especially good at creating vegetable tarts, but we can make them easily with my no-fail pastry crust that is designed just for this purpose. Use a tart pan with a fluted edge and removable bottom so you can just slide the tart out of it, leaving the lovely fluted edge intact. Your guests will think this tart came from a professional bakery! **SERVES 6**

CRUST

½ cup GF Flour Blend (see page 12)

¼ cup almond meal or flour (see Almond Meal Flour, page 240)

¼ cup sweet rice flour

1 tablespoon evaporated cane juice

1 tablespoon grated Parmesan cheese or soy Parmesan

½ teaspoon xanthan gum

½ teaspoon guar gum

¼ teaspoon table salt

6 tablespoons non-hydrogenated shortening (palm oil or soy)

2 tablespoons milk of choice

FILLING

1 tablespoon olive oil

1 large leek (white only), cut in ¼-inch slices

1 large onion, finely chopped

2 garlic cloves, minced

1 tablespoon balsamic vinegar

¼ teaspoon sea salt

¼ teaspoon freshly ground black pepper

1 tablespoon capers, rinsed and drained

½ cup store-bought pesto sauce or homemade Basil Pesto (page 252)

1 teaspoon olive oil, for brushing the crust

½ teaspoon paprika, for garnish

1. Prepare the Crust: Place the flour blend, almond meal, sweet rice flour, cane juice, Parmesan cheese, xanthan gum, guar gum, salt, and shortening in a food processor and process until crumbly. With the motor running, add the milk through the feed tube and process until the dough forms a ball. If it doesn't form a ball, use a spatula to break the dough into pieces and process again, scraping down the sides of the bowl if necessary. Remove the dough from the food processor and knead with your hands until it is pliable and as warm as your hands. Wrap the dough tightly in plastic and set aside.

2. Preheat the oven to 375°F.

3. Make the Filling: In a large skillet, heat the oil over medium heat. Swish the sliced leeks in water until they are clean, then add them and the onion to the skillet and cook, stirring occasionally, until tender, about 8 to 10 minutes. Add the garlic, vinegar, salt, pepper, and capers, and cook another minute. Set aside.

4. With your fingers, press the piecrust dough into a 6 x 10-inch rectangular or 10-inch round nonstick (gray, not black) fluted tart pan with removable sides. Spread the pesto evenly over the dough, then spread the onion-leek mixture evenly over the pesto.

5. Bake for 15 to 20 minutes or until the crust is gently browned. Remove from the oven and brush the edges lightly with olive oil for added sheen. Let stand 5 minutes, then cut into 6 slices and serve, dusted with the paprika.

Calories 360 · Fat 27g · Protein 5g · Carbohydrates 27g · Cholesterol 6mg · Sodium 374mg · Fiber 2g

---

ROMANTIC LIGHT SUPPER

Carrot-Ginger Soup with Chile-Lime Pepitas (page 133)

Onion-Leek Tart (page 80)

Mixed green salad

Breadsticks (page 177)

Tiramisù (page 236)

Summer's Bounty
Vegetable Casserole

. . . .

This dish is a perfect summertime idea to use up those delectably fresh vegetables from the farmers' market. You can vary the vegetables as you wish—perhaps very thinly sliced Russet potatoes instead of eggplant or thin slices of red bell pepper or yellow onion instead of zucchini. The pesto adds loads of flavor. **SERVES 4**

½ pound (about 2 small) green zucchini, cut in ¼-inch slices

½ pound (1 small) eggplant, cut in ¼-inch slices

½ pound tomatoes (2 large Roma or 1 large beefsteak), cut in ⅛-inch slices

¼ teaspoon sea salt, divided

¼ teaspoon freshly ground black pepper, divided

2 tablespoons homemade Basil Pesto (page 252) or GF store-bought pesto

2 tablespoons extra-virgin olive oil

⅓ cup hot water

½ cup grated low-fat mozzarella cheese or cheese alternative

½ cup grated Parmesan cheese or soy Parmesan, divided

¼ cup GF homemade Bread Crumbs (page 243) or store-bought bread crumbs

Cooking spray

1. Place a rack in the middle of the oven. Preheat the oven to 375°F. Lightly oil a 10 x 15-inch baking sheet. Coat a 9-inch round or square glass baking dish with cooking spray.

2. Arrange the zucchini and eggplant in a single layer on the baking sheet. Roast in the oven for 15 minutes. Arrange half of the zucchini, half of the eggplant, and half of the tomatoes in the baking dish. Sprinkle with half of the salt and half of the pepper. Stir the pesto, olive oil, and 2 tablespoons of the hot water together and drizzle half evenly over the vegetables. Sprinkle the mozzarella cheese evenly on top and sprinkle with half of the Parmesan cheese.

3. Repeat the layers of zucchini, eggplant, and tomato, and sprinkle with the remaining salt and pepper. Drizzle the remaining pesto-olive oil mixture evenly on top. Stir together the remaining Parmesan cheese and the bread crumbs and sprinkle evenly on top. Pour the

remaining hot water around the edges of the baking dish and spray the bread crumbs with the cooking spray.

4. Bake until the vegetables are tender and the topping is lightly browned, about 35 to 45 minutes. Serve immediately.

Calories 225 · Fat 14g · Protein 8g · Carbohydrates 17g · Cholesterol 10mg · Sodium 479mg · Fiber 3g

Southwestern Bean and Grain Casserole

This is a terrific way to eat your grains. Leftovers keep nicely in the fridge and are easily reheated. I especially like to drench it with Mexican tomato salsa and maybe a little guacamole for garnish. Heating the broth to boiling temperature saves time by speeding up the cooking process. **SERVES 4**

1 can (15 ounces) pinto beans, rinsed and drained

1/2 cup whole-grain millet

1/2 cup whole-grain quinoa

1/2 cup corn kernels

1 small onion, finely chopped

2 small carrots, peeled, cut in 1/4-inch slices

4 button mushrooms, cleaned and cut in 1/4-inch slices

1 large tomatillo, husked, peeled, and finely chopped

1/2 cup chopped fresh cilantro

1/4 cup grape tomatoes, halved, or plum tomatoes, quartered

1 small serrano pepper, finely diced, optional

2 garlic cloves, minced

1 teaspoon dried oregano, or 1 tablespoon chopped fresh

1/2 teaspoon sea salt

1 1/2 cups homemade Vegetable Broth (page 245) or GF store-bought vegetable broth, heated to boiling

1/4 cup dry white wine

1/2 cup shredded low-fat Monterey jack cheese or cheese alternative, Vegan Gourmet

1 cup store-bought salsa or your favorite GF Mexican tomato salsa

1. Preheat the oven to 375°F. Generously grease a 2-quart lidded glass or ceramic baking dish.

2. Place the beans, millet, quinoa, corn, onion, carrots, mushrooms, tomatillo, cilantro, tomatoes, serrano pepper, garlic, oregano, and salt in the baking dish. Combine the broth and wine in a separate bowl, then pour on top, stirring to evenly distribute the ingredients. Cover the baking dish tightly.

3. Bake 45 to 60 minutes, stirring halfway through the baking time. Remove the cover and sprinkle with the cheese. Return to the oven and bake another 5 minutes, uncovered, until the cheese melts. Serve immediately with the salsa.

Calories 390 · Fat 6g · Protein 18g · Carbohydrates 67g · Cholesterol 8mg · Sodium 1059mg · Fiber 11g

Black-Eyed Peas in Barbecue Sauce

Use this recipe as a starting point for wonderful variations. Serve it by itself, on brown rice, or with cooked collards. All the wonderfully flavorful ingredients in the barbecue sauce assure that this will be one of your favorites. **SERVES 4 (MAKES 5 1/2 CUPS)**

3 cans (14 ounces each) black-eyed peas, rinsed and drained

BARBECUE SAUCE

1 cup ketchup

2 tablespoons molasses (not blackstrap)

2 tablespoons dried onion flakes, or 1/2 cup diced fresh onion

2 tablespoons maple syrup

1 teaspoon dried oregano, or 1 tablespoon chopped fresh

1/2 teaspoon crushed red pepper flakes

1/2 teaspoon freshly ground black pepper

1/2 teaspoon sea salt

1 garlic clove, minced

1/2 cup orange juice

1 tablespoon canola oil

1 tablespoon red wine vinegar

1. Place a rack in the middle of the oven. Preheat the oven to 350°F.
2. Make the Barbecue Sauce: In a 2-quart saucepan with a lid and an ovenproof handle, combine all the ingredients except the black-eyed peas. Stir over medium heat until well blended, then simmer for 10 minutes to mingle the flavors. Stir in the black-eyed peas until thoroughly blended.
3. Bake, covered, for 25 to 30 minutes. Serve immediately.

Calories 335 · Fat 1g · Protein 17g · Carbohydrates 66g · Cholesterol 0mg · Sodium 398mg · Fiber 14g

Smothered Bean Burritos with Green Chile Sauce

Burritos are a staple in the Southwestern lifestyle we live here in Colorado. When gluten-free tortillas were finally introduced a few years ago, we all rejoiced! Use these suggested ingredients as just that . . . suggestions. Feel free to vary the contents as you wish. That's part of the beauty of burritos—they can be filled with virtually anything! **SERVES 4**

4 GF 8-inch brown rice flour tortillas

1 cup grated low-fat Monterey Jack cheese or vegan cheese

4 plum tomatoes, seeded and diced, for garnish

1/4 cup chopped fresh cilantro, for garnish

GREEN CHILE SAUCE (MAKES 2 CUPS)

1 tablespoon canola oil

1 small onion, peeled, finely diced

2 medium garlic cloves, minced

2 cups of homemade Vegetable Broth
    (page 245) or GF vegetable broth

1 can (4 ounces) diced green chiles,
    undrained

1/2 teaspoon ground coriander

1/2 teaspoon dried oregano, or
    2 teaspoons chopped fresh

2 tablespoons chopped fresh cilantro

1/4 teaspoon sea salt, or to taste

2 teaspoons cornstarch, whisked into 2
    tablespoons water until smooth

FILLING

2 tablespoons balsamic vinegar

3 tablespoons canola oil, divided

1 teaspoon freshly ground black pepper

8 ounces button mushrooms, cleaned
    and cut in 1/4-inch slices

1 small white onion, cut in 1/8-inch
    vertical slices

1 large red bell pepper

2 medium garlic cloves, minced

1 can (15 ounces) black beans, rinsed and
    drained

1 1/2 teaspoons dried oregano, or
    1 1/2 tablespoons chopped fresh

1/2 cup Green Chile Sauce (see above)

5 ounces baby spinach, washed and
    patted dry

1. Make the Green Chile Sauce: In a heavy skillet, heat the oil over medium-low heat and cook the onion until just tender, about 5 minutes. Add the garlic, and cook, stirring constantly, another minute. Add the broth, chiles, coriander, oregano, cilantro, and salt, and simmer, covered, for 15 to 20 minutes. Add the cornstarch mixture and bring to a boil, stirring constantly, until the mixture thickens slightly. Keep the sauce warm while making the filling or refrigerate, tightly covered, for up to one week.

2. Make the Filling: In a medium bowl, whisk together the vinegar, 2 tablespoons of the oil, and the pepper. Add the mushrooms and toss to coat thoroughly. Let stand for 10 minutes.

3. In a large heavy skillet, heat the remaining oil over medium-low heat. Add the onion and bell pepper and cook, stirring occasionally, until the onion is lightly browned, about 5 to 7 minutes. Add the mushroom mixture and the garlic and cook, stirring occasionally, until the mushroom juices have evaporated and appear dry, about 3 to 5 minutes. Add the beans, oregano, and ½ cup of the Green Chile Sauce, and stir to blend thoroughly. Layer the spinach over the top and simmer, covered, until the spinach is wilted, about 1 to 2 minutes. Stir together. You may prepare the filling up to this point, then refrigerate up to one day before using.

4. Steam each tortilla on a splatter guard set over a skillet of simmering water, covered with a lid, until soft and pliable, about 10 seconds. Place the tortillas between sheets of waxed paper to keep warm and soft while steaming the other tortillas. Place about ¾ cup of the filling in each tortilla, top with 2 tablespoons cheese, then wrap up burrito-style and place seam side down on a serving plate. Smother each burrito with a generous ⅓ cup of the remaining Green Chile Sauce, sprinkle with 2 tablespoons cheese and the diced tomatoes, and microwave on low power just until the cheese is melted. Repeat with remaining burritos, garnish with the cilantro, and serve immediately.

Calories 550 · Fat 19g · Protein 22g · Carbohydrates 76g · Cholesterol 6mg · Sodium 827mg · Fiber 11g

Soft Corn Tacos with Black Bean Burgers

You can double the recipe for the Black Bean Burgers and serve them just as you would regular hamburgers. In this dish, however, they're fried in a rectangular shape to fit into the tacos better. Those of us who live in the Southwest know that a taco recipe is just a set of suggestions, so vary these ingredients as you wish. A local restaurant taught me to use two corn tortillas together (instead of just one) to prevent them from breaking.

SERVES 6 (MAKES 12 TACOS)

24 GF white corn tortillas

2 cups shredded lettuce

¾ cup store-bought *pico de gallo* or your favorite Mexican salsa

1 cup jicama, peeled, cut in matchsticks

GUACAMOLE

1 whole avocado, peeled, seeded, and mashed

3 tablespoons chopped fresh cilantro

2 tablespoons fresh lime juice

¼ teaspoon hot pepper sauce, or more to taste

⅛ teaspoon sea salt

BLACK BEAN BURGERS

1 can (15 ounce) black beans, rinsed and drained

½ cup cornstarch

¼ cup chopped onion

2 tablespoons mayonnaise or vegan mayonnaise

2 teaspoons chili powder

⅛ teaspoon salt

⅛ teaspoon freshly ground black pepper

1 tablespoon mild-flavored oil, such as canola

1. Make the Guacamole: In a small bowl, combine the ingredients and mash with a fork until thoroughly blended. Cover and set aside.

2. Make the Black Bean Burgers: In a food processor, pulse the beans, cornstarch, onion, mayonnaise, chili powder, salt, and pepper until just blended, leaving the mixture slightly chunky. Divide the mixture into 12 portions, about 2 heaping tablespoons each. Shape each portion into a rectangular patty (which fits the tortilla better than a round patty), about 3 inches long and half an inch thick.

3. Heat the oil in a large nonstick skillet over medium heat. Add 4 patties, leaving at least 2 inches around each to allow easier turning. Cook until browned on both sides, about 5 to 6 minutes per side, turning once very gently. Repeat with remaining patties. Place on a plate and cover with foil to keep warm.

4. Wipe out the skillet and warm each tortilla in the skillet over medium heat until lightly browned and pliable. Keep turning the tortillas to check their progress; you want little brown splotches on at least one side but don't burn them.

5. To assemble, nestle two tortillas together, browned side out. Fill with 1 black bean burger and a dollop of the guacamole, and sprinkle with lettuce, *pico de gallo*, and jicama. Fold in half gently. Serve immediately.

Calories 430 · Fat 12g · Protein 11g · Carbohydrates 74g · Cholesterol 1mg · Sodium 511mg · Fiber 12g

Pinto Bean–Polenta Fajitas with Tomatillo Sauce

Fajitas are similar to tacos, except a larger (usually flour) tortilla is used instead of corn tortillas. They can be filled with anything you wish, but here we use crisp-baked polenta wedges, pinto beans, bell peppers, onions, and red cabbage slaw—all topped with salsa verde (green salsa) made from tomatillos. This may seem like a lot of ingredients, but they come together nicely in this delightful and colorful dish. *Queso fresco* is a type of fresh Mexican cheese with a crumbly texture. **SERVES 4 (MAKES 8 FAJITAS)**

8 8-inch GF flour tortillas

½ cup chopped fresh cilantro

½ cup *queso fresco* or vegan cheese (optional)

POLENTA WEDGES

1 tube (18 ounces) prepared polenta, whatever flavor you like

Cooking spray

½ teaspoon dried oregano, or 2 teaspoons chopped fresh

½ teaspoon sea salt, or to taste

RED CABBAGE SLAW

½ cup red cabbage, finely shredded

1 cup store-bought tomatillo sauce, or more as desired, divided

1 teaspoon agave nectar

PINTO BEANS

1 can (15 ounces) pinto beans, drained and rinsed

½ teaspoon dried oregano, or 2 teaspoons chopped fresh

½ teaspoon chili powder

½ teaspoon ground cumin

¼ teaspoon sea salt

1 tablespoon canola oil

3 large bell peppers (preferably red, green, and yellow for color)

½ cup sliced white onion

1 small garlic clove, minced

1. Preheat the oven to 425°F. Lightly coat a 13 x 18-inch rimmed nonstick baking sheet with cooking spray.

2. Make the Polenta Wedges: Cut the polenta tube in half crosswise, then cut each half in half, lengthwise, to form 4 pieces. Cut each piece into 6 wedges so you have 24 wedges. Arrange the wedges in a single layer on the baking sheet and coat with cooking spray.

3. Bake until the wedges are lightly browned and crisp, turning once, about 35 to 40 minutes. Remove from the oven and lightly sprinkle with oregano and salt. Keep warm while assembling tacos.

4. Make the Red Cabbage Slaw: While the polenta wedges brown, combine the red cabbage with 2 tablespoons of the tomatillo sauce, and the agave, and toss to coat thoroughly. Cover and set aside.

5. Make the Pinto Beans: In a 9-inch skillet, heat the pinto beans, oregano, chili powder, cumin, and salt over medium heat until warm. Slightly mash the beans with a fork. Transfer the beans to a bowl and cover to keep warm.

6. Make the Vegetables: Wipe out the skillet with a paper towel and heat the canola oil over medium-low heat. Add the bell peppers, onion, and garlic, and cook, stirring occasionally, until the vegetables are tender, about 5 minutes. Transfer the vegetables to a plate and cover to keep warm.

7. Wipe the skillet with a paper towel and fill with 1 inch of water. Bring the water to a boil and steam each tortilla on a splatter guard set over the skillet, covered with a lid, until soft and pliable, about 10 seconds. Although it is best to fill each tortilla right after you steam it because it is most pliable then, you can place tortillas between sheets of waxed paper to keep warm and soft while steaming other tortillas. If they become hard, steam them again.

8. To assemble the fajitas, spread a scant ¼ cup of beans in each tortilla, then divide the polenta wedges, red cabbage slaw, vegetables, cilantro, and *queso fresco* (if using) into

each and drizzle with the remaining tomatillo sauce, to taste. Roll the tortilla up and eat immediately.

Calories 820 · Fat 23g · Protein 25g · Carbohydrates 126g · Cholesterol 3mg · Sodium 1710mg · Fiber 13g

Polenta Croutons: Cut the polenta into ½-inch rounds, then cut each round into quarters and toss with 1 teaspoon Italian seasoning and ¼ teaspoon garlic powder. Bake as directed in Step 3. Serve as polenta croutons on mixed green salads.

Falafel with Dill Yogurt Sauce

Falafel is a Middle-Eastern bean fritter, made from chickpeas (garbanzo beans). Devotees fiercely defend their versions; I provide a very basic recipe here that you can customize to suit your tastes. My version is much less time-consuming than the traditional one, which starts with dried chickpeas; if you're averse to frying, you can bake the patties instead. The dill yogurt sauce is a nice alternative to the tahini sauce sometimes served with falafel.

SERVES 8 (MAKES 16 SMALL PATTIES)

DILL YOGURT SAUCE

1 cup plain yogurt (coconut, cow, or soy) or Yogurt (page 249)

1 to 2 tablespoons chopped fresh dill, or to taste

2 tablespoons chopped English cucumber

2 tablespoons chopped onion

1 small garlic clove, minced

1 tablespoon fresh lemon juice

½ teaspoon cayenne pepper

Salt and pepper

FALAFEL

1 can (15 ounces) chickpeas (1½ cups), rinsed, drained, and patted dry

¼ cup finely chopped onion

2 tablespoons chopped fresh cilantro or parsley

2 large garlic cloves, minced (or to taste)

1 teaspoon coriander

½ teaspoon cumin

½ teaspoon sea salt

⅛ teaspoon crushed red pepper flakes

2 tablespoons chickpea flour or other bean flour (navy bean, fava, or white bean)

neutral oil for frying, such as corn or grapeseed

Cooking spray, for baking the falafel patties

1. Make the Dill Yogurt Sauce: In a small bowl, whisk together all the ingredients. Refrigerate, covered, until ready to serve.
2. Make the Falafel: In a food processor, combine the chickpeas, onion, cilantro or parsley, garlic, coriander, cumin, salt, crushed red pepper flakes, and chickpea flour, and pulse a

few times to mash the beans. Scrape down the sides of the bowl and pulse again, scraping the sides again, until a coarse, thick paste forms. With wet hands, shape the mixture into 16 balls, about a generous tablespoon each, then flatten slightly into a patty.

3. Heat ½ inch of oil in a large, heavy skillet over medium heat. Fry the patties until crisp and golden brown, about 5 to 7 minutes per side. Frying time will depend on the size of the patties and the temprature of the oil, which should be about 350°F. If you prefer, bake the patties on a parchment-lined 9 x 13-inch nonstick baking sheet until dry and crisp, about 20 to 35 minutes, turning once. Lightly coat the patties with cooking spray to aid in browning.

Calories 80 · Fat 1g · Protein 5g · Carbohydrates 13g · Cholesterol 1mg ·
Sodium 87mg · Fiber 1g

Quinoa Pilaf with Pine Nuts and Dried Fruit

Quinoa is the foundation ingredient in this fragrant dish; experiment with other combinations of fruit and nuts—perhaps dried cranberries and pistachios for the holidays, or dried apricots and pine nuts for summer. It makes a large batch, perfect for a buffet table or large party. And the leftovers are just as delicious. **SERVES 8**

1 cup whole-grain quinoa

2 teaspoons olive oil

1 small yellow onion, diced

2 cups homemade Vegetable Broth (page 245) or GF store-bought vegetable broth

1 small garlic clove, minced

½ teaspoon ground cinnamon

½ teaspoon sea salt

½ cup dried cranberries

½ cup candied ginger root, chopped into ¼-inch pieces

½ cup pine nuts, toasted, plus extra for garnish

¼ cup chopped fresh parsley, plus extra for garnish

2 tablespoons white wine vinegar

2 tablespoons extra-virgin olive oil

1 tablespoon agave nectar or honey

Salt and freshly ground black pepper

1. Toast the quinoa in a heavy medium saucepan over medium heat, stirring often, until it becomes aromatic and begins to crackle, about 5 minutes.

2. Add the oil and onion to the saucepan and cook over medium heat, stirring constantly, about 1 minute. Add the broth, garlic, cinnamon, and salt. Increase the heat to high and bring to a boil. Reduce heat to medium-low and simmer, covered, until the quinoa is tender and the liquid is absorbed, about 15 to 18 minutes. Remove from the heat and let cool slightly. Drain any excess liquid. Stir in the cranberries, ginger, pine nuts, and parsley.

3. Combine the vinegar, oil, and agave nectar in a glass jar with a lid and shake until well blended. Transfer the quinoa to a medium bowl and toss with as much of the dressing as you like. Add salt and pepper to taste. Serve warm—or chill overnight, then let stand at room temperature for 20 minutes—and garnish with the parsley and pine nuts.

Calories 220 · Fat 10g · Protein 5g · Carbohydrates 29g · Cholesterol 0mg · Sodium 124mg · Fiber 2g

Warm Millet Salad

Although we call it a grain, millet is a grass seed that is very high in protein, and due to its high alkalinity, it is one of the easier grains to digest. I feel that it is one of our more underutilized gluten-free grains, so incorporate this easy, tasty dish into your diet and you'll be doing yourself a favor. **SERVES 4**

3½ cups homemade Vegetable Broth (page 245) or GF store-bought vegetable broth

1 cup whole-grain millet

1 tablespoon chopped fresh rosemary

½ teaspoon sea salt

2 tablespoons olive oil

1 small onion, diced

1 celery rib, diced

¼ cup dried cranberries

¼ cup sherry vinegar

2 tablespoons agave nectar or honey

½ cup seedless green or red grapes

¼ cup walnuts, coarsely chopped

Salt and pepper to taste

1. In a medium heavy saucepan, bring the broth to a boil. Add the millet, rosemary, and salt, and cook, covered, over low heat until the grains are soft, about 35 to 40 minutes. Drain any excess liquid.

2. Meanwhile, in a large heavy saucepan heat the olive oil over medium heat. Add the onion and celery, and cook, covered, over medium-low heat about 5 minutes, or just until the vegetables are somewhat softened.

3. Add the cooked millet mixture, cranberries, vinegar, and agave to the saucepan, and stir to coat the grains thoroughly. Stir in grapes and walnuts, and add salt and pepper to taste. Serve warm.

Calories 350 · Fat 13g · Protein 8g · Carbohydrates 52g · Cholesterol 0mg · Sodium 305mg · Fiber 5g

Moroccan Millet-Stuffed Acorn Squash

Millet by itself is delicious; combined with these fragrant Moroccan spices it is a knockout. This is also a particularly pretty dish, with the millet nestled in the lovely yellow squash. It makes a delightful meal in autumn. **SERVES 4**

2 medium acorn squash, halved crosswise

3 cups homemade Vegetable Broth (page 245) or GF store-bought vegetable broth

½ teaspoon sea salt

1 cup whole-grain millet

½ cup medium onion, finely chopped

1 teaspoon olive oil

2 garlic cloves, minced

½ cup golden raisins

¼ cup chopped fresh cilantro or Italian flat-leaf parsley

½ teaspoon ground cumin

¼ teaspoon ground turmeric

3 tablespoons pine nuts

Dash paprika

1. Preheat the oven to 400°F. Line a 9 x 13-inch glass baking dish with foil and spray with cooking spray.

2. Place the squash, cut sides down, in the dish. Bake until tender, about 35 to 40 minutes. Remove from heat to cool while cooking the millet. Leave the oven on.

3. While the squash bakes, cook the millet: In a medium saucepan, bring the broth to a boil over high heat. Add the salt, millet, and onion, and return to a boil, then reduce the heat to medium-low. Cook, covered, until the millet is tender, about 35 to 40 minutes. Remove the millet from the heat and stir in the oil to coat thoroughly, then stir in the garlic, raisins, cilantro, cumin, and turmeric.

4. With a spoon, scrape out the squashes, leaving ¼ inch of the flesh along the skin (but saving as much of the scooped-out flesh as possible, in a medium bowl, to use in the filling), to create squash bowls. Discard the seeds. Place the scooped-out squashes back in the casserole dish, cut sides up. Add the scooped-out flesh to the millet and fold it in with a spatula until well blended. Divide the millet mixture evenly in the squash shells and press it in with a spatula to create smooth, even mounds. Divide the pine nuts

among the squashes and press them into the millet mixture with your fingers. (They will toast as the squash bakes.) Lightly sprinkle with paprika.

5. Bake until the millet mixture is slightly browned, about 10 to 15 minutes. Serve hot.

Calories 395 · Fat 7g · Protein 10g · Carbohydrates 79g · Cholesterol 0mg · Sodium 249mg · Fiber 9g

AUTUMN DINNER

Cream of Tomato Soup with Crunchy Basil Bread Crumb Topping (page 141)

Moroccan Millet-Stuffed Acorn Squash (page 97)

Mixed green salad

Apple Crisp (page 232)

Sorghum Salad

I am a huge fan of whole-grain sorghum. I love its chewy texture (much like bulgur), and it is one of the more filling gluten-free grains. This recipe makes a large batch, perfect for buffet tables or large dinner parties. Whole-grain sorghum is available from Shiloh Farms (www.glutenfreemall.com). And the leftovers are terrific. You have to plan ahead to make this dish; soaking the grains overnight shortens the cooking time considerably. **SERVES 4 (MAKES 6 CUPS)**

1 cup whole-grain sorghum

3 cups homemade Vegetable Broth (page 245) or GF store-bought vegetable broth

½ teaspoon sea salt

¼ cup dried cranberries or pomegranate seeds

¼ cup chopped pecans

½ whole unpeeled Granny Smith apple, cored and cut in ½-inch pieces

½ unpeeled Honey Crisp or Gala apple, cored and cut in ½-inch pieces

2 green onions, chopped

2 tablespoons chopped fresh thyme, or 1½ teaspoons dried

2 tablespoons chopped fresh parsley or cilantro, plus more for garnish

2 tablespoons sherry vinegar or champagne vinegar

2 tablespoons fresh lemon juice

2 tablespoons extra-virgin olive oil

1 tablespoon agave nectar

1 garlic clove, minced

¼ teaspoon sea salt

⅛ teaspoon freshly ground black pepper

2 cups baby spinach

1. Soak the sorghum in water to cover overnight, then drain and discard the water. In a large pot bring the broth to a boil, add the salt and soaked sorghum, and cook, covered, until tender, about 45 to 50 minutes. Drain well.
2. Transfer the sorghum to a medium bowl and stir in the cranberries, pecans, apples, onions, thyme, and the 2 tablespoons of parsley.
3. In a small bowl, whisk together the vinegar, lemon juice, oil, agave nectar, garlic, salt, and pepper until well blended. Drizzle over the sorghum and toss to coat well, using as much of the dressing as you like. Cover and refrigerate 4 hours to meld the flavors.

4. To serve, let stand at room temperature 20 minutes. Arrange the spinach in a single layer on a large serving platter and top with the sorghum salad. Garnish with the remaining chopped parsley and serve immediately.

Calories 320 · Fat 14g · Protein 7g · Carbohydrates 49g · Cholesterol 0mg · Sodium 371mg · Fiber 9g

Wild Rice Salad

Wild rice isn't really rice at all, but the seed of a grass. It's hearty and chewy, and especially attractive in this dish with its citrusy flavors. Serve it as a buffet dish. **SERVES 4**

3 cups homemade Vegetable Broth (page 245) or GF store-bought vegetable broth

1 cup wild rice, rinsed 3 times and drained

½ teaspoon sea salt

1 cup fresh snow peas

4 green onions, chopped

½ cup chopped dried apricots

¼ cup chopped toasted walnuts

2 tablespoons fresh parsley, plus extra for garnish

¼ cup freshly squeezed orange juice

2 tablespoons sherry vinegar

2 teaspoons orange zest

1 medium garlic clove, minced

¼ teaspoon sea salt

⅛ teaspoon freshly ground black pepper

1 teaspoon extra-virgin olive oil

1. In a large saucepan, bring the broth to a boil over high heat. Add the wild rice and salt. Return to a boil, reduce the heat to low, and simmer, covered, until done, about 45 minutes. Drain any remaining liquid, then transfer the wild rice to a serving bowl.

2. While the wild rice cooks, bring a small pan of water to a boil. Add the snow peas and cook 1 minute, then drain and immerse in cold water to stop cooking. Add them to the serving bowl, along with the green onions, apricots, walnuts, and the 2 tablespoons of parsley.

3. In small bowl, whisk together the orange juice, vinegar, orange zest, garlic, salt, and pepper until well blended. Whisk in the oil until slightly thickened. Drizzle it over the salad and toss to coat well. Serve at room temperature, garnished with the remaining parsley. Or chill it for 4 hours, let stand at room temperature for 20 minutes, and then serve.

Calories 265 · Fat 6g · Protein 10g · Carbohydrates 47g · Cholesterol 0mg · Sodium 378mg · Fiber 6g

Vegetables

The world is truly a magical place when we consider how many marvelous vegetables we have on this planet. Thanks to a renewed interest in eating fresh vegetables (due in part to Michael Pollan and the new White House vegetable garden) and eating locally, it's easier to find wonderful produce in our supermarkets and farmers' markets. I developed this array of recipes to entice you to eat more vegetables. Some are prepared in familiar ways (such as Scalloped Potatoes), but others may be new to you, such as Apple-Fennel Slaw, Kale Salad, and Roasted Carrots and Parsnips. For more tasty vegetable recipes, see my other books: *Wheat-Free Recipes & Menus, Cooking Free,* and *Gluten-Free Quick & Easy.*

• COLD SALADS •

Apple-Fennel Slaw

Broccoli Salad

Kale Salad

Mediterranean Orange-Olive Salad

Spinach Salad with Cannellini

• HOT OR FRIED VEGETABLES •

Bok Choy

Scalloped Potatoes

Grilled Ratatouille Vegetable Stacks

Bistro French Fries

Sweet Potato Fries

Vegetable Tempura with Wasabi Dipping Sauce

• ROASTED VEGETABLES •

Roasted Asparagus with Mustard Cream

Roasted Brussels Sprouts in Orange-Nut Sauce

Roasted Fennel with Garlic and Thyme

Roasted Carrots and Parsnips with Sage Butter

Apple-Fennel Slaw

Apples and fennel have an affinity for each other. A mandoline makes it easier to cut both into extremely thin slices. The tarragon enhances the fennel's licorice flavor in this delicious salad. **SERVES 4**

1 small unpeeled Granny Smith apple, cored and thinly sliced

1 small unpeeled red apple (Fuji, Gala, or Honey Crisp), cored and thinly sliced

1 whole fennel bulb, cut into ¼-inch strips (reserve the fronds)

1 small yellow onion, thinly sliced

2 tablespoons chopped toasted pecans

1½ teaspoons celery seed, or to taste

1 tablespoon chopped fresh tarragon, or 1 teaspoon dried

¼ teaspoon sea salt, or to taste

2 tablespoons vinegar (sherry, champagne, or fruit-infused, such as pear)

2 tablespoons canola oil

1 tablespoon agave nectar or honey

1 teaspoon Dijon mustard

Salt and pepper to taste

1. Place the apples, fennel (plus 1 tablespoon chopped fronds), onion, pecans, celery seed, tarragon, and salt in a serving bowl.
2. In a small bowl, whisk together the vinegar, oil, agave nectar, and mustard until thoroughly blended and slightly thickened. Add the salt and pepper to taste.
3. Pour as much of the dressing as you like over the apple-fennel mixture and toss until it is thoroughly coated. Add salt and pepper to taste, if desired. Refrigerate for 2 hours. Serve cold.

Calories 170 · Fat 10g · Protein 2g · Carbohydrates 22g · Cholesterol 0mg · Sodium 167mg · Fiber 4g

Broccoli Salad

Blanching the broccoli preserves its vibrant green color and makes for a prettier salad. Broccoli is one of the most healthful vegetables on earth, so make it a habit to enjoy it often. This salad is a great place to start. **SERVES 4**

$2/3$ cup mayonnaise or vegan
   mayonnaise

2 tablespoons agave nectar or honey

1 tablespoon red wine vinegar

4 cups broccoli florets

$1/2$ cup dried cranberries

$1/2$ cup slivered almonds

$1/4$ cup diced red onion

1. In a small bowl, whisk together the mayonnaise, agave nectar, and vinegar. Set aside.
2. Have a bowl of ice water ready. Bring a pan of salted water to a boil. Cook the broccoli for 1 minute, then plunge it into the ice water to stop the cooking. Pat the broccoli dry and cut the florets into bite-size pieces. Place them in a serving bowl.
3. Add the cranberries, almonds, and onion to the serving bowl with the broccoli. Add the dressing and toss to coat thoroughly. Refrigerate for 1 to 2 hours before serving. Toss again and serve chilled.

Calories 255 · Fat 17g · Protein 6g · Carbohydrates 24g · Cholesterol 10mg · Sodium 221mg · Fiber 4g

Kale Salad

Kale is a dark green leafy member of the cabbage family. It is chock-full of nutrients and something I recently learned to eat. Now it's a staple in my diet, and I even toss it into my morning smoothies. If you can't find Tuscan, or lacinato, kale (which has smoother blue-green leaves) you may substitute the more common curly kind instead. Use crunchy peanut butter if you like the texture; otherwise go for creamy for a smoother feel. **SERVES 4**

5 cups shredded Tuscan kale (about 1 bunch), cut in 1/8-inch strips

1 medium red bell pepper, seeded, ribs removed, and thinly sliced

1 carrot, peeled and cut in 1/8-inch slices

1/4 cup peanut oil

1/4 cup seasoned rice vinegar

1 tablespoon fresh ginger root, peeled, coarsely chopped

1 tablespoon creamy or crunchy natural peanut butter

1 tablespoon packed light brown sugar

1/4 teaspoon sea salt

2 tablespoons chopped peanuts, for garnish

1. Place the kale strips in a large serving bowl. Add the bell pepper and carrot.
2. In a blender, process the oil, vinegar, ginger, peanut butter, brown sugar, and salt until very smooth. Pour over the kale and toss well to thoroughly coat it with dressing. Serve immediately, garnished with the peanuts.

Calories 240 · Fat 18g · Protein 5g · Carbohydrates 17g · Cholesterol 0mg · Sodium 177mg · Fiber 3g

Mediterranean Orange-Olive Salad

This is a very showy salad, so use your prettiest serving platter to showcase it. It is great for buffets since it can stand at room temperature for a couple of hours. I prefer this salad garnished with cilantro, but you can use parsley instead. **SERVES 6**

4 medium navel oranges, peeled and cut horizontally into ¼-inch rounds

¼ cup toasted slivered almonds

¼ cup stuffed green olives, sliced crosswise

2 tablespoons sliced black olives

2 tablespoons chopped canned pimientos

2 tablespoons minced red onion

Salt and freshly ground black pepper to taste

2 tablespoons white wine vinegar

2 tablespoons extra-virgin olive oil

1 tablespoon grated orange zest

1 tablespoon agave nectar or honey

2 tablespoons chopped fresh cilantro or parsley, for garnish

1. Arrange the oranges in a single layer on the serving platter. Sprinkle the almonds, olives, pimiento, and red onion on top. Season to taste with the salt and pepper. You can cover the salad and refrigerate until serving time.

2. To make the dressing, whisk together the vinegar, oil, orange zest, and agave nectar in a small bowl until thickened. Pour it over the oranges. Sprinkle with the cilantro and serve immediately.

Calories 140 · Fat 9g · Protein 2g · Carbohydrates 16g · Cholesterol 0mg · Sodium 115mg · Fiber 3g

Spinach Salad with Cannellini

Use the spinach as the basis for many variations on this nutritious dish. You can substitute your favorite beans for the cannellini (white kidney beans) if you wish. See below for suggested beans and the spice blends that complement them. **SERVES 4**

1 can (15 ounces) cannellini beans, rinsed and drained

2 plum or Roma tomatoes, or 6 grape tomatoes, diced

½ cup black olives, halved horizontally

½ small red onion, thinly sliced

1 tablespoon vinegar (sherry, red wine, or white wine)

2 teaspoons Dijon mustard

½ teaspoon Italian seasoning (or your favorite seasoning)

1 small garlic clove, minced

3 tablespoons extra-virgin olive oil

¼ teaspoon sea salt, or to taste

¼ teaspoon freshly ground black pepper, or to taste

8 cups baby spinach

1. In a large salad bowl, combine the beans, tomatoes, olives, and onion.
2. In a small jar with a tight-fitting lid, combine the vinegar, mustard, Italian seasoning, and garlic, and shake vigorously until combined. Add the olive oil and shake vigorously until thoroughly blended and slightly thickened. Add the salt and pepper, to taste. Toss with the bean mixture.
3. Just before serving, add the spinach to the salad bowl and toss gently to thoroughly coat the spinach leaves. Serve immediately.

Calories 235 · Fat 13g · Protein 9g · Carbohydrates 24g · Cholesterol 0mg · Sodium 336mg · Fiber 7g

FLAVOR VARIATIONS:

Cajun: black-eyed peas, green beans, and Creole seasoning

Greek: butter beans, feta cheese, oregano, and capers

Mexican: pinto beans, avocados, and Fajita or taco seasoning

Bok Choy

Bok choy is a leafy green from the cabbage family, with bulbous white stems. It can be prepared in a variety of ways; this technique uses an Asian theme with crunchy peanuts. I'm especially fond of baby bok choy, which is a miniature version of the larger variety. Use three baby bok choy instead of a single large one, if you wish—green leaves and all.

SERVES 4

3 tablespoons gluten-free tamari soy sauce

1 tablespoon Thai Kitchen sweet red chili sauce

1/4 cup orange juice

2 tablespoons peanut oil

2 tablespoons toasted sesame oil

1 tablespoon peeled, grated fresh ginger root

1 large bok choy (about 2 pounds), trimmed and sliced in 1-inch strips

1/4 cup chopped peanuts

1. In a small bowl, whisk together the soy sauce, chili sauce, and orange juice. Set aside.

2. In a large skillet or wok, heat the peanut oil and sesame oil over medium heat. Add the ginger and bok choy and cook for 2 minutes, stirring and tossing constantly. Add the soy sauce mixture, cover, and simmer for 2 minutes. Serve hot, sprinkled with the peanuts.

Calories 190 · Fat 18g · Protein 4g · Carbohydrates 4g · Cholesterol 0mg · Sodium 768mg · Fiber 1g

Scalloped Potatoes

Yukon Gold potatoes are the perfect choice for this down-home dish because they are creamier than other potato varieties when cooked. **SERVES 4**

2 cups milk of choice, divided

2 tablespoons sweet rice flour

2 tablespoons butter or buttery spread

2 tablespoons Parmesan cheese or soy
  Parmesan, divided

1 tablespoon Dijon mustard

1 tablespoon minced onions

1 teaspoon onion powder

1 teaspoon sea salt

1/4 teaspoon freshly ground black pepper

1/8 teaspoon freshly grated nutmeg

1 pound Yukon Gold potatoes
  (3 to 4 medium)

1/2 teaspoon paprika, for garnish

1. Place a rack in the middle of the oven. Preheat the oven to 375°F. Generously grease a 9 x 9-inch glass baking dish with at least 2-inch sides.

2. Place 1½ cups of the milk in a 2-quart saucepan. In a small bowl, whisk the sweet rice flour into the remaining ½ cup of milk until very smooth and then whisk it into the saucepan. Add the butter, 1 tablespoon of the Parmesan cheese, the Dijon mustard, minced onions, onion powder, salt, pepper, and nutmeg.

3. Place the pan over medium heat and cook, stirring constantly, until the mixture thickens slightly, about 4 to 5 minutes. Remove from the heat and let the sauce cool slightly while preparing the potatoes.

4. Peel the potatoes and cut them into 1/8-inch slices (a mandoline makes quick work of this task). Arrange a third of the potatoes in the bottom of the dish, overlapping the slices slightly. Pour a third of the sauce over the potatoes. Repeat two more times, ending with the sauce. Dust with the remaining tablespoon of Parmesan cheese. Cover the dish with aluminum foil and place on a rimmed baking sheet to catch any spillovers.

5. Bake until the potatoes are tender, about 40 to 45 minutes. Remove the foil and bake until the top is lightly browned, about 10 minutes. Serve hot, dusted with the paprika for garnish.

Calories 235 · Fat 8g · Protein 8g · Carbohydrates 32g · Cholesterol 22mg · Sodium 633mg · Fiber 2g

Grilled Ratatouille Vegetable Stacks

Remember the scene in the movie *Ratatouille* where the restaurant critic eats Remy's version of this home-style French classic? He probably would have been surprised at this decidedly modern version, but your guests will admire its beauty even before they take their first bite. The more definite the grill marks, the prettier the stacks will look. **SERVES 4**

1 medium eggplant, unpeeled and sliced in ¼-inch rounds

Salt and pepper

1 medium green zucchini, unpeeled, cut in ¼-inch rounds

1 medium yellow zucchini, cut in ¼-inch rounds

1 small red onion, cut in ¼-inch rounds but rings not separated

1 medium tomato, cut in ¼-inch rounds

⅓ cup extra-virgin olive oil, divided

¼ cup sherry vinegar or red wine vinegar

4 tablespoons minced fresh basil

2 tablespoons minced fresh parsley

1 tablespoon minced fresh thyme

2 small garlic cloves, minced

4 teaspoons grated Parmesan cheese or soy Parmesan

1. Sprinkle the eggplant rounds with salt and place them in a colander to drain for 20 minutes. Pat them dry with paper towels. Lightly brush the eggplant, zucchini, onion, and tomatoes with some of the olive oil.

2. Preheat a grill to medium-high. Grill the vegetables, turning only once, until done and grill marks are visible. Grilling times will vary; tomatoes may take just a few seconds, while eggplant, onion, and zucchini may take 2 to 4 minutes per side.

3. Whisk together the remaining oil, vinegar, basil, parsley, thyme, and garlic until smooth, adding more salt and pepper to taste, if desired. (If you wish, prepare the dressing 30 minutes ahead to let the herbs meld together.)

4. Stack the vegetables on 4 salad plates, starting with a round of eggplant, then the green zucchini, the red onion, the yellow zucchini, and the tomato. Drizzle generously with the dressing and dust each stack with a teaspoon of the Parmesan cheese. Serve hot or at room temperature.

Calories 245 · Fat 19g · Protein 4g · Carbohydrates 18g · Cholesterol 1mg · Sodium 46mg · Fiber 6g

Bistro French Fries

Homemade French fries are so easy to make and allow us to avoid the conundrum in restaurants where they're often fried in the same oil as gluten-containing items. Serve them bistro-style according to the suggestion below. Even though we often favor fresh parsley, this is one dish where dried parsley works far better because its small, dry, delicate texture doesn't overwhelm the fries. **SERVES 4**

4 medium russet potatoes, peeled and cut in ½-inch strips

2 tablespoons olive oil

1 teaspoon sea salt, divided

1 teaspoon onion powder

1 tablespoon dried parsley, for garnish

1. Preheat the oven to 450°F. Line a 10 x 15-inch rimmed baking sheet (not nonstick) with parchment paper.
2. Toss the potatoes with the oil. Combine half of the salt and all of the onion powder, sprinkle on the potatoes, and toss again to coat thoroughly. Arrange the slices in an even layer on the baking sheet.
3. Bake until the potatoes are tender, about 30 minutes, turning once. Remove from the oven and sprinkle with the remaining salt and the parsley. Serve immediately.

Calories 120 · Fat 7g · Protein 2g · Carbohydrates 14g · Cholesterol 0mg · Sodium 476mg · Fiber 1g

Everyday to Elegant

Serve in a wire French-fry holder or use a wire bread basket or a wide-mouthed drinking glass or a pint mason jar. Wrap a piece of white parchment paper into a scroll and place it in the container. Arrange the hot French fries inside the scroll, ends up, and dust with dried parsley for garnish. Serve immediately.

Sweet Potato Fries

This is a much healthier way to enjoy sweet potatoes than frying them in oil. Try the ancho chile powder for a really flavorful punch, but if it doesn't agree with you, then try either the thyme or coriander instead. **SERVES 4**

4 small sweet potatoes, peeled and cut in ½-inch strips

2 tablespoons olive oil

1 teaspoon sea salt, divided

½ teaspoon ancho chile powder (or dried thyme or ground coriander)

1. Preheat the oven to 450°F. Line a 10 x 15-inch rimmed baking sheet (not nonstick) with parchment paper.
2. Toss the potatoes with the oil. Combine half of the salt and all of the ancho chile powder and sprinkle on the potatoes. Toss to coat thoroughly. Arrange the slices in an even layer on the baking sheet.
3. Bake until the potatoes are tender, about 30 minutes, turning once. Remove from the oven and sprinkle with the remaining salt. Serve immediately.

Calories 195 · Fat 7g · Protein 2g · Carbohydrates 32g · Cholesterol 0mg · Sodium 490mg · Fiber 4g

Vegetable Tempura with Wasabi Dipping Sauce

This dish is best served as soon as the vegetables are fried. So it makes a great choice for dinner parties where everyone gathers in the kitchen around the cook (at a safe distance to escape hot bubbling oil!) and then eats in stages, along with a frosty mug of gluten-free beer or sake. This makes a light meal; for a heartier main course, double the vegetables.

SERVES 4 FOR A LIGHT MEAL

WASABI DIPPING SAUCE

1½ tablespoons low-sodium gluten-free tamari soy sauce

1 tablespoon rice wine vinegar

1 tablespoon mirin (rice wine)

1 tablespoon fresh lemon juice

1 teaspoon wasabi powder, or to taste

VEGETABLES

1 small sweet potato, peeled and cut in ¼-inch slices

1 small eggplant, halved lengthwise and cut in ¼-inch slices

1 cup button mushrooms, cleaned and cut in ¼-inch slices

1 small red bell pepper, seeded and cut in ¼-inch slices

12 thin asparagus spears, trimmed of woody ends

BATTER

1½ cups white rice flour, divided

1 cup cornstarch

2 teaspoons baking powder

½ teaspoon sea salt

1½ cups club soda or sparkling water, or more to thin batter

Peanut oil for frying

1. Make the Wasabi Dipping Sauce: In a small bowl, whisk together the soy sauce, rice wine vinegar, mirin, lemon juice, and wasabi powder until smooth. Set aside.
2. Prepare the vegetables and pat them dry with a paper towel so the batter will stick to them. Line a rimmed baking sheet with paper towels for draining the fried vegetables.
3. Make the Batter: In a shallow bowl, whisk together 1 cup of the rice flour, the cornstarch, baking powder, and salt. Whisk in the club soda until the batter is smooth. It should be the consistency of melted ice cream.
4. Heat 2 to 3 inches of the peanut oil to 375°F in a wok or deep fryer. Dust the vegetables with the remaining ½ cup of rice flour and shake off any excess. Working in batches, dip the vegetables into the batter and gently shake off any excess, then gently place 4 or 5 pieces of the same type of vegetable in the hot oil. Do not overcrowd the vegetables. Fry until light golden brown, then remove to the lined baking sheet to drain. Serve immediately with the dipping sauce.

Calories 465 · Fat 1g · Protein 9g · Carbohydrates 101g · Cholesterol 0mg · Sodium 1487mg · Fiber 8g

Roasted Asparagus
with Mustard Cream

While Dijon mustard sounds more elegant, good old ballpark yellow mustard makes a prettier, more full-flavored sauce for this asparagus, which becomes mellower in flavor when roasted. **SERVES 4**

1 pound fresh asparagus, preferably medium-size stalks

1 tablespoon extra-virgin olive oil

½ teaspoon coarse salt

¼ teaspoon freshly ground black pepper

MUSTARD CREAM

¼ cup nonfat sour cream or vegan sour cream

1 tablespoon yellow mustard

2 tablespoons fresh lemon juice, or enough to make a thin sauce

Salt and freshly ground black pepper, to taste

1. Preheat the oven to 400°F.
2. With your hands, break off the tough ends from the asparagus spears. Place them on a 9 x 13-inch baking sheet, drizzle with the olive oil, then toss to coat the asparagus completely. Make sure the asparagus is in a single layer for even roasting and then sprinkle with the salt and pepper.
3. Roast the asparagus for 20 minutes, or until tender but still crisp. Do not over-roast.
4. While the asparagus roasts, whisk together the sour cream, mustard, and lemon juice until smooth. Add the salt and pepper to taste. Serve the asparagus hot, drizzled with the mustard cream.

Calories 60 · Fat 4g · Protein 3g · Carbohydrates 5g · Cholesterol 2mg · Sodium 298mg · Fiber 1g

Everyday to Exceptional

Sprinkle 1½ teaspoons rinsed and drained capers on top of the asparagus just before serving. Their salty, briny flavor and chewiness contrast nicely with the mellow roasted asparagus.

Roasted Brussels Sprouts in Orange-Nut Sauce

Blanching the sprouts briefly in boiling water helps preserve their lovely green color. If you don't have time or don't mind the loss of color, you can skip Step 2.

1 pound Brussels sprouts

2 tablespoons olive oil

¼ teaspoon sea salt

¼ teaspoon freshly ground black pepper

3 tablespoons orange marmalade

1½ tablespoons sherry vinegar

¼ cup chopped toasted walnuts

1. Place a rack in the middle of the oven. Preheat the oven to 400°F. Line a 9 x 13-inch baking sheet with parchment paper. Have a medium bowl of water and ice cubes ready.
2. Bring a large pot of water to a boil. Remove any bruised outer leaves from the Brussels sprouts and cut them in half through the stem end. Cook in boiling water for 3 minutes. Remove them from the water with a slotted spoon and immediately submerge them in the ice water for 2 minutes to stop the cooking, then blot dry with paper towels.
3. In a medium bowl, toss the Brussels sprouts with the olive oil and arrange on the baking sheet, cut side down. Sprinkle with the salt and pepper.
4. Roast until caramelized, about 25 to 30 minutes. Transfer to a serving bowl. Whisk the marmalade and vinegar together and then toss with the Brussels sprouts. Sprinkle with the toasted nuts and serve immediately.

Calories 194 · Fat 12g · Protein 5g · Carbohydrates 21g · Cholesterol 0mg · Sodium 150mg · Fiber 6g

Roasted Fennel with Garlic and Thyme

If you've never tried roasted fennel, you're in for a treat. I grew it in my garden pots for the first time last summer and used the anise-flavored fronds in many dishes. While it is delicious raw in salads, roasting elevates it to a whole new level of flavor. **SERVES 4**

2 whole fennel bulbs, sliced (about 3 cups), plus 3 tablespoons chopped fronds

2 tablespoons extra-virgin olive oil

2 tablespoons fresh thyme, or 2 teaspoons dried

½ teaspoon sea salt

¼ teaspoon freshly ground black pepper

2 garlic cloves, minced

1 tablespoon sherry vinegar

1. Preheat the oven to 450°F.
2. Combine the fennel, 2 tablespoons of the chopped fronds, and the oil, thyme, salt, and pepper in a large bowl and toss to thoroughly coat. Spread the fennel evenly on a 9 x 13-inch rimmed baking sheet (not nonstick).
3. Roast for 12 to 15 minutes, or until the fennel just starts to brown. Stir in the garlic and continue roasting another 5 minutes. Toss with the remaining tablespoon of fennel fronds, drizzle with the sherry vinegar, and toss to coat thoroughly. Serve immediately.

Calories 100 · Fat 7g · Protein 2g · Carbohydrates 10g · Cholesterol 0mg · Sodium 296mg · Fiber 4g

Roasted Carrots and Parsnips with Sage Butter

During my travels in Europe, I observed that parsnips are far more popular there. I hope this recipe convinces you to give them a try. If your parsnips are especially large, slice away the core, which tends to be woody. Both carrots and parsnips become much sweeter when roasted. I've even eaten roasted parsnips for breakfast at a world-famous spa, so feel free to serve them anytime. **SERVES 4**

½ pound parsnips, peeled and thinly sliced in ¼-inch strips

½ pound carrots, peeled and thinly sliced in ¼-inch strips

1 tablespoon extra-virgin olive oil

½ teaspoon sea salt

¼ teaspoon freshly ground black pepper

1½ tablespoons unsalted butter or buttery spread

10 fresh sage leaves, chopped, or ½ teaspoon dried, plus extra for garnish

1. Place a rack in the middle of the oven. Preheat the oven to 375°F. Line a 9 x 13-inch baking sheet (not nonstick) with parchment paper.
2. In a large bowl, toss the parsnips and carrots with the oil until well coated. Add the salt and pepper and toss to coat thoroughly, then arrange in a single layer on the baking sheet.
3. Roast until tender and lightly browned, about 20 to 25 minutes.
4. While the vegetables roast, melt the butter in a small saucepan over medium heat. Add the sage and cook just until it is slightly crispy, being careful not to burn the butter.
5. Transfer the vegetables to a serving bowl, drizzle the sage-butter mixture over them, and toss gently to coat thoroughly. Garnish with the remaining sage leaves and serve hot.

Calories 130 · Fat 8g · Protein 1g · Carbohydrates 14g · Cholesterol 12mg · Sodium 258mg · Fiber 4g

Soups and Stews

Soups and stews may sound innocent enough, but in reality they're often huge stumbling blocks for gluten-free diets because they can contain hidden thickeners such as wheat flour. And they're often laden with dairy as well. So rest easy and enjoy these wonderful dishes that use other ways to make thick, creamy, and delicious soups. Of course, you can use cream or half-and-half if you wish, but I suggest using plain coffee creamers made of soy or coconut instead. For more soup and stew recipes, see my other books: *Wheat-Free Recipes & Menus, Cooking Free,* and *Gluten-Free Quick & Easy.*

· BEANS, PEAS, AND LENTILS ·

Cincinnati Chili

Lentil Soup

Minestrone

Creamy Asparagus Soup with Crispy Bread Crumbs

Borscht (Beet Soup)

Cream of Broccoli Soup

Butternut Squash Soup with Chipotle Cream

Carrot-Ginger Soup with Chile-Lime Pepitas

Chilled and Dilled Cucumber-Apple Soup

Gazpacho Shooters (see the Little Meals or Appetizers chapter)

Miso Soup with Wakame

Cream of Mushroom Soup

Spring Green Pea Soup

Creamy Potato-Leek Soup with Dill

Cream of Tomato Soup with Crunchy Basil Bread Crumb Topping

Thai Corn Chowder

Posole with Crispy Tortilla Strips

Vegetable Soup with Dumplings

Cincinnati Chili

Even better when reheated the next day, this classic is filling, and satisfies our craving for hearty food. What sets it apart from traditional Southwestern chili is the fact that it's eaten over spaghetti and can be adorned with many garnishes. It's also a good way to get more fiber into your diet in the form of beans. **SERVES 6**

1 tablespoon olive oil

1 large onion, chopped

1 large garlic clove, minced

1 small red bell pepper or green bell pepper, seeded and diced

1 large can (28 ounces) tomatoes, preferably fire-roasted, undrained

1 cup water

1 can (15 ounces) dark red kidney beans, rinsed and drained

1 can (15 ounces) light red kidney beans, rinsed and drained

1 tablespoon yellow mustard

1 tablespoon chili powder

1 teaspoon ground cumin

1 teaspoon sea salt, or to taste

1/2 teaspoon dried oregano, or 2 teaspoons chopped fresh

1/4 teaspoon ground cinnamon

1/4 teaspoon ground cloves

1/8 teaspoon freshly grated nutmeg or ground allspice

8 ounces GF spaghetti

4 whole green onions, finely chopped, for garnish

1 cup shredded low-fat cheddar cheese or vegan cheese, for garnish

1/2 cup chopped cilantro, for garnish

1. In a medium saucepan, heat the oil over medium heat. Add the onion and cook, stirring occasionally, until tender, about 4 minutes. Add the garlic and bell pepper, and cook another minute, stirring constantly.
2. Add the tomatoes (including juices), water, beans, mustard, chili powder, cumin, salt, oregano, cinnamon, cloves, and nutmeg. Bring to a boil, reduce the heat to low, and simmer, covered, for 45 minutes.
3. Cook the spaghetti according to package directions until done; drain thoroughly and keep warm.
4. Serve the chili over bowls of spaghetti, garnished with the green onions, cheese, and cilantro.

Calories 425 · Fat 6g · Protein 24g · Carbohydrates 72g · Cholesterol 4mg · Sodium 679mg · Fiber 13g

Lentil Soup

It is sad that lentils aren't a staple in Americans' diets; they should be. They're chock-full of nutrients, provide important fiber, and are fairly mild in flavor, which makes them the perfect tableau on which to base many dishes. You'll love the depth provided by the smoked paprika, so give it a try. If you use any lentils other than brown ones, the cooking time and amount of water required may vary. **SERVES 4 (MAKES 4 CUPS)**

1 tablespoon canola oil

1 small onion, finely chopped

1 large carrot, peeled, sliced in 1/8-inch coins

2 celery ribs, cut in 1-inch cubes

1 cup brown lentils

5 cups homemade Vegetable Broth (page 245) or GF store-bought vegetable broth

1 1/2 teaspoons herbes de Provence or fines herbes

1/2 teaspoon sea salt, or more to taste

1/2 teaspoon freshly ground black pepper

1/2 teaspoon smoked paprika, optional

1 teaspoon sherry vinegar, optional

1/4 cup chopped fresh parsley, for garnish

1. In a medium saucepan, heat the oil over medium heat. Add the onion, carrot, and celery, and cook, stirring constantly, until the onion is tender, about 5 minutes. Add the lentils, broth, herbes de Provence, salt, pepper, and smoked paprika.

2. Bring the mixture to a boil, reduce the heat to low, and simmer, covered, until the lentils are tender, about 45 to 60 minutes. Add more broth if the mixture becomes dry. Stir in the vinegar, and more salt and pepper, if desired. Serve hot, garnished with parsley.

Calories 215 · Fat 4g · Protein 14g · Carbohydrates 33g · Cholesterol 0mg · Sodium 265mg · Fiber 16g

Minestrone

This is Italian comfort food at its best, perfect for a cold winter's night. This classic allows you to load up on vegetables and savor all the wonderful herbs that make this soup so flavorful. Feel free to use whatever vegetables you have on hand. Use this soup as a way to incorporate the highly nutritious edamame (young green soybeans) into your diet.

SERVES 6 (MAKES 10 CUPS)

1 tablespoon olive oil

1 small onion, chopped

2 garlic cloves, minced

1 large can (28 ounces) tomatoes, preferably fire-roasted, undrained

1 small carrot, cut in ½-inch diagonal slices

4 cups homemade Vegetable Broth (page 245) or GF store-bought vegetable broth

¼ pound green beans, cut in 1-inch pieces, or frozen edamame, thawed (about 1 cup)

2 small new potatoes, unpeeled, cut in ½-inch cubes

¼ teaspoon crushed red pepper flakes

1 teaspoon dried basil

1 teaspoon dried thyme

½ teaspoon dried sage

½ teaspoon dried oregano, or 2 teaspoons chopped fresh

½ teaspoon sea salt, or to taste

¼ teaspoon freshly ground black pepper

1 can (15 ounces) white kidney beans, rinsed and drained

1 small yellow zucchini, sliced in ¼-inch coins

1 cup fresh baby spinach

¼ cup GF elbow macaroni

½ cup Parmesan cheese or soy Parmesan, divided

1. In a 6-quart saucepan, heat the olive oil over medium-low heat. Add the onion and cook, covered, stirring occasionally, until tender, about 5 minutes. Add the garlic, tomatoes, carrot, broth, green beans, potatoes, red pepper flakes, basil, thyme, sage, oregano, salt, and pepper. Bring to a boil, reduce the heat to low, and simmer, covered, 15 minutes.

2. Add the kidney beans, zucchini, spinach, macaroni, and ¼ cup of the Parmesan cheese. Bring to a boil, reduce the heat to low, and simmer, covered, until the pasta is done, about 10 minutes. Taste and add more salt and seasonings, if necessary.

3. Ladle the soup into 6 bowls and garnish each with a heaping tablespoon of Parmesan.

Calories 375 · Fat 5g · Protein 22g · Carbohydrates 63g · Cholesterol 5mg · Sodium 502mg · Fiber 14g

Creamy Asparagus Soup with Crispy Bread Crumbs

Lovely and green, this soup is especially nice when made with the first asparagus of spring. Potatoes may seem an odd ingredient in asparagus soup, but their role is to make the soup thick and creamy without any additional thickeners (like the typical wheat flour often used). As you'll see, it works beautifully. **SERVES 4 (MAKES 6 CUPS)**

1½ teaspoons sea salt, divided

1 pound asparagus (about 1 bunch), trimmed and chopped in 2-inch pieces

2 tablespoons butter or buttery spread

1 small onion, or 1 whole leek (white part only), cleaned and chopped

2 cups russet potatoes, peeled, chopped in 1-inch cubes

2 garlic cloves, chopped

½ cup chopped fresh parsley, plus more for garnish

¼ cup chopped fresh thyme

1 whole bay leaf

½ cup fat-free half-and-half or plain coffee creamer (soy or coconut)

1 tablespoon dry vermouth, white wine, dry sherry, or red wine vinegar

Freshly ground black pepper

1 tablespoon capers, rinsed and drained, for garnish

4 tablespoons Crunchy Bread Crumbs (page 141; omit the basil)

Hungarian hot paprika, for garnish

1. Place a medium bowl containing ice water and ½ teaspoon salt by the cooktop. Bring a large pot of water to a boil and add ½ teaspoon salt. Working in 2 batches, add the asparagus to the boiling water and cook until just tender, about 3 minutes per batch. With a slotted spoon, quickly transfer the asparagus to the bowl of ice water. Drain. Reserve 3½ cups of the cooking liquid in a large measuring cup or bowl.

2. Return the large pot to the cooktop and melt the butter over medium heat. Add the onion and cook, covered, stirring occasionally, until soft, about 5 minutes. Pour in the reserved asparagus cooking liquid, bring to a boil, and add the final ½ teaspoon salt. Add the potatoes, garlic, parsley, thyme, and bay leaf, and bring to a boil again. Reduce the heat to low and simmer, covered, until the potatoes are done, about 10 to 15 minutes. Discard the bay leaf and add the asparagus.

3. Transfer half of the asparagus mixture to a blender, add ¼ cup of the half-and-half, and puree until smooth. Repeat with the remaining half of the asparagus mixture and half-and-half. Return the puree to the pot and bring to serving temperature over medium heat, stirring constantly.

4. Stir in the vermouth and taste, adding additional salt and the pepper to taste, if necessary. Divide among warmed soup bowls, sprinkle each soup with a few capers, and garnish with a tablespoon of the bread crumbs. Dust with the hot paprika and serve immediately.

Calories 215 · Fat 10g · Protein 4g · Carbohydrates 27g · Cholesterol 16mg · Sodium 817mg · Fiber 4g

Borscht (Beet Soup)

Borscht is the Russian word for beet soup. This recipe is extraordinarily simple because it starts with canned beets, which will save you time in the kitchen. Of course, you can still use fresh beets if you wish. **SERVES 4 (MAKES 6 CUPS)**

1 tablespoon butter or buttery spread

1 small red onion, chopped

2 cans (15 ounces each) red beets, undrained

1 cup orange juice

2 tablespoons chopped fresh tarragon, or to taste

¼ teaspoon sea salt, or more to taste

¼ teaspoon freshly ground black pepper, or more to taste

1 teaspoon sherry vinegar, port wine, or dry sherry

½ cup nonfat sour cream or vegan sour cream, divided, plus 4 teaspoons for garnish

4 teaspoons chopped fresh chives, for garnish

1 tablespoon finely chopped toasted walnuts, for garnish

1. In a large soup pot, melt the butter over medium heat. Cook the onion, stirring occasionally, until tender, about 5 minutes.

2. Add the beets, orange juice, tarragon, salt, and pepper. Bring the soup to a boil, reduce the heat to low, and simmer, covered, 20 minutes. Stir in the vinegar.

3. Place half of the soup in a blender, add half of the sour cream, and puree, placing a towel over the opening to prevent splatters. Repeat with the remaining soup and sour cream. Taste, and add more salt and pepper, if desired. Return the soup to the pot and reheat.

4. Serve the soup hot in warmed bowls, each garnished with a teaspoon of sour cream, a teaspoon of chives, and a dusting of chopped walnuts.

Calories 155 · Fat 3g · Protein 5g · Carbohydrates 29g · Cholesterol 11mg · Sodium 595mg · Fiber 4g

Cream of Broccoli Soup

A lovely shade of light green, this soup packs a wallop of nutrients from the cruciferous family. As with my other soups, the potatoes and half-and-half lend creaminess. **SERVES 6 (MAKES 8 CUPS)**

2 tablespoons butter or buttery spread

1 large shallot, finely chopped

2 garlic cloves, minced

½ cup russet potatoes, peeled and chopped

1 bunch broccoli florets, about 3 cups

6 cups homemade Vegetable Broth (page 245) or GF store-bought vegetable broth

½ teaspoon sea salt

¼ teaspoon freshly ground black pepper

½ cup fat-free half-and-half or plain coffee creamer (soy or coconut)

⅛ teaspoon freshly grated nutmeg

2 tablespoons fresh lemon juice

Salt and freshly ground black pepper, to taste

Fresh chopped chives, for garnish

Dash of paprika, for garnish

1. In a large pot, melt the butter over medium heat and cook the shallot until tender, about 2 to 3 minutes. Add the garlic and potatoes and toss to coat with the butter. Add the broccoli, broth, salt, and pepper, and bring to a boil. Reduce the heat to low and cook, covered, until the potatoes and broccoli are tender, about 15 to 20 minutes.

2. Place half of the soup in a blender, add half of the half-and-half, and puree until very smooth. Repeat with remaining soup and half-and-half. Return the soup to the pot, add nutmeg, lemon juice, and more salt and pepper, if desired. Bring to serving temperature over medium heat, stirring constantly. Serve hot, garnished with the chives and paprika.

Calories 70 · Fat 4g · Protein 2g · Carbohydrates 7g · Cholesterol 10mg · Sodium 227mg · Fiber 1g

Butternut Squash Soup with Chipotle Cream

Apple juice provides just the right touch of sweetness to balance the spices in this vibrant soup. I love the rich orange color, and it looks so professional with its drizzle of Chipotle Cream. **SERVES 4 (MAKES 4 CUPS)**

2 cups apple juice

2 boxes (12 ounces each) frozen butternut squash

1 large onion, chopped

2 large garlic cloves, minced

1 tablespoon canola oil

2 teaspoons ground coriander

1 teaspoon ground cumin

1 teaspoon ground mustard

1/4 teaspoon freshly grated nutmeg

1/2 teaspoon sea salt

1/4 teaspoon crushed red pepper flakes, optional

1 tablespoon lemon juice

2 tablespoons chopped fresh chives or parsley, for garnish

CHIPOTLE CREAM

1/4 cup low-fat mayonnaise or vegan mayonnaise

1/4 cup nonfat sour cream or vegan sour cream

2 tablespoons lime juice

1/4 teaspoon agave nectar

1/8 teaspoon chipotle chile powder

1. In a large pot, combine all of the soup ingredients except the lemon juice and chives. Bring to a boil, then reduce the heat to low and simmer, covered, 30 minutes. Stir the mixture occasionally to break up the frozen chunks of squash.

2. While the soup simmers, make the Chipotle Cream: In a small bowl, whisk together the mayonnaise, sour cream, lime juice, agave nectar, and chipotle chile powder. Set aside.

3. With a handheld immersion blender, puree the soup in the pot until very smooth. Stir in the lemon juice and serve hot, garnished with the chives and a drizzle of the Chipotle Cream. Refrigerate any unused Chipotle Cream, tightly covered, for a week.

Calories 220 · Fat 7g · Protein 3g · Carbohydrates 40g · Cholesterol 5mg · Sodium 333mg · Fiber 3g

Carrot-Ginger Soup with Chile-Lime Pepitas

Brightly colored soups like this one are the perfect place for sneaking a bit of a healthy orange-colored herb called turmeric into your diet. Pepitas (raw, hulled pumpkin seeds) are a common ingredient in Southwestern cooking, and bring a nice crunch to this otherwise smooth, creamy soup. **SERVES 4 (MAKES 6 CUPS)**

1 tablespoon butter or buttery spread

1 medium onion, diced

1 tablespoon fresh ginger root, finely chopped

2 cups peeled and chopped carrots

2 cups peeled and chopped russet potatoes (1-inch pieces)

3 cups homemade Vegetable Broth (page 245) or GF store-bought vegetable broth

1 cup orange juice

3/4 teaspoon sea salt, divided, plus more to taste

1/2 teaspoon ground turmeric

1/2 cup fat-free half-and-half or plain coffee creamer (soy or coconut)

1 tablespoon agave nectar or honey

1 tablespoon dry sherry or dry white wine

1/8 teaspoon freshly grated nutmeg

Dash freshly ground black pepper

Dash white pepper

2 tablespoons chopped fresh parsley, for garnish

CHILE-LIME PEPITAS

1/2 cup raw hulled pumpkin seeds (aka *pepitas*)

2 tablespoons fresh lime juice

1/8 teaspoon New Mexico red chile powder

1/8 teaspoon sea salt, optional

1. Heat the butter in a large pot over medium-low heat, add the onion and ginger, and cook, stirring constantly, until the onion is soft, about 5 minutes.

2. Add the carrots, potatoes, broth, orange juice, 1/2 teaspoon of the salt, and the turmeric. Bring to a boil, reduce the heat to low, and simmer, covered, until the vegetables are tender, about 35 to 40 minutes.

3. While the soup simmers, make the Chile-Lime Pepitas. Heat a 10-inch skillet over medium heat. Add the pumpkin seeds and cook, stirring occasionally, until they turn brown and begin to make popping sounds, about 2 to 3 minutes. Add the lime juice, chile powder, and salt (if using), and cook until the juice evaporates. Remove from the heat and transfer to a plate.

4. Transfer half of the carrot mixture to a blender, add ¼ cup of the half-and-half, and puree until smooth. Repeat with the remaining half of the carrot mixture and half-and-half. Return the puree to the pot. Bring to serving temperature over medium heat, stirring constantly. Add the agave nectar, sherry, nutmeg, the remaining ¼ teaspoon salt, and the pepper.

5. Serve hot, garnished with the parsley and Chile-Lime Pepitas.

Calories 230 · Fat 5g · Protein 5g · Carbohydrates 42g · Cholesterol 0mg · Sodium 508mg · Fiber 5g

Chilled and Dilled Cucumber-Apple Soup

Cool and refreshing as an entrée for a summer luncheon, or served in espresso cups as an appetizer before dinner, this super-easy soup is absolutely tantalizing. The sweetness of the apple juice both balances and accentuates the dill. Dried dill won't cut it here; use the real thing. **SERVES 4 AS A MAIN COURSE, 8 AS AN APPETIZER**

3 medium Granny Smith apples, peeled, cored, and cut in $\frac{1}{2}$-inch pieces

1 cup apple juice

1 tablespoon fresh lemon juice

2 tablespoons agave nectar or honey

$\frac{1}{4}$ teaspoon sea salt

2 cups English cucumber, unpeeled, chopped, plus some for garnish

1 cup nonfat sour cream or vegan sour cream

1 tablespoon fresh dill, chopped, plus extra dill sprigs for garnish

1. In a medium saucepan, combine the apples, apple juice, lemon juice, agave nectar, and salt. Bring to a boil over medium heat and simmer, covered, for 8 to 10 minutes, or until the apples are tender. Let cool for 10 minutes.

2. Place the apple mixture, cucumber, sour cream, and dill in a blender and process until very smooth. Chill overnight, or for at least 3 hours, to meld the flavors. Serve chilled, garnished with thin slices of cucumber and a small dill sprig.

Calories 165 · Fat 0g · Protein 5g · Carbohydrates 38g · Cholesterol 6mg · Sodium 163mg · Fiber 3g

Miso Soup with Wakame

Miso is made from fermented soybeans, but be sure to check the label since some brands may contain wheat or barley. Wakame is dried seaweed. Together, they create umami, sometimes called the fifth taste in Japan (the others are sweet, salty, sour, and bitter). This soup is perfect for an Asian meal. **SERVES 4 (MAKES ABOUT 6 CUPS)**

1 tablespoon toasted sesame oil

4 green onions, white part only, reserve green tops

2 teaspoons ginger, minced

2 garlic cloves, minced

4 cups water

½ cup dried wakame, chopped

2 ounces dried shiitake mushrooms

¼ cup GF light miso

4 ounces extra-firm tofu, cut in ½-inch cubes

1. Heat the oil in a heavy medium saucepan over medium heat. Add the white parts of the onion, and the ginger and garlic. Cook, stirring constantly, for 1 minute.

2. Add the water, wakame, mushrooms, and miso, and simmer gently for 10 to 15 minutes or until the wakame and mushrooms are hydrated and tender. Add the tofu and cook for another 5 minutes. Ladle into 4 warmed soup bowls. Finely chop the reserved green parts of the onions, sprinkle them on the soup, and serve immediately.

Calories 145 · Fat 6g · Protein 6g · Carbohydrates 19g · Cholesterol 0mg · Sodium 728mg · Fiber 3g

Cream of Mushroom Soup

Ever so much better than buying it in a can, this fresh soup is perfect for a cold winter's night. For best results, use only fresh mushrooms, not canned. If you're not a fan of nutmeg, try the same amount of dried marjoram instead. **SERVES 4, SMALL SERVINGS (MAKES 4½ CUPS)**

1 tablespoon butter or buttery spread

1 garlic clove, minced

½ cup chopped onion

2 cups fresh mushrooms, trimmed and cut into quarters

1 tablespoon fresh lemon juice

1½ cups homemade Vegetable Broth (page 245) or GF store-bought vegetable broth

1 tablespoon sweet rice flour

½ cup fat-free half-and-half or plain coffee creamer (soy or coconut)

1 tablespoon dry sherry or red wine vinegar

¼ teaspoon freshly grated nutmeg or dried marjoram

¼ teaspoon sea salt, or to taste

⅛ teaspoon freshly ground black pepper, or to taste

4 teaspoons chopped fresh chives, for garnish

4 teaspoons toasted slivered almonds, for garnish

1. Heat the butter in a 2-quart saucepan over medium-low heat. Add the garlic and onion, and cook, covered, for 4 to 5 minutes. Toss the mushrooms with the lemon juice and add to the saucepan. Cook, stirring occasionally, for 5 minutes.

2. Add 1 cup of the vegetable broth to the saucepan. Whisk the sweet rice flour into the remaining ½ cup of broth until smooth, and whisk it into the pan. Bring the mixture to a boil, reduce the heat to low, and simmer, covered, 20 minutes.

3. Transfer half of the soup to a blender, add ¼ cup of the half-and-half, and puree until very smooth. Repeat with the remaining soup and half-and-half. Return the soup to the pan and stir in the sherry, nutmeg, salt, and pepper. Bring to serving temperature and serve in warmed soup bowls, each garnished with a teaspoon of the fresh chives and a teaspoon of the toasted almonds.

Calories 355 · Fat 18g · Protein 6g · Carbohydrates 43g · Cholesterol 47mg · Sodium 542mg · Fiber 5g

Spring Green Pea Soup

Frozen peas work very well in this lovely soup that shouts "springtime" and "ladies' luncheon." However, if you have fresh peas, it is even more delectable. No tarragon? Try the same amount of fresh mint. **SERVES 4 (MAKES 6 CUPS)**

1 tablespoon butter or buttery spread

1 cup leeks, chopped, or chopped shallots

3½ cups green peas, fresh or frozen

3 cups homemade Vegetable Broth (page 245) or GF store-bought vegetable broth

2 tablespoons chopped fresh tarragon, or 1 teaspoon dried, plus more for garnish

½ teaspoon sea salt, or more to taste

¼ teaspoon freshly ground black pepper, or more to taste

½ cup fat-free half-and-half or plain coffee creamer (soy or coconut)

1 tablespoon lemon juice or red wine vinegar

2 tablespoons plain yogurt (coconut, dairy, or soy) or Yogurt (page 249), thinned with water to drizzling consistency

½ teaspoon paprika, for garnish

1. In a large heavy soup pot, heat the butter over medium heat. Swish the chopped leeks in water to clean them, then add to the pot and cook, covered, stirring occasionally, until they are tender, about 5 minutes.
2. Add the peas, broth, tarragon, salt, and pepper. Bring to a boil, then reduce the heat to medium-low and simmer, covered, until the peas are tender, about 5 to 7 minutes.
3. Transfer half of the pea mixture to a blender, add ¼ cup of the half-and-half, and puree until smooth. Repeat with the remaining soup and half-and-half. Return the soup to the pot, add the lemon juice, and bring to serving temperature.
4. Serve hot in warmed bowls, garnished with the tarragon, a drizzle of the yogurt, and a dash of the paprika.

Calories 160 · Fat 4g · Protein 7g · Carbohydrates 24g · Cholesterol 0mg · Sodium 3mg · Fiber 6g

Creamy Potato-Leek Soup with Dill

....

This is American comfort food at its best, wonderfully comforting in winter, yet delightfully refreshing when served chilled in summer. If you prefer a whiter soup, tie the dill in a square of cheesecloth so you can remove it from the soup before pureeing. **SERVES 4 (MAKES 6 CUPS)**

2 tablespoons butter or buttery spread

2 small leeks, white parts only, chopped

2 cups peeled and chopped russet potatoes (1-inch cubes)

2 tablespoons chopped fresh dill, plus 2 teaspoons for garnish

1/8 teaspoon freshly grated nutmeg

3 cups homemade Vegetable Broth (page 245) or GF store-bought vegetable broth

1/2 teaspoon sea salt, plus more to taste

1/4 teaspoon freshly ground black pepper, plus more to taste

1 cup fat-free half-and-half or plain coffee creamer (soy or coconut)

1. Heat the butter in a large soup pot over medium-low heat. Swish the chopped leeks in water to clean them, add them to the pot, and cook, stirring occasionally, until they are just tender, about 5 minutes.

2. Add the potatoes, dill, nutmeg, broth, 1/2 teaspoon of the salt, and the pepper. Bring the soup to a boil over high heat, then reduce the heat to low and simmer, covered, until the potatoes are tender, about 20 minutes.

3. Transfer half of the soup and half of the half-and-half to a blender and puree until smooth, covering the opening with a towel to prevent splatters. Repeat with the remaining soup and half-and-half. Return the soup to the pot and heat to serving temperature. Taste and add more salt and pepper, if desired.

4. Serve in warmed bowls, garnished with the remaining 2 teaspoons of fresh dill.

Calories 180 · Fat 6g · Protein 2g · Carbohydrates 26g · Cholesterol 16mg · Sodium 132mg · Fiber 2g

CELEBRATION DINNER

Creamy Potato-Leek Soup with Dill (page 139)

Savory Leek-Onion Bread Pudding (page 40)

Wild Rice Salad (page 101)

Mixed green salad

All-American Cherry Pie (page 238)

Cream of Tomato Soup with Crunchy Basil Bread Crumb Topping

Tomato soup is an all-American crowd-pleaser, and the crunchy bread crumb topping takes it to new heights. The smoked paprika adds more depth, so use it if you can. **SERVES 4 (MAKES 4 CUPS)**

1 tablespoon olive oil

¼ cup chopped shallots or white onion

1 large garlic clove, chopped

2 tablespoons tomato paste

1 large can (28 ounces) tomatoes, preferably fire-roasted

1¼ cups homemade Vegetable Broth (page 245) or GF store-bought vegetable broth

¼ cup orange juice

1 small bay leaf

1 tablespoon chopped fresh basil, divided

¼ teaspoon smoked paprika, optional

½ cup half-and-half or plain coffee creamer (soy or coconut)

1 teaspoon sherry vinegar or champagne vinegar

CRUNCHY BASIL BREAD CRUMB TOPPING

2 tablespoons olive oil

½ cup GF Bread Crumbs (page 243) or GF store-bought bread crumbs

¼ teaspoon dried basil

⅛ teaspoon sea salt

⅛ teaspoon freshly black ground pepper

2 tablespoons chopped fresh basil, for garnish

1. Heat the oil in a medium saucepan over medium heat. Add the shallots and cook, stirring occasionally, until tender, about 3 to 4 minutes. Add the garlic and tomato paste, and cook, stirring constantly, for 1 minute. Add the tomatoes, broth, orange juice, bay leaf, half of the basil, and the paprika. Bring to a boil, reduce the heat to low, and simmer, covered, 15 minutes.

2. While the soup simmers, make the Crunchy Basil Bread Crumb Topping: Heat the olive oil in a skillet over medium-high heat. Add the bread crumbs and cook, stirring constantly,

until they are toasted and golden brown, about 2 minutes. Transfer to a bowl, toss with the dried basil, salt, and pepper, and cool. Set aside.

3. Remove the bay leaf from the soup, add the half-and-half, and, working in batches, puree the soup in a blender until smooth, covering the top with a dishtowel to prevent splatters. Strain the soup through a sieve; discard solids.

4. Return the soup to the saucepan and add the vinegar. Bring to serving temperature. Serve immediately in warmed soup bowls, garnished with 2 tablespoons of the crumb topping and a sprinkling of the remaining fresh basil.

Calories 220 · Fat 11g · Protein 4g · Carbohydrates 26g · Cholesterol 0mg · Sodium 573mg · Fiber 3g

Thai Corn Chowder

During the summer, freshly cut corn from the cob is delicious in this soup. But you can make it year-round using frozen corn instead. The amount of red pepper flakes you use determines the heat in this soup, so taste it first before adding more. **SERVES 4 (MAKES ABOUT 6 CUPS)**

2 cups yellow corn (fresh or frozen)

2 cups unpeeled diced red potatoes

½ cup finely diced yellow onion

2 tablespoons grated ginger root

1 small garlic clove, chopped

2 cups homemade Vegetable Broth (page 245) or GF store-bought vegetable broth

½ teaspoon sea salt

⅛ teaspoon crushed red pepper flakes, or to taste

1 tablespoon grated lemon zest

1 can (15 ounces) light coconut milk

10 large fresh basil leaves, chopped

10 large fresh mint leaves, chopped

¼ cup chopped fresh cilantro, divided

Salt and freshly ground black pepper, to taste

2 whole limes, halved

1. In a heavy medium saucepan, bring the corn, potatoes, onion, ginger, garlic, broth, salt, red pepper flakes, and lemon zest to a boil over high heat, adding water, if necessary, to cover. Reduce the heat to low and simmer, covered, for 25 to 30 minutes or until the potatoes are tender. With a potato masher, mash enough of the mixture to create a thicker, creamier soup. If a thin soup is more to your liking, skip this step.

2. Add the coconut milk, basil, mint, and half of the cilantro, and bring to serving temperature. Add salt and pepper to taste. Serve in warmed soup bowls, garnished with the remaining cilantro and the lime halves.

Calories 185 · Fat 4g · Protein 5g · Carbohydrates 37g · Cholesterol 0mg · Sodium 270mg · Fiber 4g

Posole with Crispy Tortilla Strips

Posole, or pozole, is a traditional southwestern soup and is made with hominy, a form of corn. The crisp tortilla strips are also traditional, so be sure to use them. **SERVES 4**

2 tablespoons olive oil

1 medium onion, finely chopped

2 medium carrots, peeled and diced

2 celery ribs, cut in ½-inch pieces

2 medium garlic cloves, chopped

2 teaspoons ground cumin

1 tablespoon chopped fresh oregano, or 1 teaspoon dried

½ teaspoon ancho chile powder

1 can (15 ounces) chopped tomatoes, preferably fire-roasted, undrained

1 can (15 ounces) white hominy, drained

3 cups homemade Vegetable Broth (page 245) or GF store-bought vegetable broth

½ cup chopped fresh cilantro, divided

CRISPY TORTILLA STRIPS

Vegetable oil, for frying tortilla strips

3 yellow corn tortillas, cut in ¼-inch strips

Salt to taste

Garnishes: chopped avocado, sliced radishes, shredded cabbage, lime wedges, sour cream or vegan sour cream, and tomato salsa

1. In a Dutch oven or soup pan, heat the oil over medium heat. Cook the onion, carrots, and celery, stirring often, until the vegetables soften, about 5 minutes. Add the garlic, cumin, oregano, and ancho chile powder and cook another 2 minutes, stirring constantly.

2. Add the tomatoes, hominy, broth, and ¼ cup of the cilantro, and cook over medium-low heat, covered, about 1 hour. Taste, and add salt if necessary.

3. While the Posole cooks, make the Crispy Tortilla Strips: In a small saucepan, heat 1 inch of the vegetable oil until very hot. Fry the corn tortilla strips a few at a time until crisp. Remove from the oil with a slotted spoon and drain on paper towels, then sprinkle with the salt. Or arrange the tortilla strips in a single layer on a parchment-lined baking

sheet, coat with cooking spray, and bake until lightly browned and crisp, about 7 to 10 minutes, stirring occasionally.

4. Serve the soup in warmed bowls, sprinkled with tortilla strips, the remaining cilantro, and your choice of garnishes.

Calories 235 · Fat 9g · Protein 5g · Carbohydrates 36g · Cholesterol 0mg · Sodium 300mg · Fiber 7g

Vegetable Soup with Dumplings

Vegetable soup and dumplings just seem to go together, don't they? Dumplings are quite easy to make and satisfy your need for something homey and filling. **SERVES 4**

1 tablespoon canola oil

1 large onion, chopped

2 medium carrots, peeled and cut in
    ½-inch slices

2 celery ribs, diced

1 medium zucchini, cut in ¼-inch slices

3 cups homemade Vegetable Broth (page 245)
    or GF store-bought vegetable broth

1 tablespoon chopped fresh thyme, or
    1 teaspoon dried

1 tablespoon chopped fresh parsley, plus
    additional for garnish

Salt and freshly ground black pepper, to taste

DUMPLINGS

½ cup GF Flour Blend (page 12)

1 teaspoon baking powder

¼ teaspoon baking soda

¼ teaspoon sea salt

¼ teaspoon xanthan gum

2 teaspoons butter or buttery spread

¼ cup milk of choice

2 tablespoons chopped fresh flat-leaf
    parsley, optional

1. Heat the oil in a Dutch oven over medium heat. Add the onion, carrots, and celery, and cook, covered, until they are tender, about 5 minutes. Add the zucchini, broth, thyme, parsley, salt, and pepper, and cook, covered, 20 minutes. Let the soup simmer while preparing the dumplings.

2. Make the Dumplings: In a small bowl, whisk together the flour blend, baking powder, baking soda, salt, and xanthan gum until well blended. With a fork, cut in the butter until the mixture resembles peas. Stir in the milk until the mixture thickens slightly and a soft dough forms. Stir in the parsley.

3. Drop the dough by teaspoonfuls into the simmering soup, and cook, covered, 15 to 20 minutes. You can also cook the dumplings separately in broth, if you wish. Serve immediately in warmed soup bowls, garnished with the fresh parsley.

Calories 150 · Fat 6g · Protein 3g · Carbohydrates 24g · Cholesterol 6mg ·
Sodium 380mg · Fiber 3g

Little Meals
or Appetizers

Sometimes you just want a small meal or an appetizer before a bigger meal. This chapter offers you some highly nutritious options for those occasions. For more appetizer recipes, see my other books: *Wheat-Free Recipes & Menus*, *Cooking Free*, and *Gluten-Free Quick & Easy*.

· VEGETABLES ·

Baked Kale Chips

Gazpacho Shooters

Greek Salad Skewers with Greek Salad Dressing

Potatoes (Patatas Bravas) with Mustard Cream

Stuffed Mushrooms

· DIPS ·

Caponata

Hummus

· BREADS OR BREADED APPETIZERS ·

Mini Corn Dogs

Crostini

Roasted Red Pepper Panini with White Truffle Aioli

· MISCELLANEOUS ·

Cereal and Popcorn Snack Mix

Veggie Spring Rolls

Baked Kale Chips

I always thought of kale as something you cooked like collard greens, so I was delighted to learn about these little chips, which are addictive. You may use curly kale or Tuscan kale (sometimes called lacinato kale) in this recipe, whichever type you can find. **SERVES 4**

4 cups kale (1 bunch), stems removed, torn into chip-size pieces

1 tablespoon olive oil

¼ teaspoon sea salt

1. Place a rack in the middle of the oven. Preheat the oven to 350°F. Line a 10 x 15-inch baking sheet (not nonstick) with parchment paper.
2. Wash the kale and trim the stems from each piece. Spin it dry in a salad spinner and blot any remaining moisture with paper towels.
3. In a large bowl, toss the kale with the olive oil until thoroughly coated. For curly kale, you may need to massage the pieces with your hands to work the oil into the crevices. Toss with the salt. Spread the kale in a single layer on the baking sheet.
4. Bake until the chips are crispy, about 15 minutes. Watch carefully so they don't burn. Cool the pan on a wire rack until the chips are cool. Serve immediately.

Calories 65 · Fat 4g · Protein 2g · Carbohydrates 7g · Cholesterol 0mg · Sodium 146mg · Fiber 1g

Gazpacho Shooters

Soup in a shot glass? Your guests will love this clever idea. Make the gazpacho ahead of time, fill the shot glasses, and refrigerate them on a tray. Then wait for the "oohs" and "aahs" when you carry the tray of these gorgeous little treats to your guests. **SERVES 12 AS SHOOTERS, 4 AS SMALL ENTRÉES**

2 1/2 cups tomato juice, divided

1/4 cup diced yellow onion

1/2 to 1 jalapeño pepper, seeds and veins removed, coarsely chopped (or to taste)

1 large garlic clove, minced

1 tablespoon fresh lime juice

1/2 unpeeled English cucumber, plus 12 very thin half-slices for garnish

1 celery rib, diced

3 tablespoons chopped fresh cilantro, divided

1. In a food processor, puree 1 cup of the tomato juice along with the onion, jalapeño, garlic, and lime juice.
2. Transfer to a large bowl and stir in the cucumber, celery, 2 tablespoons of the cilantro, and the remaining tomato juice. Divide evenly among 12 shot glasses (2 ounces each) and serve chilled, garnished with a half-slice of cucumber and the remaining cilantro.

Calories 15 · Fat 0g · Protein 1g · Carbohydrates 3g · Cholesterol 0mg · Sodium 187mg · Fiber 1g

Everyday to Exceptional

To keep these little shooter gems cool in summer, freeze a 6-ounce can of tomato juice in mini ice cube trays. Drop one cube into each shooter just before serving. They will melt quickly, cooling the soup without diluting its flavor.

Greek Salad Skewers
with Greek Salad Dressing

These colorful little skewers are perfect for a hot summer day when cooking seems like way too much work. If you can find cocktail-size marinated artichoke hearts, they can be used in place of the feta cheese if you don't want dairy. Look for the skewers in party stores, grocery stores, or online, and tailor how many items you put on the skewer to its length. You want guests to be able to hold the skewer in their fingers easily. **SERVES 6 (MAKES 12 SKEWERS)**

12 short wooden skewers

24 red grape tomatoes

1/4 small red onion, cut in 1/2-inch cubes

12 whole pitted Kalamata olives, or regular black olives

3 ounces feta cheese, cut in 1/2-inch cubes

12 whole Spanish olives

GREEK SALAD DRESSING

1 tablespoon red wine vinegar

1 tablespoon fresh lemon juice

1 tablespoon chopped fresh oregano

1 small garlic clove, minced

2 tablespoons extra-virgin olive oil

Salt and pepper, to taste

1 tablespoon chopped fresh thyme, for garnish

1. To assemble the skewers, place the ingredients on each skewer in this order: tomato, onion, Kalamata olive, cheese, Spanish olive, and tomato. Place the skewers on a shallow serving platter.

2. Make the Dressing: In a bowl, whisk together the vinegar, lemon juice, oregano, garlic, and olive oil until thoroughly blended. Season the dressing to taste with salt and pepper, then drizzle over the skewers, turning to coat evenly. Sprinkle with the chopped thyme and serve immediately at room temperature.

Calories 215 · Fat 12g · Protein 6g · Carbohydrates 26g · Cholesterol 13mg · Sodium 399mg · Fiber 6g

Potatoes (Patatas Bravas) with Mustard Cream

Patatas Bravas is a traditional tapa served in Spain with many variations. Here it is served with a velvety Mustard Cream. Deeply browning the potatoes produces a more flavorful and colorful dish, so take the time for this important step. Smoked hot paprika is worth tracking down for this recipe because of its full-bodied flavor. **SERVES 8 (MAKES 16)**

16 small new red potatoes, unpeeled

2 tablespoons olive oil

Salt and freshly ground black pepper, to taste

1 teaspoon smoked hot paprika

2 teaspoons chopped fresh rosemary, for garnish

2 tablespoons chopped pimientos, for garnish

MUSTARD CREAM

½ cup nonfat cream cheese or vegan cream cheese, softened

1 small garlic clove, minced

1 pinch sea salt

1 tablespoon chopped chives

1 teaspoon Dijon mustard

1 teaspoon fresh lemon juice

1 pinch cayenne pepper

1 pinch freshly ground black pepper

1. Place a rack in the middle of the oven. Preheat the oven to 425°F. Line a 9 x 13-inch nonstick (gray, not black) baking sheet with parchment paper.

2. Wash and pat the potatoes dry. Cut into ¾-inch coins (discard ends or use for soup) and toss with olive oil until well coated. Place in a single layer on the baking sheet, then sprinkle with the salt and pepper. Cover tightly with foil.

3. Bake the potatoes until tender, about 15 to 20 minutes. Discard the foil, turn the potatoes over gently with a fork, and sprinkle evenly with the paprika. Continue baking until deep golden brown, about 5 to 8 minutes. Cool the potatoes while making the Mustard Cream.

4. Make the Mustard Cream: Place the cream cheese in a small bowl. Stir in the garlic, salt, chives, mustard, lemon juice, cayenne, and black pepper until well blended.

5. To serve, top each potato slice with a small dollop of the Mustard Cream and then garnish with a sprinkle of the rosemary. Top with a strip of the pimiento and serve immediately.

Calories 240 · Fat 4g · Protein 7g · Carbohydrates 45g · Cholesterol 1mg · Sodium 114mg · Fiber 4g

Stuffed Mushrooms

This traditional American appetizer has been around forever, and it is so good that it will never go out of style. The size of the mushrooms determines how much stuffing each holds; use just enough stuffing to lightly mound on the mushrooms—too much and it will fall out. **SERVES 6**

1 pound button mushrooms or
  large cremini

½ cup GF Bread Crumbs (page 243)

½ cup grated Parmesan cheese or
  soy Parmesan

2 tablespoons Dijon mustard

1 tablespoon extra-virgin olive oil

½ cup chopped fresh parsley

1 large garlic clove, minced

½ teaspoon Italian seasoning

¼ teaspoon sea salt

¼ teaspoon freshly ground black pepper

¼ teaspoon paprika, for garnish

1. Place a rack in the middle of the oven. Preheat the oven to 400°F. Lightly oil a 9 x 13-inch glass baking dish.

2. Clean the mushrooms and cut the stems off, dicing them finely, but leaving the caps intact.

3. In a small bowl, combine the diced stems with the bread crumbs, Parmesan cheese, mustard, oil, parsley, garlic, Italian seasoning, salt, and pepper, and mix together with a spatula until well blended. Stuff the mushrooms with this mixture and place, filled side up, in the baking dish.

4. Bake until the mushrooms are tender and the filling is lightly browned, about 15 to 20 minutes. Remove from the oven, dust with the paprika, and serve immediately.

Calories 110 · Fat 5g · Protein 6g · Carbohydrates 11g · Cholesterol 5mg · Sodium 349mg · Fiber 2g

Caponata

This dip, based primarily on eggplant and seasoned with Italian herbs, is an extremely tasty way to incorporate eggplant into your diet. **SERVES 8 (MAKES 2 CUPS)**

1 small eggplant, about 1/2 pound

1/3 cup extra-virgin olive oil, divided

1 cup celery, finely diced

1/2 cup red, yellow, and green bell peppers, finely diced

1 small onion, diced

1 can (8 ounces) tomato sauce

1/2 cup Spanish olives, thinly sliced

1/4 cup red wine vinegar

1 tablespoon capers, rinsed and drained

1 large garlic clove, minced

1 teaspoon agave nectar

1/2 teaspoon dried oregano, or 2 teaspoons chopped fresh

1/2 teaspoon sea salt, or to taste

1/2 teaspoon freshly ground black pepper

1. Wash eggplant, peel, and cut in 1/2-inch cubes. Heat 3 tablespoons of the oil in a large heavy skillet over medium-low heat and sauté the eggplant until tender and lightly browned, about 5 minutes. Transfer the eggplant to a plate.
2. Add the remaining olive oil to the skillet and sauté the celery, bell peppers, and onion over medium-low heat until tender, about 3 to 5 minutes.
3. Return the eggplant to the skillet, add the tomato sauce, and bring to a boil. Reduce the heat to low and simmer, covered, 15 minutes. Stir in the olives, vinegar, capers, garlic, agave nectar, oregano, salt, and pepper, and simmer on low, covered, for another 15 minutes, stirring occasionally. Taste, and add more salt and oregano if necessary.
4. Refrigerate overnight. Serve slightly warm or at room temperature on gluten-free crackers, toasted gluten-free bread, or as a dip for vegetables.

Calories 125 · Fat 10g · Protein 1g · Carbohydrates 10g · Cholesterol 0mg · Sodium 388mg · Fiber 3g

Hummus

Hummus is a thick spread or paste made from mashed chickpeas, which originated in the Middle East. Americans are developing a strong liking for hummus, and we now see it on restaurant menus and in a variety of flavors at the supermarket. Typically flavored with lemon juice and tahini paste (made from ground sesame seeds), it is extremely easy and relatively inexpensive to make at home. Its high protein and fiber content make it a healthy part of any diet. **SERVES 6 (MAKES 1½ CUPS)**

1 can (15 ounces) garbanzo beans
   (chickpeas), rinsed and drained

2 garlic cloves, chopped

3 tablespoons extra-virgin olive oil

¼ cup fresh lemon juice

¼ cup tahini (sesame paste)

½ teaspoon sea salt, or to taste

1 teaspoon ground cumin

2 tablespoons chopped fresh cilantro

½ teaspoon freshly ground black pepper

¼ teaspoon crushed red pepper flakes

Water, if needed

Place all ingredients in a food processor and puree until smooth. Scrape down the sides of the bowl often. If the mixture is too thick, add water, 1 tablespoon at a time, to reach desired consistency. Serve immediately with fresh vegetables or your favorite gluten-free crackers. Refrigerate, covered, for up to 1 week.

Calories 215 · Fat 13g · Protein 6g · Carbohydrates 21g · Cholesterol 0mg · Sodium 395mg · Fiber 4g

Mini Corn Dogs

These little treats will remind you of summertime and county fairs, but you can serve them to your most discriminating guests and they'll be delighted at any time of the year.

SERVES 8 (MAKES 16)

1 cup GF corn bread mix

¾ cup milk of choice

2 teaspoons apple cider vinegar

8 meatless soy franks, patted dry

¼ cup white rice flour, for dusting

16 round toothpicks

1½ cups peanut oil, for frying

Mustard and ketchup, for dipping

1. In a 2-cup measuring cup, whisk together the corn bread mix, milk, and vinegar until the batter is very smooth. Let the batter stand 5 minutes. It should be the consistency of cake batter, thick enough to coat a spoon. If the batter is too stiff, add more milk, a tablespoon at a time.

2. Cut each soy frank in half crosswise, then toss with white rice flour so the batter will stick better, and insert a toothpick into one end of each one.

3. Heat the oil to a depth of 3 inches in a heavy-duty one-quart saucepan over medium-high heat. Holding the end of a toothpick with tongs, dip the frank in the batter, and roll to coat it thoroughly. Gently immerse the frank (toothpick and all) in the oil and fry until lightly browned, about 1 to 2 minutes, turning to assure even browning. They brown very quickly, so remove them before they burn.

4. Remove the corn dogs from the oil with a slotted spoon and drain on paper towels. Serve immediately with the mustard and ketchup.

Calories 150 · Fat 7g · Protein 7g · Carbohydrates 17g · Cholesterol 1mg · Sodium 390mg · Fiber 2g

Crostini

Crostini means "little crusts" in Italian; these little toasts can be topped with anything you like, but this colorful mélange of Mediterranean vegetables will be one of your favorites. For best results, slice the bread about ½ inch thick. **SERVES 6 (MAKES 12 CROSTINI)**

12 thin slices of French Baguette (page 181)

2 large garlic cloves, sliced in half

2 tablespoons olive oil, divided

Coarse salt and pepper to taste

12 large Kalamata olives, pitted and chopped

12 red grape tomatoes, chopped

3 tablespoons capers, rinsed and drained

3 tablespoons chopped fresh basil, or your favorite herb

1 tablespoon red wine vinegar

1. Toast the bread slices in a regular toaster or toaster oven until lightly browned on both sides.
2. Immediately, rub the warm bread with the cut side of the garlic clove, then brush 1 tablespoon of the oil over the slices. Sprinkle with the salt and pepper.
3. Toss together the remaining oil, the olives, tomatoes, capers, basil, and vinegar until well blended. Spoon onto the toasts and serve immediately.

Calories 250 · Fat 9g · Protein 7g · Carbohydrates 38g · Cholesterol 0mg · Sodium 485mg · Fiber 4g

Roasted Red Pepper Panini with White Truffle Aioli

Panini is the Italian for "sandwiches"; one sandwich is a *panino*. Gluten-free bread is usually small, so these are very cute little sandwiches. Aioli is garlic-flavored mayonnaise. The white truffle oil (which has a slight garlic taste and is available in natural food stores) gives the dip a flavorful lift, but a little goes a long way. So use it with a light hand. **MAKES 4 PANINI**

8 slices GF sandwich bread

4 roasted red peppers, cut in ¼-inch strips, then patted dry

4 slices low-fat mozzarella cheese or cheese alternative

4 small lettuce leaves

WHITE TRUFFLE AIOLI

½ cup mayonnaise or vegan mayonnaise

1 large garlic clove, minced

Pinch sea salt

1½ tablespoons chopped chives

½ teaspoon Dijon mustard

1½ teaspoons fresh lemon juice

¼ teaspoon white truffle oil

Pinch cayenne pepper

Pinch freshly ground black pepper

PANINI FILLING

2 ounces (about ¼ of a tub) nonfat cream cheese or vegan cream cheese, softened

2 tablespoons homemade Basil Pesto (page 252) or store-bought pesto

1 tablespoon dry mustard

⅛ teaspoon crushed red pepper flakes

1. Make the Aioli: Put the mayonnaise in a small bowl. Add the garlic to the salt with a sharp knife until a paste forms. Add the paste to the mayonnaise, along with the chives, mustard, lemon juice, white truffle oil, cayenne, and pepper. Whisk until well blended. Refrigerate until ready to use; keep leftovers refrigerated for up to one week.

2. Make the Panini Filling: In a small bowl, stir together the cream cheese, pesto, mustard, and crushed red pepper flakes until thoroughly blended.

3. Heat a panini machine according to the manufacturer's directions. Spread 1 tablespoon of the cream cheese mixture on one side of each of the bread slices. Place the red pepper strips on top of four slices, then the cheese, and the lettuce leaf. Top with the remaining bread slices, cream cheese side down.

4. Grill the sandwiches until lightly browned following the manufacturer's directions. Serve immediately with the White Truffle Aioli for dipping.

Calories 520 · Fat 22g · Protein 22g · Carbohydrates 60g · Cholesterol 17mg · Sodium 1366mg · Fiber 3g

---

SUMMER LUNCHEON

Chilled and Dilled Cucumber-Apple Soup (page 135)

Roasted Red Pepper Panini with White Truffle Aioli (page 159)

Fresh melon (cantaloupe, honeydew, or watermelon) wedges

Cereal and Popcorn Snack Mix

You can vary the cereals in this old-fashioned treat; just be sure to read the labels on the cereal package to make sure your choice is safe. I like Corn Chex because it is sturdy and holds its shape. **SERVES 18 (MAKES ABOUT 9 CUPS)**

4 cups GF Corn Chex

1 cup whole unsalted pecans or walnuts

1 cup whole unsalted almonds

1/2 cup hulled, unsalted sunflower seeds

1/4 cup butter or buttery spread, melted

1 tablespoon gluten-free tamari soy sauce

2 teaspoons Italian seasoning, or your favorite seasoning

1/2 teaspoon onion powder

1/2 teaspoon garlic powder

1/2 cup Parmesan cheese or soy Parmesan

1 teaspoon paprika

2 cups plain popped corn (unflavored)

4 ounces GF pretzels

Sea salt

1. Preheat the oven to 300°F. Line a 10 x 15-inch rimmed baking sheet (not nonstick) with foil or parchment paper.

2. Combine the cereal, nuts, and seeds in a bowl large enough to hold 9 cups. Combine the melted butter and soy sauce and toss it with the cereal mixture to coat thoroughly. In a small bowl, whisk together the Italian seasoning, onion powder, garlic powder, Parmesan cheese, and paprika. Add to the cereal mixture and toss to coat thoroughly. Spread the mixture on the baking sheet.

3. Bake until the cereal is lightly browned and the nuts and seeds are toasted and fragrant, about 30 to 35 minutes (browning time will vary depending on the cereal, so watch carefully). Stir every 10 minutes to assure even browning. Return the mixture to the large bowl and add the popped corn and pretzels. Toss to coat thoroughly. Taste, and add more salt if desired. Serve at room temperature.

Calories 225 · Fat 16g · Protein 5g · Carbohydrates 17g · Cholesterol 7mg · Sodium 244mg · Fiber 2g

KIDS' PARTY

Mini Corn Dogs (page 157)

Cereal and Popcorn Snack Mix (page 161)

Veggie Pizza (page 41)

Vegetable sticks (carrots, celery, bell peppers)

Chocolate Brownies (page 211)

Veggie Spring Rolls

These are non-fried spring rolls using rice paper sheets (found in Asian restaurants), and they are surprisingly simple to make. The more you practice rolling the rice papers, the better you will get; eventually you will be a pro. The fresher the ingredients, the better these rolls will be. So if you can't find really fresh bean sprouts, substitute very finely chopped, peeled cucumber instead. **MAKES 8 SPRING ROLLS**

8 (8-inch) round rice paper sheets

½ cup chopped fresh cilantro leaves

½ cup chopped fresh basil

½ cup chopped fresh mint

2 cups very thinly sliced Bibb lettuce leaves (use the soft, bright green parts only)

1 large carrot or 2 medium carrots, peeled and coarsely shredded

2 cups (2 ounces) cooked and drained cellophane noodles (sometimes called bean threads)

1 cup fresh bean sprouts

¼ cup green onions (including green ·tops), very thinly sliced

Thai Kitchen Sweet Red Chili Sauce for Dipping

1. Working with one rice paper sheet at a time, immerse each in 1 inch of hot water until soft and pliable, about 30 seconds. Transfer to a flat surface and, leaving a 1-inch margin around the edge of the rice paper, layer with 1 tablespoon cilantro, 1 tablespoon basil, and 1 tablespoon mint. Top with ¼ cup lettuce, 2 tablespoons carrots, ¼ cup noodles, 2 tablespoons bean sprouts, and 1 teaspoon green onions.

2. Fold both sides of the rice paper sheet over the filling, then roll up as tightly as possible without tearing—starting with the side close to you—like a burrito. Place on a serving plate, seam side down, and cover to prevent drying while you prepare the remaining rolls. Serve immediately with the red chili dipping sauce.

Calories 200 · Fat 1g · Protein 3g · Carbohydrates 47g · Cholesterol 0mg · Sodium 195mg · Fiber 4g

Quick Breads and Yeast Breads

Bread is the mainstay of any diet, and most of us simply take it for granted—until gluten gets in the way. Then, the familiar becomes foreign and we have to learn new techniques and ingredients. The simple, versatile recipes in this chapter give you a set of basic breads that you can adapt to your own lifestyle.

Some of these yeast bread recipes utilize a technique that is not really new but is certainly rocking the baking world. All you do is make the yeast dough ahead of time, refrigerate it, and bake it the next day or a few days later. The crust is smooth and the bread has a soft crumb; try the French Baguettes (page 181) and see for yourself.

For more bread recipes, see my other books: *Wheat-Free Recipes & Menus*, *Cooking Free*, and *Gluten-Free Quick & Easy*.

· QUICK BREADS ·

Basic Muffins with Fruit and Nut Variations
Banana Oatmeal Muffins with Streusel Topping
Hearty Bran Muffins
Corn Bread and Corn Bread Muffins
Basic Scones with Drizzle

• YEAST BREADS •

Angel Pan Biscuits

Breadsticks

Rosemary Focaccia with Onion Marmalade

French Baguettes

Hearty Flax Bread

Basic Muffins with Fruit and Nut Variations

A simple, basic muffin is the foundation of many delicious options. Here is your basic recipe: Follow the variations below to suit your tastes. These muffins freeze beautifully; put them in individual containers, grab one when you leave the house, and you'll have a great treat waiting for you later in the day. These muffins are better with butter or buttery spread because of the buttery flavor, but you can use canola oil if you wish. **MAKES 12 MUFFINS**

2 cups GF Flour Blend (page 12)

²/₃ cup evaporated cane juice, plus extra for sprinkling

1 tablespoon baking powder

1 teaspoon xanthan gum

¼ teaspoon baking soda

½ teaspoon sea salt

1¼ cups hot (120°F) milk of choice

½ cup butter or buttery spread, melted, or canola oil

1 teaspoon pure vanilla

1. Place a rack in the middle of the oven. Preheat the oven to 375°F. Generously grease a standard 12-cup nonstick (gray, not black) metal muffin pan or use paper liners.

2. In a large mixing bowl, whisk together the flour blend, the ⅔ cup of the evaporated cane juice, and the baking powder, xanthan gum, baking soda, and salt until well blended. Add the hot milk, melted butter, and vanilla, and mix with an electric mixer on low speed just until blended. Beat for 30 seconds on medium-low speed, scraping down the sides of the bowl with a spatula. Stir in the fruit and nuts, if using (see the variations that follow). Divide the batter evenly in the muffin pan and sprinkle with evaporated cane juice.

3. Bake until the muffins are firm and slightly cracked on top, and a toothpick inserted into the center comes out clean, about 20 to 25 minutes. Cool the muffins in the pan on a wire rack for 15 minutes. Remove the muffins from the pan and serve warm.

Calories 200 · Fat 8g · Protein 2g · Carbohydrates 31g · Cholesterol 22mg · Sodium 240mg · Fiber 1g

Blueberry-Lemon Muffins: Add 1 cup fresh or frozen blueberries and 1 tablespoon grated lemon zest to the batter.

Cranberry-Orange Muffins: Add ¾ cup dried cranberries and 1 tablespoon grated orange zest to the batter.

Everyday to Elegant

Transform your muffins into elegant creations by using tulip muffin papers instead of regular paper liners. They are available at kitchen stores, but you can also make your own: Cut 5-inch squares of parchment paper (either white or brown). Turn your muffin pan over and shape each paper around a cup, folding the paper at least 4 times to make it fit tightly. Flip the pan over, put a tulip paper in each mold, fill with batter, and bake. Your muffins will look like they came from a professional bakery.

Banana Oatmeal Muffins with Streusel Topping

Homey, wholesome, and hearty, these are stick-to-your-ribs muffins. The Streusel Topping is very versatile and can be used on other muffins as well as on scones or cakes. It will also work on fruit crisps. **MAKES 12 MUFFINS**

2 cups GF Flour Blend (page 12)

⅓ cup GF quick-cooking oats*

1 tablespoon baking powder

1½ teaspoons xanthan gum

1 teaspoon ground cinnamon

¾ teaspoon sea salt

2 small ripe bananas, mashed

1 cup milk of choice

⅓ cup canola oil

⅔ cup evaporated cane juice

1 teaspoon pure vanilla

¼ cup finely chopped walnuts

STREUSEL TOPPING

3 tablespoons GF quick-cooking oats*

1 tablespoon finely chopped walnuts or pecans

1 tablespoon packed light brown sugar

¼ teaspoon baking powder

1 tablespoon butter or buttery spread

Check with your physician before eating gluten-free oats.

1. Place a rack in the middle of the oven. Preheat the oven to 375°F. Generously grease a standard 12-cup nonstick (gray, not black) metal muffin pan. Set aside.
2. In a medium bowl, whisk together the flour blend, oats, baking powder, xanthan gum, cinnamon, and salt until well blended.
3. In a small bowl, beat the bananas, milk, oil, evaporated cane juice, and vanilla with an electric mixer on low speed until thoroughly blended.
4. With the mixer on low speed, gradually beat the banana mixture into the dry ingredients until the batter is smooth and no flour is visible. Stir in the nuts. Divide the batter evenly in the muffin pan. Let stand 10 minutes.

5. Make the Streusel Topping: In a small bowl, whisk together the oats, nuts, brown sugar, and baking powder, then cut in the butter with a fork, pressing until the mixture forms clumps. Sprinkle evenly on the muffin tops and press it lightly into the batter with your fingertips.

6. Bake until the muffins tops are firm and a toothpick inserted into the center comes out clean, about 35 to 40 minutes. Cool the muffins in the pan on a wire rack for 10 minutes, then remove the muffins from the pan and cool another 10 minutes on the wire rack. Serve slightly warm.

Calories 240 · Fat 10g · Protein 3g · Carbohydrates 38g · Cholesterol 3mg · Sodium 288mg · Fiber 2g

Hearty Bran Muffins

Wholesome and filling, these delicious muffins help you meet a portion of your daily requirements for fiber. Draining the applesauce concentrates the pectins, slightly improving the muffins' texture. If you don't have time, skip this step but remember to do it next time. **MAKES 12 MUFFINS**

1²/₃ cups GF Flour Blend (page 12)

½ cup rice bran or Montina Pure Baking Supplement

²/₃ cup evaporated cane juice, plus 2 tablespoons for the muffin tops

2 teaspoons baking powder

¼ teaspoon baking soda

1 teaspoon cinnamon

¼ teaspoon freshly grated nutmeg

¼ teaspoon allspice

½ teaspoon sea salt

1 teaspoon xanthan gum

1 cup hot (120°F) milk of choice

⅓ cup canola oil

¼ cup applesauce, drained for 20 minutes (discard juice)

1 teaspoon pure vanilla

2 teaspoons grated orange zest, optional

¼ cup raisins or currants

¼ cup chopped walnuts, plus 2 tablespoons for topping

1. Place a rack in the lower third of the oven. Preheat the oven to 375°F. Generously grease a 12-cup standard nonstick (gray, not black) metal muffin pan or use paper liners.

2. In a medium bowl, whisk together the flour blend, rice bran, evaporated cane juice, baking powder, baking soda, cinnamon, nutmeg, allspice, salt, and xanthan gum until well blended.

3. In a 2-cup measuring bowl, whisk the hot milk, oil, applesauce, vanilla, and orange zest together, then gradually beat it into the flour mixture with an electric mixer on low speed. Increase the speed to medium and beat until the batter thickens slightly, about 30 seconds. Stir in the raisins and ¼ cup of the walnuts. Place about ⅓ cup batter in each muffin cup. Combine the remaining 2 tablespoons of evaporated cane juice and 2 tablespoons of walnuts, then gently press the mixture on the muffin tops. Let stand 10 minutes.

4. Bake until the muffins tops are lightly browned and firm, and a toothpick inserted into the center comes out clean, about 30 to 35 minutes. Place the pan on a wire rack to cool for 15 minutes. Remove the muffins and serve warm.

Calories 215 · Fat 9g · Protein 3g · Carbohydrates 34g · Cholesterol 1mg · Sodium 197mg · Fiber 2g

Corn Bread
and Corn Bread Muffins

Corn bread is the perfect accompaniment to a hearty winter soup or to round out a light dinner salad. Freeze the leftover corn bread for corn bread stuffing. For a higher, lighter corn bread, replace ¼ cup of the flour blend with modified tapioca starch, known as Expandex (see page 267). **MAKES 12 SERVINGS**

1 cup GF Flour Blend (page 12)

¾ cup GF yellow cornmeal

⅓ cup evaporated cane juice

1 tablespoon baking powder

¼ teaspoon baking soda

½ teaspoon xanthan gum

½ teaspoon guar gum

½ teaspoon sea salt

1¼ cups milk of choice

¼ cup canola oil

1. Place a rack in the lower third of the oven. Preheat the oven to 350°F. Grease a 9-inch round nonstick (gray, not black) metal pan.
2. In a small bowl, whisk together the flour blend, cornmeal, evaporated cane juice, baking powder, baking soda, xanthan gum, guar gum, and salt until well blended.
3. In a large mixing bowl, beat the milk, and oil with an electric mixer on low speed until well blended, about 15 seconds. Gradually beat in the flour mixture on low speed; increase the speed to medium and beat until the batter thickens slightly, about 30 seconds. Spread the batter evenly in the pan.
4. Bake until the top is firm and a toothpick inserted into the center comes out clean, about 20 to 25 minutes. Cool the corn bread in the pan on a wire rack for 15 minutes. Cut into 12 wedges and serve warm.

Calories 140 · Fat 5g · Protein 2g · Carbohydrates 23g · Cholesterol 1mg · Sodium 218mg · Fiber 1g

For a lighter texture, beat in one large egg with the liquid ingredients until smooth.

Corn Bread Muffins: Line a standard 12-cup nonstick (gray, not black) metal muffin pan with paper liners. Fill each liner with ¼ cup batter. Bake until a toothpick inserted into the center of a muffin comes out clean, about 18 to 20 minutes. Serve slightly warm.

Basic Scones with Drizzle

Scones are so easy to make, especially this version. They start out as a mound of dough on a baking sheet, then you cut them into wedges after baking. But they are even easier if you bake them in a nonstick scone pan with 8 individual indentations (available at kitchen stores). And who says you can't have chocolate for breakfast? Be sure to try the variations to this versatile recipe. **SERVES 8**

1¾ cups GF Flour Blend (page 12)

⅓ cup evaporated cane juice, plus 1 tablespoon for sprinkling on scones

1 tablespoon baking powder

¼ teaspoon baking soda

1 teaspoon xanthan gum

½ teaspoon sea salt

5 tablespoons butter or buttery spread, at room temperature, cut in 5 pieces

¾ cup warm (110°F) milk of choice, plus 2 tablespoons for brushing

Zest of 1 orange; reserve 1 teaspoon for drizzle

1 teaspoon pure vanilla extract or orange-flavored extract

¼ cup currants or golden raisins

DRIZZLE

½ cup powdered sugar

1 tablespoon milk of choice or enough to form a thin frosting

1. Preheat the oven to 400°F. Line 9 x 13-inch baking sheet (not nonstick) with parchment paper.

2. In a food processor, pulse together the flour blend, evaporated cane juice, baking powder, baking soda, xanthan gum, and salt until thoroughly blended. Add the butter, milk, orange zest, and vanilla, and pulse just until mixed. Add the currants and pulse a few times to incorporate. The dough will be soft.

3. Transfer the dough to the baking sheet. With a wet spatula, pat the dough into a very smooth 7-inch circle, ¾-inch thick, with straight rather than sloped edges. Brush the top with 1 tablespoon of the milk.

4. Bake for 15 to 20 minutes or until golden brown. Remove from the oven, brush with the remaining tablespoon of milk, sprinkle with the remaining tablespoon of evaporated cane

juice, cut into 8 wedges, and slide the wedges an inch from each other so the sides can brown. Return to the oven for another 5 to 8 minutes of baking. Cool the pan on a wire rack for 10 minutes.

5. Prepare the Drizzle: Add the reserved teaspoon of orange zest and the milk to the powdered sugar and stir until a thin frosting forms, adding more milk, if necessary, to reach desired consistency. Drizzle over the scones, allow the frosting to firm up for 10 minutes, and serve immediately while the scones are still slightly warm.

Calories 250 · Fat 9g · Protein 2g · Carbohydrates 43g · Cholesterol 3mg · Sodium 337mg · Fiber 2g

Lemon-Blueberry Scones with Lemon Drizzle: Replace the currants with dried blueberries and the orange zest with lemon zest. Use lemon zest instead of orange zest in the Drizzle.

Chocolate Chip Scones with White Chocolate Drizzle: Stir 1 cup of chocolate chips into the batter. Bake as directed. Cool for 15 minutes. Drizzle with melted white chocolate.

Everyday to Exceptional

Soak the currants in 2 tablespoons of a complementary-flavored liqueur for 30 minutes before assembling the recipe:

Orange-Currant Scones: Triple-Sec, Cointreau, or Grand Marnier
Lemon-Blueberry Scones: Limoncello

Angel Pan Biscuits

Called "angel" biscuits because the yeast makes them rise higher, these biscuits will be your breakfast staple. Slathered with butter, jam, or jelly, they're divine. Increase the sweetener, bake as directed, and they become shortcake for Strawberry Shortcake (see the variation following the recipe). **MAKES 12 BISCUITS**

White rice flour for dusting

1 teaspoon active dry yeast

1 tablespoon apple cider vinegar or lemon juice

¾ cup warm (110°F) milk of choice

½ cup GF Flour Blend (page 12)

½ cup potato starch

½ cup cornstarch

2 tablespoons evaporated cane juice

2 tablespoons baking powder

½ teaspoon baking soda

½ teaspoon xanthan gum

½ teaspoon sea salt

5 tablespoons unsalted butter, buttery spread, or shortening, divided

1. Generously grease an 8-inch round cake pan and dust with white rice flour.
2. Stir the yeast and vinegar into the warm milk. Set aside for 5 minutes.
3. Place the flour blend, potato starch, cornstarch, evaporated cane juice, baking powder, baking soda, xanthan gum, and salt in a food processor and pulse to blend thoroughly. Add 4 tablespoons of the butter and pulse until the mixture forms a few balls.
4. With the motor running, add the yeast-milk mixture through the tube and process until a very soft dough forms.
5. Dip a #30 metal ice cream scoop or a 2-tablespoon measuring cup into hot water, scoop out a ball of dough, and drop it into the pan, rounded side up. Continue with the remaining dough, wetting the scoop with water each time, and place all 12 balls very close to each other so the biscuits rise rather than spreading out. Melt the remaining tablespoon of butter and brush it on the tops of the biscuits. Cover the pan with plastic wrap and let stand 20 minutes in a warm place (85°F) while the oven preheats.
6. Place a rack in the lower third of the oven. Preheat the oven to 375°F.

7. Remove plastic covering and bake until the tops of the biscuits are lightly browned, about 15 to 20 minutes. Transfer the biscuits to a wire rack and cool for 10 minutes, then serve warm.

Calories 235 · Fat 10g · Protein 2g · Carbohydrates 37g · Cholesterol 27mg · Sodium 715mg · Fiber 1g

Shortcake: Increase the evaporated cane juice to ⅓ cup. Use the sweet dough as the basis for your favorite Strawberry Shortcake recipe.

Breadsticks

Bread bakers across the United States are raving about a new technique that produces fantastic bread. The secret? Simply make the dough a day or so ahead and refrigerate; magical enzymes work on the refrigerated dough, elevating it to a better flavor and texture. It works perfectly here, but if you can't wait that long, make the dough with warm (110°F) milk and bake it right away, starting with Step 3. **MAKES 12 BREADSTICKS**

1 tablespoon instant (quick-rise) yeast

1 cup cold milk of choice

2 teaspoons evaporated cane juice

½ cup brown rice flour

½ cup tapioca flour

2 teaspoons xanthan gum

½ teaspoon sea salt

½ cup grated Parmesan cheese or soy Parmesan

1 teaspoon onion powder

1 tablespoon olive oil, plus more for brushing

2 teaspoons sesame seeds

1. In a small bowl, combine the yeast, milk, and cane juice. Set aside for 5 minutes.

2. In a medium mixer bowl, blend the flours, xanthan gum, salt, Parmesan cheese, and onion powder with an electric mixer on low speed. Add the yeast mixture and olive oil. Beat on high speed for 30 seconds. Place the dough in a heavy-duty 1-quart resealable bag and refrigerate overnight or up to 3 days, then let the dough stand in the bag at room temperature for 30 minutes before going to Step 4. To bake immediately, proceed to Step 3.

3. Place a rack in the middle of the oven. Preheat the oven to 200°F for 4 minutes, then turn it off. Line a 9 x 13-inch metal baking sheet (not nonstick) with parchment paper.

4. With scissors, cut a ½-inch opening in one bottom corner of the bag of dough. Squeeze the dough onto the baking sheet in strips, 1 inch wide by 6 inches long. Brush lightly with the olive oil, then sprinkle with the sesame seeds. Cover lightly with aluminum foil, but don't let it touch the breadsticks.

5. Place the breadsticks in the oven to rise for 20 minutes. Remove the foil but leave the breadsticks in the oven and turn the oven temperature to 400°F. Bake until the

breadsticks are golden brown, about 20 to 25 minutes. Switch the position of the baking sheet halfway through baking to assure even browning. Cool 10 minutes on the wire rack and serve warm.

Calories 85 · Fat 3g · Protein 3g · Carbohydrates 12g · Cholesterol 3mg · Sodium 152mg · Fiber 1g

Rosemary Focaccia with Onion Marmalade

....

This is the bread typically served in Italian restaurants, often with a balsamic vinegar–olive oil dipping sauce. Called a flatbread because it doesn't rise very high, focaccia is a cross between bread and pizza. Serve it warm, fresh from the oven, spread with the savory Onion Marmalade for a real treat. Or cool it and slice in half horizontally for very flavorful sandwich bread. **SERVES 12**

2¼ teaspoons (1 packet) instant (quick-rising) yeast

½ teaspoon golden ground flax meal

1 cup hot (120°F) milk of choice

1 cup potato starch

½ cup GF Flour Blend (page 12)

4 teaspoons evaporated cane juice

1 teaspoon xanthan gum

½ teaspoon sea salt

⅛ teaspoon baking soda

1½ tablespoons chopped fresh rosemary, or 1 teaspoon dried, divided

2 tablespoons olive oil, divided

Coarse salt for sprinkling, optional

2 tablespoons grated Parmesan cheese or soy Parmesan, for topping

ONION MARMALADE (MAKES ABOUT 1¼ CUPS)

1 tablespoon canola oil

3 large yellow onions, peeled and thinly sliced

⅓ cup packed light brown sugar, or more to taste

1 medium garlic clove, minced

½ cup white wine vinegar

1 tablespoon chopped fresh thyme, optional

¼ to ½ teaspoon sea salt, or to taste

⅛ teaspoon freshly ground black pepper

1. Generously grease an 8 x 8-inch nonstick (gray, not black) metal pan.
2. In a small bowl, dissolve the yeast and ground flax meal in the hot milk. Set aside.
3. In a medium mixing bowl, whisk together the potato starch, flour blend, evaporated cane juice, xanthan gum, salt, baking soda, and 2 teaspoons of the fresh rosemary (½ teaspoon of the dried) until well blended. Add 1 tablespoon of the oil to the yeast

mixture and pour it into the dry ingredients. With an electric mixer on low speed, beat until the dough is slightly thickened, about 30 seconds. The dough will be soft and sticky.

4. Spread the dough very evenly in the pan with a wet spatula. Brush the dough with the remaining tablespoon of olive oil and sprinkle with the remaining rosemary and the coarse salt, if using. Cover with a foil tent and let rise in a warm place (80 to 85°F) until the dough is level with the top of the pan, about 45 to 50 minutes. Remove the foil tent before baking. Place a rack in the lower third of the oven. Preheat the oven to 375°F.

5. Bake until the focaccia is golden brown and an instant-read thermometer registers 205°F when inserted into the center of the loaf, about 35 to 40 minutes. Lay the foil tent over the bread after 15 minutes of baking if it browns too quickly. Remove the pan from the oven and sprinkle with the Parmesan cheese. Return the pan to the oven and bake until the Parmesan is melted, about 3 to 5 minutes. Cool the focaccia in the pan on a wire rack for 15 minutes.

6. While the bread rises, bakes, and cools, make the Onion Marmalade: In a heavy medium saucepan, heat the oil over medium heat. Add the onions, brown sugar, garlic, vinegar, and thyme (if using), and cook, covered, stirring occasionally, until the onions are very soft, about 30 minutes. Add the ¼ teaspoon of salt and the pepper, and continue to cook until the onions absorb the juices and reach the texture of marmalade. The onions will reduce as they cook, but watch carefully to avoid scorching. Taste and add more brown sugar and salt, if desired. Set aside to cool slightly. Cut the focaccia into 12 slices and serve warm with the marmalade. Refrigerate any leftover marmalade in a glass jar for up to one week.

Calories 130 · Fat 4g · Protein 2g · Carbohydrates 23g · Cholesterol 1mg · Sodium 195mg · Fiber 1g

French Baguettes

Hot bread, fresh from the oven! You'll make this recipe over and over, I guarantee. Baguettes are smaller than French bread loaves and bake more quickly because a baguette pan typically has 3 indentations, compared to two for French bread. Use the leftovers for Crostini (page 158), stuffing, or bread pudding. For spectacular texture and flavor, mix the dough with cold ingredients a day ahead, refrigerate overnight, then shape and bake right before dinner. If you simply can't wait, use warm (110°F) milk and immediately go to Step 4. For a higher rise, replace the cornstarch with the same amount of modified tapioca starch, known as Expandex (see page 267). **SERVES 8 (MAKES 3 7-INCH BAGUETTES)**

½ teaspoon golden ground flax meal, stirred into ¼ cup boiling water, then cooled to room temperature

2¼ teaspoons (1 packet) active dry yeast

4 teaspoons evaporated cane juice, divided

⅔ cup cold milk of choice

¾ cup potato starch

½ cup GF Flour Blend (page 12)

⅓ cup cornstarch

½ teaspoon sea salt

½ teaspoon xanthan gum

½ teaspoon guar gum

3 tablespoons butter or buttery spread, melted and cooled to room temperature, divided

1 teaspoon apple cider vinegar

1 teaspoon sesame seeds

1. Line a French baguette pan with parchment paper. Stir the ground flax meal and boiling water together and set aside to cool to room temperature, stirring occasionally.

2. In a small bowl, dissolve the yeast and 1 teaspoon of the cane juice in the milk. Set aside.

3. In a medium bowl, whisk together the potato starch, flour blend, cornstarch, salt, xanthan gum, guar gum, and remaining evaporated cane juice until blended. Add the yeast-milk mixture, flax mixture, 2 tablespoons of the melted butter, and the vinegar, and beat on low speed with an electric mixer until thoroughly blended, about 30 seconds. Refrigerate the dough, tightly covered, for up to three days.

4. Transfer the dough to the pan. With a wet spatula, shape the dough into three blunt-ended 7-inch logs. Brush the tops with the remaining tablespoon of melted butter. Sprinkle with the sesame seeds. Cover the dough and put in a warm place (80 to 85°F) to rise until doubled in size. Place a rack in the middle of the oven. Preheat the oven to 375°F.

5. With kitchen scissors, make 3 diagonal snips (⅛ inch deep) or a series of snips down the center of each loaf so steam can escape during baking. Bake until the loaves are firm and lightly browned, about 25 to 30 minutes or until an instant-read thermometer registers 205°F when inserted into the center of a loaf.

6. Remove the bread from the pan and cool 15 minutes on a wire rack before slicing with an electric knife or serrated knife. For the best flavor and texture, serve immediately, slightly warm.

Calories 155 · Fat 5g · Protein 2g · Carbohydrates 28g · Cholesterol 12mg · Sodium 173mg · Fiber 1g

For lighter, softer baguettes, replace the cornstarch with an equal amount of dried egg whites.

Cold-Oven Start for Small Breads

You may start smaller breads—like French bread, baguettes, breadsticks, or pizza—to bake in a cold oven, immediately after shaping the dough (do not let it rise). Place it in a cold oven, turn the oven to 375°F, and bake as directed, perhaps extending baking time by 5 to 10 minutes. The dough rises as the oven preheats, and this pre-heating session produces a smoother loaf with a crispy crust. This method does not work well with full-sized bread loaves because they need more rising time than this method allows.

Boosting the Nutrient and Fiber Content

To boost the nutrients and fiber of these French baguettes, try these tips:

INSIDE THE LOAF

Add ¼ cup whole teff, amaranth, quinoa cereal flakes, almond meal, or Montina Pure Baking Supplement to the dough. If you use amounts beyond these suggestions, you may have to increase the amount of liquid in the recipe.

OUTSIDE THE LOAF

Sprinkle 2 tablespoons of GF rolled oats,* hulled millet, or unroasted and hulled sunflower seeds evenly on the parchment paper in each pan indentation before shaping the dough. After shaping, sprinkle the tops of each loaf with another 2 tablespoons, pressing them into the dough slightly with your fingers.

*Check with your physician before eating gluten-free oats.

Hearty Flax Bread

This earthy bread is heavy, dense, and chock-full of fiber and nutrients. Definitely not for sissies! I love it toasted and slathered with Earth Balance buttery spread, while I sip a cup of freshly brewed coffee. It makes a very filling sandwich, too. Like most other recipes, this one is amazingly versatile. Instead of the flax meal, try the same amount of Montina Pure Baking Supplement or almond meal. Instead of agave nectar, try molasses or maple syrup. Each substitution yields a slightly different look and texture, so feel free to experiment with this amazing bread. **MAKES 14 SERVINGS**

1 tablespoon active dry yeast

1 tablespoon ground flax meal

1¼ cups warm (110°F) milk of choice

2 cups GF Flour Blend (page 12)

1 cup potato starch

⅓ cup whole flaxseeds

¼ cup sunflower seeds (or finely chopped nuts of choice)

1 tablespoon chia seeds, optional (or whole-grain teff or rice bran)

1½ teaspoons xanthan gum

1½ teaspoons sea salt

¼ cup canola oil

¼ cup agave nectar

1 teaspoon apple cider vinegar

1. Generously grease three 4 x 6-inch nonstick (gray, not black) metal pans.
2. In a small bowl, dissolve the yeast and ground flax meal in the warm milk. Set aside.
3. In a medium mixing bowl, whisk together the flour blend, potato starch, flaxseeds, sunflower seeds, chia seeds (if using), xanthan gum, and salt. Add the yeast-milk mixture, oil, agave nectar, and vinegar. With an electric mixer on low speed, beat until the dough is well blended, about 30 seconds. The dough will be soft and sticky.
4. Spread the dough very evenly in the pans with a wet spatula. Cover lightly with an oiled foil tent and let rise in a warm place (80 to 85°F) until the dough is level with the top of the pans, about 45 to 60 minutes.
5. Place a rack in the lower third of the oven. Preheat the oven to 375°F. Bake until the crust is hard and an instant-read thermometer registers 205°F when inserted into the center of a loaf, about 40 to 45 minutes. Lay a foil tent over the bread if it browns too quickly. Cool the bread in the pans on a wire rack for 15 minutes. Transfer the

bread to the wire rack to cool completely before slicing with a serrated knife or electric knife.

Calories 200 · Fat 7g · Protein 4g · Carbohydrates 32g · Cholesterol 1mg · Sodium 215mg · Fiber 3g

Flaxseeds and Chia Seeds

Whole flaxseeds are not digested, because their tough hull makes it impossible for our bodies to break them down. But they supply interesting texture and visual appeal in breads like this one. Flax meal, on the other hand, is ground flaxseeds, and the important nutrients are easily absorbed in this form. Chia is a member of the mint family; the seeds do not need to be pulverized to be absorbed, so leave them whole, but grind them with a spice grinder if you want to reduce their grittiness.

Breakfast

Because our American breakfast is typically laden with wheat, this meal is often the one that is most perplexing to people on a gluten-free diet and even more so to vegetarians and vegans. The recipes here are basics, designed to give you the most essential breakfast dishes. If you're a lacto-ovo vegetarian, you will enjoy all the recipes. If you are a vegan, you'll enjoy all the recipes except the Breakfast Strata, Eggs Benedict, Mediterranean Frittata, and Quiche. For more breakfast dishes, see my other books: *Wheat-Free Recipes & Menus*, *Cooking Free*, and *Gluten-Free Quick & Easy*.

• ON THE GRIDDLE •

Pancakes

Waffles

• CEREALS AND GRAINS •

Amaranth Porridge

Granola

Granola Bars

Whole Grains for Breakfast (or Any Time of Day)

• EGGS AND CASSEROLE DISHES •

Breakfast Egg Strata

Crispy Potato Cakes with Herb Cream Sauce

Asparagus (or Eggs) Benedict with Hollandaise Sauce

Mediterranean Frittata

Quiche

Grilled Herb Tofu with Chimichurri on Toast

Pancakes

Pancakes were made for weekends, when the breakfast pace is more leisurely. If you want to serve them during the week, mix the batter and store it, tightly covered, in the refrigerator. Add ½ teaspoon fresh lemon juice to the batter right before cooking to revive the leavening. Mixing the batter in a blender incorporates air into these pancakes and makes them lighter. If you want to use an egg, see below. **SERVES 4, 3 PANCAKES EACH (MAKES 1¼ CUPS BATTER)**

1 cup GF Flour Blend (page 12)

½ cup potato starch

1 cup hot (120°F) milk of choice

1 teaspoon fresh lemon juice

½ teaspoon apple cider vinegar

1½ tablespoons evaporated cane juice

1½ teaspoons baking powder

¼ teaspoon sea salt

⅛ teaspoon xanthan gum

1 teaspoon butter or buttery spread, melted

½ teaspoon vanilla extract

Canola oil for frying, or melted butter or buttery spread

1. Whirl all the ingredients except the oil in a blender until thoroughly blended, about 1 minute.
2. Heat the oil in a large nonstick skillet over medium heat. For each 4-inch pancake, pour 3 tablespoons batter (a scant ¼ cup) into the skillet and cook until the top is bubbly all over, about 2 to 3 minutes. Turn and cook until the bottom is golden brown, about another minute. Repeat until all batter is used. Serve immediately.

Calories 235 · Fat 2g · Protein 4g · Carbohydrates 51g · Cholesterol 2mg · Sodium 333mg · Fiber 1g

For a lighter texture, add one large egg to the blender and reduce the milk to ¾ cup. Blend, let stand for 5 minutes, then adjust consistency if necessary by adding more flour blend or more milk, a tablespoon at a time.

Waffles

• •

Cornstarch lightens these waffles, and cornmeal adds a nice crunch. Using an egg (see below) enhances their texture, but these waffles will delight everyone, with or without eggs. **MAKES 4 WAFFLES**

1¼ cups GF Flour Blend (page 12)

½ cup cornstarch

1 tablespoon GF cornmeal

1½ tablespoons evaporated cane juice

½ teaspoon baking soda

¼ teaspoon sea salt

¼ teaspoon xanthan gum

1¼ cups buttermilk or 1¼ cups milk of choice with 1 tablespoon apple cider vinegar stirred in, at room temperature

2 tablespoons butter or buttery spread, melted

½ teaspoon pure vanilla

1. In a medium bowl, whisk together the flour blend, cornstarch, cornmeal, evaporated cane juice, baking soda, salt, and xanthan gum until thoroughly blended. In a measuring cup, whisk together the buttermilk, butter, and vanilla until well blended and then pour it in a steady stream into the flour mixture, stirring constantly with a spatula until a thick, smooth batter forms.

2. Heat a waffle iron. Following the manufacturer's directions, pour the appropriate amount of batter into the waffle iron (usually about ¼ of the batter for 4 waffles, which would be one-half cup per waffle for this recipe). Close and bake until the steaming stops, about 4 to 6 minutes. Repeat with the remaining batter. Serve immediately.

Calories 155 · Fat 3g · Protein 2g · Carbohydrates 30g · Cholesterol 9mg · Sodium 208mg · Fiber 1g

For a lighter texture, whisk in one large egg with the liquid ingredients before adding them to the dry ingredients.

Amaranth Porridge

Historians tell us that amaranth was a primary food for the ancient Aztecs. Known as one of the most nutritious grains on earth, it is an excellent choice for the gluten-free diet. Here, it is cooked into a hearty porridge. Make a batch and refrigerate it; eat it throughout the week for a good start to your day. **SERVES 4 (MAKES 3 CUPS)**

3 cups water

1 cup whole amaranth grain

1 teaspoon butter or buttery spread

¼ teaspoon sea salt, or to taste

3 tablespoons pure maple syrup

1 teaspoon ground cinnamon

¼ teaspoon freshly grated nutmeg

½ cup unsweetened coconut flakes, optional

¼ cup chopped walnuts or pecans

1. Bring the water to a boil in a medium saucepan. Add the amaranth, butter, and salt, and bring to a boil again. Reduce the heat to low and simmer, covered, 20 to 25 minutes. Remove from the heat.

2. Stir in the maple syrup, cinnamon, and nutmeg until smooth. Serve in 4 cereal bowls, each garnished with 2 tablespoons coconut flakes (if using) and 1 tablespoon walnuts.

Calories 325 · Fat 12g · Protein 9g · Carbohydrates 48g · Cholesterol 0mg · Sodium 169mg · Fiber 9g

Granola

Granola is one of the more versatile and nutritious options you can choose for breakfast. This version is intentionally simple; dress it up with your favorite nuts, dried fruits, and additional spices like grated nutmeg or a dash of allspice. Sprinkle it on ice cream, pudding, or yogurt. Take it to work for a quick snack, or add a few nuts and candies and you have a trail mix for your next hike. **SERVES 6 (MAKES 4 CUPS)**

3 cups GF rolled oats*

1 cup large unsweetened coconut flakes
    (not shredded coconut)

2 tablespoons packed dark brown sugar

1 teaspoon ground cinnamon

½ teaspoon sea salt

¼ cup pure maple syrup

¼ cup canola oil

1 tablespoon pure vanilla

Check with your physician before eating gluten-free oats.

1. Preheat the oven to 275°F. Line a 10 x 15-inch rimmed metal baking sheet (not non-stick) with parchment paper.
2. In a large bowl, whisk together the oats, coconut, brown sugar, cinnamon, and salt until blended.
3. In a measuring cup, whisk together the maple syrup, oil, and vanilla, and pour it over the oat mixture. Toss until thoroughly coated. Spread the granola evenly on the baking sheet.
4. Bake the granola for 45 to 60 minutes, stirring every 15 minutes to promote even browning. Remove the baking sheet from the oven and cool the granola on the sheet on a wire rack. Transfer to an airtight container and store, covered, up to one week.

Calories 345 · Fat 16g · Protein 7g · Carbohydrates 47g · Cholesterol 0mg · Sodium 225mg · Fiber 5g

Granola Bars

Hearty granola bars are wonderful for breakfast when everyone is running late and can't sit down to eat. They're portable, and can be eaten on the school bus or in the backseat of the car during a mad dash to school. Freeze a few bars individually and grab them as you head out the door. I always have at least one in my carry-on bag for plane or car trips.

SERVES 18

2 cups GF rolled oats*

3/4 cup chopped walnuts, sunflower
    seeds, or almonds

3/4 cup chopped dried fruit such as
    apricots, cranberries, dates, figs,
    currants, raisins, or plums

1/2 cup sweetened shredded
    coconut

2 tablespoons rice bran

2 tablespoons packed light brown
    sugar

1 teaspoon ground cinnamon

1/2 teaspoon sea salt

1/4 teaspoon xanthan gum

2 tablespoons ground flax meal

2 teaspoons pure vanilla

1/4 cup boiling water

1/3 cup agave nectar or honey

1/3 cup canola oil

Check with your physician before eating gluten-free oats.

1. Place a rack in the middle of the oven. Preheat the oven to 325°F. Line a 9 x 13-inch metal cake pan with aluminum foil, letting the foil extend over the edges.

2. Spread the oats in the pan and toast them in the oven, stirring occasionally, just until they become fragrant, about 10 minutes. Transfer the oats to a large bowl and coat the foil-lined pan with cooking spray. Set the pan aside.

3. In the large bowl, toss the oats with the nuts, dried fruit, coconut, bran, brown sugar, cinnamon, salt, and xanthan gum until thoroughly mixed. In a small bowl, whisk the flax meal and vanilla into the boiling water and let stand until slightly thickened, about 5 minutes. Whisk the agave nectar and oil into the flax mixture until thoroughly blended and then pour it over the oat mixture. Toss with a spatula until the oats are thoroughly coated. Press the mixture evenly in the pan.

4. Bake until the granola is crisp and lightly browned, about 25 to 30 minutes. Cool the granola in the pan, then invert the pan onto a large cutting board, remove the foil, and cut the granola into 18 squares, approximately 4 x 1½ inches each. Serve at room temperature. Store, tightly covered, in the refrigerator for one week or freeze up to one month.

Calories 155 · Fat 9g · Protein 3g · Carbohydrates 18g · Cholesterol 0mg · Sodium 56mg · Fiber 3g

Whole Grains for Breakfast
(or Any Time of Day)

Whole grains play a critical role in the gluten-free diet, since they are required to supply important nutrients we no longer get when we avoid wheat. Technically, some of the grains are actually seeds but I call them grains for easier discussion. The Whole Grains Council urges us to get at least three to five servings of whole grains per day. Go to www. wholegrainscouncil.org/whole-grains-101 for more information on the definition of whole grains and our daily requirements.

Try these delicious and nutritious substitutions for breakfast or as a side dish at any meal. The following table gives you basic guidelines on how to cook these grains. Use sea salt as you wish. Serves 4.

Note: Check with your physician before eating gluten-free oats.

GRAIN (1 CUP)	WATER	COOKING TIME
Amaranth seed[1]	2 cups	15 to 20 minutes
Brown rice	2 ½ cups	30 to 45 minutes
Buckwheat (whole groats)[1]	1 cup	15 to 20 minutes
Corn grits[1]	3 cups	5 minutes
Millet seed[1]	3 ½ to 4 cups	35 to 45 minutes
Oats (rolled)[1]	2 cups	15 to 20 minutes
Oats (quick-cooking)[2]	2 cups	5 to 10 minutes
Oats (steel-cut) [1]	2 cups	10 to 20 minutes
Quinoa seeds[1]	2 cups	12 to 15 minutes

(continued)

GRAIN (1 CUP)	WATER	COOKING TIME
Sorghum grains[3] (soak overnight)	2 cups	40 to 45 minutes
Teff grains[4]	3 cups	20 minutes
Wild rice seeds	4 cups	40 minutes

1. Available at www.BobsRedMill.com or www.NuWorldAmaranth.com.

2. Available at www.BobsRedMill.com.

3. Available at www.ShilohFarms.com.

4. Available at www.BobsRedMill.com or www.theteffcompany.com.

Breakfast Egg Strata

This is the classic breakfast casserole served at brunches. It is super-simple to make and quite versatile, and never fails to please your guests. It is especially good for entertaining because you make it the night before and bake it the next day, leaving you free to focus on your guests instead of being in the kitchen. **SERVES 4**

4 cups GF bread (about 8 slices sandwich bread), cut in 1/2-inch cubes

2 tablespoons olive oil

1 small onion, finely diced, or 1 small leek, white parts only, finely chopped

1 small garlic clove, minced

1 cup grated Monterey Jack cheese or cheese alternative

1 jar (6 ounces) marinated artichoke hearts, drained and coarsely chopped

1 tablespoon capers, drained and rinsed

8 tablespoons Parmesan cheese or soy Parmesan, divided

3 large eggs

1 1/2 cups milk of choice

1/4 cup dry white wine (or milk of choice)

1 tablespoon Dijon mustard

2 tablespoons chopped fresh basil, tightly packed, or 2 teaspoons dried

1/2 teaspoon sea salt

1/4 teaspoon freshly grated nutmeg

1/4 teaspoon freshly ground black pepper

2 tablespoons chopped fresh parsley

1/2 teaspoon paprika, for garnish

1. Grease an 8 x 8-inch glass baking dish. Arrange the bread cubes in the bottom of the dish.

2. In a heavy skillet, heat the oil over medium-low heat. Cook the onion and garlic, covered, stirring occasionally, until the onion is tender and lightly browned, about 5 minutes. Add to the dish, along with the cheese, artichoke hearts, and capers, and toss gently to mix thoroughly. Sprinkle with 6 tablespoons of the Parmesan cheese.

3. In a medium bowl, whisk together the eggs, milk, wine, mustard, basil, salt, nutmeg, pepper, and parsley until well combined, then pour evenly over the bread mixture. Press the bread down lightly with a spatula. Cover tightly with foil and refrigerate overnight or at least 4 hours.

4. Place a rack in the lower third of the oven. Preheat the oven to 350°F.

5. Bake with the foil on for 45 minutes. Discard the foil, sprinkle with the remaining 2 tablespoons of Parmesan cheese, and bake another 15 minutes or until the top is nicely browned. Let cool 5 minutes before serving, dusting with the paprika for garnish. Serve hot.

Calories 390 · Fat 21g · Protein 23g · Carbohydrates 25g · Cholesterol 167mg · Sodium 917mg · Fiber 2g

Crispy Potato Cakes with Herb Cream Sauce

One of the textures I missed the most when I went gluten-free was "crispiness." If you're like me, then you'll love biting into the crispy potatoes, accentuated by the smooth, creamy sauce. You can use these potato cakes instead of English muffins in Asparagus (or Eggs) Benedict with Hollandaise Sauce (page 201). **MAKES 6 CAKES**

3 medium russet potatoes (about 1 pound), peeled and grated

6 tablespoons butter or buttery spread, melted

1 tablespoon olive oil

1 tablespoon cornstarch

Salt and freshly ground black pepper, to taste

HERB CREAM SAUCE

1 small onion, finely chopped

3 sprigs fresh rosemary or dill, chopped finely, plus more for garnish

½ cup nonfat sour cream or vegan sour cream

3 tablespoons fresh lemon juice

½ teaspoon freshly grated nutmeg

½ teaspoon sea salt, or to taste

½ teaspoon freshly ground black pepper, or to taste

1. Preheat the oven to 250°F. Line a 9 x 13-inch baking sheet with paper towels.
2. Squeeze the potatoes in a linen towel or press through a sieve to remove all liquid. The drier the potatoes, the crispier the potato cakes.
3. Combine the butter and oil and toss the grated potatoes in 5 tablespoons of the mixture. Toss the potatoes with the cornstarch and season with the salt and freshly ground pepper.
4. Heat a 10-inch cast-iron skillet over medium heat. Add the remaining 2 tablespoons of the butter-oil mixture to the skillet. Divide the potatoes into six mounds and drop two mounds into the skillet at a time, using a metal spatula to form them into a uniform shape and thickness. Fry until golden brown on the bottom, about 5 minutes, then turn and fry until crispy, about 4 minutes more. Place on the paper towel–lined baking sheet and keep warm in the oven while frying the remaining potato cakes.

5. While the potato cakes are in the oven, prepare the Herb Cream Sauce: In a bowl, mix together well the onions, rosemary, sour cream, lemon juice, nutmeg, salt, and pepper.

6. Remove the potato cakes from the oven. Serve immediately, topped with a dollop of the cream sauce, garnished with a sprinkle of fresh rosemary or dill.

Calories 290 · Fat 21g · Protein 3g · Carbohydrates 24g · Cholesterol 2mg · Sodium 449mg · Fiber 2g

Asparagus (or Eggs) Benedict with Hollandaise Sauce

For this dish, look for English muffins by Food for Life. Or use slices of GF toast or the Crispy Potato Cakes (page 199) instead. If you prefer the traditional Eggs Benedict, place a poached egg on top instead of the asparagus (or use both). See page 202 for how to poach eggs. **SERVES 4**

8 ounces soft silken tofu, drained

2 tablespoons fresh lemon juice

2 tablespoons butter or buttery spread

1/4 teaspoon ground turmeric

1/4 teaspoon ground mustard

1/4 teaspoon sea salt

1/8 teaspoon xanthan gum

1/8 teaspoon cayenne pepper

1/8 teaspoon white pepper

1/4 cup hot (120°F) water

1 pound asparagus (thin spears work best, or peel stems if thick)

1 tablespoon butter or buttery spread

4 GF English muffins

1/2 teaspoon paprika, for garnish

1. Make the Hollandaise Sauce: Place the tofu, lemon juice, butter, turmeric, mustard, salt, xanthan gum, cayenne pepper, white pepper, and water in a blender, and process until the mixture is very smooth. Scrape down the sides of the blender with a spatula, as needed, adding more hot water, a tablespoon at a time, if necessary to reach the consistency of syrup. The sauce can be made a day ahead; to serve, heat on low power in the microwave. If it is too thick, add hot water a tablespoon at a time to reach desired consistency.

2. Trim the asparagus. In a skillet, toss it with the butter and cook over medium heat just until the spears are tender, about 2 to 3 minutes (depending on size).

3. Toast the muffins and place each, cut side up, on a plate. Top with asparagus spears, drizzle with the hot Hollandaise Sauce, garnish with the paprika, and serve immediately.

Calories 260 · Fat 11g · Protein 9g · Carbohydrates 32g · Cholesterol 23mg · Sodium 475mg · Fiber 3g

HOW TO POACH EGGS

In a large shallow skillet, bring salted water and a teaspoon of apple cider vinegar (to help whites solidify) to a boil. Reduce the heat to maintain a slow simmer. Carefully slip four eggs into the water (it helps to put them in small bowls beforehand, then gently slip them into the water) and let them cook, using a spoon to ladle water over the tops if needed. Cook until just done. Remove with a slotted spoon, draining well. Serve immediately.

Mediterranean Frittata

Frittatas are made of eggs, but they are also a great way to get more vegetables into our diets, as with the roasted red pepper used here. And they are a good way to use up cooked potatoes—perfect for weekend breakfasts. Or do as the Spanish do and cut them into bite-size squares to serve as tapas, or appetizers. The smoked paprika adds lovely depth to this dish, so be sure to use it. **SERVES 4 AS A MAIN COURSE, 6 AS AN APPETIZER**

3 tablespoons olive oil

2 large white onions, or 6 large shallots, finely diced

4 small new potatoes, unpeeled, cooked, and cut in 1/4-inch slices

1/2 teaspoon hot smoked paprika

1/2 teaspoon sea salt, divided

1/2 teaspoon freshly ground black pepper, divided

1/2 cup roasted red pepper, chopped

1/4 cup sliced black olives

6 large eggs

1/2 cup chopped fresh parsley, divided

1. Place a rack in the middle of the oven. Preheat the oven to 425°F.
2. In an ovenproof 9- or 10-inch nonstick or cast-iron skillet (preferably with straight rather than rounded sides), heat the oil over medium-low heat. Cook the onions until they are lightly browned, stirring occasionally, about 7 to 8 minutes.
3. Layer the potatoes evenly on top of the onions in the skillet. Whisk together the paprika, salt, and pepper until well blended. Sprinkle 1/2 teaspoon over the potatoes, then layer the red pepper and black olives on top.
4. In a medium bowl, whisk the eggs until light and fluffy. Whisk in 1/2 teaspoon of the paprika mixture and 1/4 cup of the parsley. Pour into the skillet and cook until the eggs start to set around the edges, about 3 to 5 minutes.
5. Put the skillet in the oven and bake until the eggs are set and lightly browned, about 7 to 10 minutes. Remove from the oven, loosen the edges with a heat-proof spatula, and slide onto a serving platter. Cut into wedges and serve hot, garnished with the remaining parsley.

Calories 285 · Fat 21g · Protein 16g · Carbohydrates 8g · Cholesterol 331mg · Sodium 713mg · Fiber 3g

Quiche

Quiche is perfect for brunch or a light supper, served with fruit or a salad of mixed greens. Using room-temperature ingredients means the filling will cook more quickly, saving you time. This crust is a breeze to handle; you'll serve it often. **SERVES 8**

CRUST

1 cup GF Flour Blend (page 12)

1/3 cup sweet rice flour

2 tablespoons almond meal or flour (see Almond Meal Flour, page 240)

1 tablespoon evaporated cane juice

1/4 teaspoon xanthan gum

1/4 teaspoon guar gum

1/4 teaspoon onion powder

1/8 teaspoon sea salt

1/4 cup non-hydrogenated shortening (palm or soy oil)

1 tablespoon butter or buttery spread

2 tablespoons milk of choice

FILLING

1 teaspoon canola oil

1 medium onion, diced

1 tablespoon cornstarch

1/2 teaspoon sea salt

1/8 teaspoon nutmeg

1/8 teaspoon white pepper

4 large eggs, room temperature

1 cup fat-free half-and-half or coffee creamer (soy or coconut), heated to 110°F

1 1/2 cups diced or shredded low-fat Swiss cheese, or cheese alternative

2 tablespoons Parmesan cheese or soy Parmesan

1. Make the Crust: In a food processor, mix the flour blend, sweet rice flour, almond meal, evaporated cane juice, xanthan gum, guar gum, onion powder, salt, shortening, and butter until well blended and crumbly. Add the milk and process until the mixture forms a ball. Break up the ball, scrape the sides of the bowl, and process until the mixture forms a ball again. Remove the dough from the bowl, massage it with your hands until it is

smooth, flatten it into a 4-inch disk, and refrigerate, tightly covered, while you make the filling. You can make the dough a day ahead and refrigerate it, tightly wrapped.

2. Make the Filling: In a heavy medium skillet, heat the oil over medium-low heat. Add the onion and cook, stirring occasionally, until it is lightly browned, about 5 to 7 minutes. In a large bowl, whisk together the cornstarch, salt, nutmeg, and pepper until blended. Whisk in the eggs, half-and-half, Swiss cheese, and Parmesan cheese until blended. Let the filling stand while shaping the crust.

3. Position racks in the bottom and middle positions of the oven. Preheat the oven to 425°F. Massage the dough between your hands until it doesn't feel cold, making the crust easier to handle. With a rolling pin, roll the dough into a 10-inch circle between two pieces of heavy-duty plastic wrap. (Use a damp paper towel between the countertop and bottom plastic wrap to prevent slipping.) Move the rolling pin from the center of the dough to the outer edge, moving around the circle in clockwise fashion to assure uniform thickness.

4. Remove the top plastic wrap and invert the crust, centering it over a 9-inch nonstick (gray, not black) metal pie pan. Remove the remaining plastic wrap and press the dough into place. Trim the edges to an even overhang all around the pan. Shape a decorative edge to the crust with your fingers around the rim. Pour the filling into the crust and place the pan on a 9 x 13-inch baking sheet.

5. Bake the quiche on the lower rack for 15 minutes, then shift to the middle rack, reduce the heat to 325°F, and bake until the filling is lightly browned and puffy, about 25 to 30 minutes. Cool the quiche in the pan for 10 minutes on a wire rack, then cut into slices, and serve hot.

Calories 300 · Fat 18g · Protein 11g · Carbohydrates 22g · Cholesterol 118mg · Sodium 219mg · Fiber 1g

Quiche in Crispy Potato Crust: Toss 3 cups of hash-brown potatoes (if fresh, pressed dry; if frozen, thawed and squeezed dry) with 1 tablespoon canola oil and press evenly on the bottom and high up on the sides of the pan to form a crust (the potatoes will shrink down a bit as they bake). Bake at 425°F until lightly browned, about 30 minutes. Remove from the oven, add the filling, reduce the heat to 325°F, and bake until the filling is lightly browned and puffy, about 25 to 30 minutes.

Everyday to Exceptional

· ·

Serve each wedge of Quiche with a dollop of Basil Pesto (page 252) thinned with hot water to pouring consistency.

Grilled Herb Tofu with Chimichurri on Toast

Perfect for brunch or a lazy weekend breakfast, this hearty and colorful dish will delight your guests. Chimichurri is an herb-based green sauce originating in Argentina or Uruguay, but many countries have similar versions of their own. It is extremely flavorful and versatile, and can be drizzled on vegetables as well. **SERVES 4**

1 package (15 ounces) extra-firm tofu

CHIMICHURRI

½ cup red onion, minced

⅓ cup extra-virgin olive oil

¼ cup finely chopped fresh basil

¼ cup finely chopped Italian flat-leaf
   parsley

¼ cup sherry or champagne
   vinegar

2 tablespoons finely chopped fresh oregano

1 small garlic clove, minced

1 teaspoon sea salt

⅛ teaspoon hot pepper sauce

4 slices GF bread of choice

Very thin slices of pimiento or red bell
   pepper, for garnish

1. Remove the tofu from the container and discard the liquid. On a cutting board, cut the block of tofu in half lengthwise, then cut it in half again to yield 4 equal pieces. Place the pieces in a large colander or sieve (or on paper towels) to drain for 30 minutes.
2. Meanwhile, in a shallow bowl large enough to hold the tofu in a single layer, make the Chimichurri: Combine the red onion, oil, basil, parsley, vinegar, oregano, garlic, salt, and hot pepper sauce, and stir to blend completely. Reserve ½ cup to use as a garnish.
3. Remove the tofu from the colander and marinate it in the Chimichurri for 1 hour.
4. Heat a large nonstick skillet over medium heat. Cook the tofu, removed from the marinade, until lightly browned on both sides, about 3 to 4 minutes per side.

5. Just before serving, toast the bread and place a slice on each of 4 serving plates. Place one piece of the tofu on each bread slice, top with the remaining Chimichurri, garnish with the pimiento or red bell pepper, and serve immediately.

Calories 340 · Fat 24g · Protein 11g · Carbohydrates 19g · Cholesterol 0mg · Sodium 621mg · Fiber 2g

SUNDAY BRUNCH

Basic Scones with Drizzle (page 173)

Grilled Herb Tofu with Chimichurri on Toast (page 207)

Fruit salad

No-Bake Cheesecake (page 227)

Desserts

Desserts play a gratifying role in any diet. They satisfy our quest for something sweet, allow us to indulge once in a while, and often serve as the focal point for celebrations of all kinds. The collection I have here includes mostly the basics, which can be modified much like the little black dress—dressed up for guests, or simple for every day. For more dessert recipes, see my other books: *Wheat-Free Recipes & Menus*, *Cooking Free*, and *Gluten-Free Quick & Easy*.

· BARS AND COOKIES ·

Chocolate Brownies

Oat, Blueberry, and Walnut Bars

Chocolate Cookies

Ginger-Molasses Cookies

Oatmeal Chocolate-Chip Cookies

Golden Vanilla Cookies

• CAKES AND CHEESECAKE •

Almond Vanilla Cake and Cupcakes

Chocolate Cake and Cupcakes

Gingerbread with Warm Lemon Sauce

No-Bake Cheesecake

• FRUIT, PUDDING, AND ICE CREAM DESSERTS •

Chocolate Mousse

Vanilla Bean Pudding

Apple Crisp

Ice Cream Pie with Granola and Fresh Fruit Sauce

Tiramisù

All-American Cherry Pie

Chocolate Brownies

Nothing against apples, but the story of Adam and Eve would be a lot more compelling if chocolate was involved . . . like, maybe these wickedly dense and fudgy brownies? Serve them plain, dress them up with a dusting of powdered sugar, or slather them with fudge frosting. Or make them into a Brownie Sundae (see page 212). **MAKES 16 BROWNIES**

1 cup boiling water

1 tablespoon ground flax meal

1 cup sorghum flour

1 cup garbanzo (chickpea) flour

1¼ cups evaporated cane juice

¾ cup unsweetened cocoa powder (not Dutch)

½ teaspoon baking powder

⅛ teaspoon baking soda

¾ teaspoon sea salt

½ teaspoon xanthan gum

½ cup melted butter or buttery spread or corn oil

2 teaspoons pure vanilla

½ cup chopped walnuts

½ cup chocolate chips

1. Place a rack in the middle of the oven. Preheat the oven to 350°F. Generously grease the bottom of a 7 × 11-inch nonstick (gray, not black) metal pan or line with parchment paper for easy removal.

2. In a small bowl, whisk together the boiling water and flax meal and let stand for 5 minutes. In a large mixing bowl, whisk together the sorghum flour, garbanzo flour, evaporated cane juice, cocoa powder, baking powder, baking soda, salt, and xanthan gum. With an electric mixer on low speed, beat in the flax mixture, butter (or spread or oil), and vanilla until well blended. Stir in the walnuts and chocolate chips. The butter will be stiff. Spread the batter evenly in the pan and smooth the top with a wet spatula.

3. Bake until a toothpick inserted in the center comes out almost clean, about 20 to 25 minutes. For a fudgy texture, do not overbake. Cool brownies completely in the pan on a wire rack. When cool, either cut the brownies into 16 pieces or invert the pan on a plate, discard the parchment paper from the bottom of the brownies, and invert onto a serving platter before cutting into 16 pieces.

Calories 265 · Fat 12g · Protein 5g · Carbohydrates 39g · Cholesterol 16mg · Sodium 189mg · Fiber 3g

Chocolate-Espresso Brownies: Stir ½ teaspoon instant espresso powder into the batter.

Chocolate-Peppermint Brownies: Stir 1 teaspoon peppermint extract into the batter, and immediately after baking, sprinkle ½ cup chopped peppermint candies on top and lightly press in with your fingers.

Everyday to Exceptional

Make Brownie Sundaes by cutting the brownies into 9 squares and placing each square on a serving plate. Top each with a scoop of vanilla ice cream, drizzle with chocolate syrup, and top with chocolate shavings or chocolate-covered espresso beans. Drizzle with Caramel Sauce (page 246) and serve immediately.

Oat, Blueberry, and Walnut Bars

Berries, cinnamon, and nuts team up with rolled oats to make a hearty, flavorful bar. You can also feel free to change the jam—it is equally delicious using raspberry, fig, or strawberry jam. **SERVES 16**

½ cup butter or buttery spread, melted

2 teaspoons pure vanilla, divided

1 cup GF Flour Blend (page 12)

1 cup GF rolled oats*

½ cup packed light brown sugar

¼ cup walnuts, finely chopped

1½ teaspoons xanthan gum

1 teaspoon baking powder

½ teaspoon sea salt

¼ teaspoon ground cinnamon

⅔ cup blueberry jam

Check with your physician before eating gluten-free oats.

1. Place a rack in the middle of the oven. Preheat the oven to 375°F. Generously grease an 8 x 8-inch square nonstick (gray, not black) metal pan. Or line the pan with parchment paper, leaving a 2-inch overhang for easy removal. Grease the paper.

2. In a medium bowl, combine the melted butter and 1 teaspoon of the vanilla. Stir in the flour blend, oats, brown sugar, walnuts, xanthan gum, baking powder, salt, and cinnamon until thoroughly blended.

3. Press 1 packed cup of the oat mixture firmly in the bottom of the pan.

4. Stir the remaining teaspoon of vanilla into the blueberry jam until smooth, then spread the jam evenly in the pan.

5. Sprinkle the remaining oat mixture over the jam, then pat firmly to make it smooth and even.

6. Bake until the top is lightly browned and firm, about 20 to 25 minutes. Cool the bars in the pan for 30 minutes on a wire rack. If using parchment paper, invert the pan onto a large cutting board and remove the parchment before cutting into 16 squares. Otherwise, serve the bars directly from the pan.

Calories 160 · Fat 7g · Protein 2g · Carbohydrates 224g · Cholesterol 16mg · Sodium 97mg · Fiber 1g

Chocolate Cookies

This basic recipe will be your chocolate cookie standby. Stash away at least a dozen in your freezer and you're always ready to make a chocolate crumb crust (which typically takes about 1½ cups of crumbs for a 9-inch piecrust). Of course, you can devour them immediately, fresh from the oven. The garbanzo flour gives the cookies a good protein and fiber boost, but you'll never know it's there. **MAKES 18 SMALL COOKIES, 24 IF USING CHOCOLATE CHIPS AND NUTS (SEE PAGE 215)**

1 tablespoon ground flax meal

⅓ cup boiling water

½ cup butter or buttery spread, at room temperature (but not melted)

⅔ cup packed light brown sugar

1 teaspoon pure vanilla

1 cup garbanzo (chickpea) flour

½ cup GF Flour Blend (page 12)

½ cup unsweetened cocoa powder (not Dutch)

¼ teaspoon xanthan gum

¼ teaspoon baking powder

¼ teaspoon baking soda

¼ teaspoon sea salt

¼ teaspoon instant espresso powder (optional)

1 tablespoon evaporated cane juice, for sprinkling

1. Place a rack in the lower third of the oven. Preheat the oven to 375°F. Line a 9 x 13-inch metal baking sheet (not nonstick) with parchment paper.

2. In a small bowl, stir the flax meal into the boiling water and set aside, stirring occasionally.

3. In a medium mixing bowl, beat the butter, brown sugar, vanilla, and flax mixture with an electric mixer on low speed until smooth and well blended. In a medium bowl, whisk together the garbanzo flour, flour blend, cocoa powder, xanthan gum, baking powder, baking soda, salt, and espresso powder (if using) until well blended. Gradually beat the flour mixture into the butter mixture on low speed until thoroughly blended.

4. With a #50 (1¼-tablespoon) metal ice cream scoop, drop 9 balls of dough at least 2 inches apart on the baking sheet and, for thinner cookies, flatten to ⅓ inch thick with a wet spatula. Sprinkle with evaporated cane juice.

5. Bake until the cookies are slightly cracked on top, about 8 to 12 minutes. Do not over-bake. Cool the cookies for 10 minutes on the baking sheet on a wire rack. Transfer the cookies to the wire rack to cool completely. Repeat with remaining dough.

Calories 105 · Fat 6g · Protein 2g · Carbohydrates 13g · Cholesterol 0mg · Sodium 116mg · Fiber 2g

Chocolate Chocolate-Chip Cookies: Add ¼ cup each chocolate chips and chopped walnuts to the batter.

Chocolate Ice Cream Sandwich Cookies: For each cookie sandwich, place 1 to 2 tablespoons of softened ice cream of choice between two cookies and gently press together. Roll edges of ice cream sandwiches in finely chopped walnuts or pecans. Place on a plate and freeze for 2 hours. Let stand for 10 minutes before serving.

Ginger-Molasses Cookies

Moist and very flavorful, these little gems are perfect for eating by themselves or processing into crumbs for a crumb crust (about 1½ cups for a 9-inch piecrust). Adding the optional black pepper turns them into Pfeffernüsse, a traditional German treat served during the Christmas holidays. **MAKES 18 COOKIES**

½ cup butter or buttery spread

¼ cup molasses (not blackstrap)

¾ cup packed light brown sugar

1 teaspoon pure vanilla

1 cup sorghum flour

½ cup garbanzo (chickpea) flour

1 teaspoon ground ginger

1 teaspoon ground cinnamon

½ teaspoon xanthan gum

½ teaspoon freshly grated nutmeg

½ teaspoon ground cloves

¼ teaspoon baking soda

¼ teaspoon sea salt

¼ teaspoon freshly ground black pepper, optional

2 tablespoons evaporated cane juice, for rolling

1. Place a rack in the lower third of the oven. Preheat the oven to 375°F. Line a 9 x 13-inch metal baking sheet (not nonstick) with parchment paper.

2. In a medium mixing bowl, beat the butter, molasses, brown sugar, and vanilla with an electric mixer on low speed until well blended. Add the sorghum flour, garbanzo flour, ginger, cinnamon, xanthan gum, nutmeg, cloves, baking soda, salt, and black pepper (if using) and beat until well blended.

3. With a #50 (1¼-tablespoon) metal ice cream scoop, shape 9 balls, roll each into a smooth ball with your hands, and roll each in the evaporated cane juice. Place them at least two inches apart on the baking sheet.

4. Bake until the cookies look firm and began to show little cracks on top, about 8 to 10 minutes. Do not overbake. Cool the cookies on the baking sheet on a wire rack for 5 minutes, then transfer to the wire rack to cool completely. Repeat with the remaining dough.

Calories 130 · Fat 6g · Protein 2g · Carbohydrates 20g · Cholesterol 14mg · Sodium 51mg · Fiber 1g

Everyday to Elegant

If you're giving Ginger-Molasses Cookies (or any other cookie) as a gift, stack 4 to 6 cookies and enclose in plastic wrap. Tie a colorful ribbon vertically around the stack, and fasten with a bow at the top. This looks especially pretty when placed in a basket along with other gift items.

Oatmeal Chocolate-Chip Cookies

Oatmeal cookies are the all-American choice, and this recipe is your basic starting point. Instead of chocolate chips, use white chocolate chips, raisins, or dried cranberries, or see the Peanut Butter variation on page 219. Fortunately—for those nights when you learn at eight p.m. that you need cookies tomorrow for a Cub Scout meeting, birthday party, or whatever your family forgot to tell you about—you can make these cookies in less than 30 minutes. **MAKES 16 COOKIES**

2 cups GF rolled oats*

1/3 cup evaporated cane juice

1/4 cup packed light brown sugar

2 tablespoons cornstarch

3/4 teaspoon xanthan gum

1/2 teaspoon ground cinnamon

1/2 teaspoon baking soda

1/2 teaspoon sea salt

1/4 cup butter or buttery spread, at room temperature (not melted)

1 teaspoon pure vanilla

1/3 cup milk of choice

1/2 cup chocolate chips, plus 16 for garnish

Check with your physician before eating gluten-free oats.

1. Place a rack in the middle of the oven. Preheat the oven to 375°F. Line a 9 x 13-inch baking sheet (not nonstick) with parchment paper.

2. In a food processor, pulse the oats, evaporated cane juice, brown sugar, cornstarch, xanthan gum, cinnamon, baking soda, and salt 10 times to partially grind the oats and blend the ingredients. Add the butter and vanilla, and process until the mixture is crumbly. Add the milk and process until the milk is blended in. Add the 1/2 cup of chocolate chips and pulse just until blended. Massage the dough into a smooth ball with your hands. Shape half of the dough into 8 balls with your wet hands, 1 1/2 to 2 tablespoons each, and place them at least 2 inches apart on the baking sheet. Flatten with a spatula to 1/2 inch thick.

3. Bake until the cookies are lightly browned around the edges, about 12 to 15 minutes. Do not overbake. Remove the cookies from the oven and place the baking sheet on a rack. Immediately press a chocolate chip into the middle of each cookie. Finish cooling the cookies on the baking sheet on a wire rack for 10 minutes. Transfer the cookies to the wire rack to cool completely. Repeat with remaining dough to make another 8 cookies.

Calories 130 · Fat 6g · Protein 2g · Carbohydrates 19g · Cholesterol 8mg · Sodium 130mg · Fiber 2g

Peanut Butter Oatmeal Cookies: Add ¼ cup creamy or chunky peanut butter with the butter and vanilla, and process to blend. Bake as directed.

Golden Vanilla Cookies

This not-too-sweet cookie is great by itself but also perfect for drizzling with frosting or filling with jam, for Jam Thumbprints (see below). Keep 10 in the freezer so you can make cookie crumb crusts at a moment's notice (about 1½ cups of crumbs for a 9-inch piecrust). Lyle's Golden Syrup makes a nice substitute for the agave nectar if you can find it. **MAKES 15 COOKIES**

1 cup almond meal or flour (See Almond Meal Flour, page 240)

¾ cup GF Flour Blend (page 12)

¼ cup packed light brown sugar

¼ teaspoon xanthan gum

¼ teaspoon baking soda

⅛ teaspoon sea salt

¼ cup agave nectar

¼ cup coconut oil, melted

1 teaspoon pure vanilla

½ teaspoon almond extract (optional)

2 tablespoons evaporated cane juice for sprinkling

1. Place a rack in the bottom third of the oven. Preheat the oven to 375°F. Line a 13 x 18-inch rimmed metal baking sheet (not nonstick) with parchment paper.

2. In a medium mixing bowl, whisk together the almond meal, flour blend, brown sugar, xanthan gum, baking soda, and salt until well blended. Add the agave nectar, coconut oil, and vanilla and almond extracts. With an electric mixer on low speed, beat until thoroughly blended, about 30 seconds. With a #50 (1¼-tablespoon) metal ice cream scoop, shape 15 balls and place them at least two inches apart on the baking sheet. Sprinkle each cookie with ⅛ teaspoon evaporated cane juice.

3. Bake until the cookies are slightly puffy and just starting to brown around the edges, about 8 to 10 minutes. Do not overbake. Cool the cookies on the baking sheet on a wire rack for 5 minutes, then transfer to the wire rack to cool completely.

Calories 130 · Fat 5g · Protein 4g · Carbohydrates 18g · Cholesterol 0mg · Sodium 39mg · Fiber 1g

Snickerdoodles: Whisk together 2 tablespoons evaporated cane juice and ¼ teaspoon ground cinnamon. Just before baking, sprinkle ⅛ teaspoon of this mixture on each cookie. Bake as directed.

Jam Thumbprints: Just before baking, make an indentation in each cookie with the bottom of a ½-teaspoon measuring spoon and place ½ teaspoon of your favorite (thick) jam in it. Bake as directed.

Almond Vanilla Cake and Cupcakes

This pretty little cake will be your "go-to" recipe for a simple yet elegant dessert. It practically decorates itself because you dress it up before you put it in the oven, and the almonds toast while the cake bakes, making it look like it came straight from a professional bakery. You can vary the fruit depending on the season (see page 222), although especially juicy fruits may increase the baking time. **SERVES 8 (MAKES AN 8-INCH ROUND CAKE)**

2 cups GF Flour Blend (page 12)

¼ cup almond meal or flour (see Almond Meal Flour, page 240)

1 tablespoon baking powder

1 teaspoon xanthan gum

½ teaspoon sea salt

¼ teaspoon baking soda

¾ cup agave nectar

½ cup unsweetened applesauce

⅓ cup coconut oil, melted

2 teaspoons almond extract

⅔ cup boiling water

¼ cup sliced almonds

Fruit (optional; see page 222)

Powdered sugar, for dusting

1. Place a rack in the middle of the oven. Preheat the oven to 350°F. Generously grease an 8-inch or 9-inch round nonstick (gray, not black) metal cake pan and line the bottom with parchment paper.

2. In a medium bowl, whisk together the flour blend, almond meal, baking powder, xanthan gum, salt, and baking soda until well blended. Add the agave nectar, applesauce, coconut oil, and almond extract, and beat on low speed just until blended. Pour in the boiling water and beat on medium speed until the water is completely blended in, about 30 seconds. Spread the batter evenly in the pan. Scatter the almonds over the top, pressing them in slightly with your fingers. Press the fruit, if using, into the batter (see page 222).

3. Bake until the cake is lightly browned and a toothpick inserted into the center comes out clean, about 35 to 40 minutes for the 8-inch pan, 30 to 35 minutes for the 9-inch pan. Cool the cake in the pan for 15 minutes on a wire rack. Run a sharp knife around the edge of the pan to release the cake. Gently slide the cake onto a serving platter, almond side up. Dust with powdered sugar and serve immediately.

Calories 470 · Fat 13g · Protein 4g · Carbohydrates 92g · Cholesterol 0mg ·
Sodium 343mg · Fiber 2g

Almond-Berry Cake: Scatter ¼ cup fresh raspberries or blueberries on top, gently pressing them halfway into the batter with your fingers. Bake as directed.

Almond-Plum Cake: Arrange 3 halved and pitted Italian plums on top, cut side down, gently pressing them halfway into the batter with your fingers. Bake as directed.

Almond-Cherry Cake: Arrange 12 pitted, well-drained dark cherries on top, gently pressing them halfway into the batter with your fingers. Bake as directed.

ALMOND CUPCAKES

1. Line a standard nonstick (gray, not black) 12-cup metal muffin pan with paper liners. Follow Steps 1 and 2, but divide the batter evenly in the muffin pan.

2. Bake until a toothpick inserted into the center comes out clean, about 20 to 22 minutes. Cool the cupcakes in the pan on a wire rack for 10 minutes. Remove the cupcakes from the pan and cool on the wire rack.

Chocolate Cake
and Cupcakes

Did you know that cupcakes accounted for $1 billion in U.S. retail sales in 2008 and could reach $1.3 billion by 2013? We don't want to be left out of this trend, do we? So, chocoholics, this will be an extremely valuable recipe for you. Serve it plain as cake, or as cupcakes—dressed up with a variety of frostings. At our house, we're especially fond of fudge frosting, but it's also enchanting with a simple white powdered sugar frosting. Add a couple of tablespoons of coffee or chocolate-flavored liqueur to the batter for an intriguing flavor.

SERVES 12

2 cups GF Flour Blend (page 12)

1 cup evaporated cane juice

3/4 cup unsweetened cocoa powder
   (not Dutch)

2 1/2 teaspoons baking powder

1 teaspoon baking soda

1 teaspoon xanthan gum

3/4 teaspoon sea salt

1/2 cup melted butter or buttery spread
   or cane oil

1 tablespoon pure vanilla

2 cups water, room temperature

1. Place a rack in the middle of the oven. Preheat the oven to 350°F. Generously grease two 8-inch round nonstick (gray, not black) pans. Line each with parchment paper or waxed paper and grease again.

2. In a medium mixing bowl, whisk together the flour blend, evaporated cane juice, cocoa powder, baking powder, baking soda, xanthan gum, and salt. Add the butter (or spread or oil) and vanilla, then pour the water on top and beat with an electric mixer on low speed just until blended, about 20 seconds. Spread the batter evenly in the pans with a wet spatula.

3. Bake 25 to 30 minutes or until a toothpick inserted into the center of the cakes comes out clean. Cool the cakes in the pans 10 minutes on a wire rack. Remove the cakes from the pans with a thin metal spatula, invert onto plates, discard the parchment paper, and cool completely on the wire rack. Ice with your favorite frosting to make a layer cake.

CHOCOLATE CUPCAKES

1. Line a standard nonstick (gray, not black) 12-cup metal muffin pan with paper liners. Follow Steps 1 and 2, but divide the batter evenly in the muffin pan.

2. Bake until a toothpick inserted into a cupcake center comes out clean, about 20 to 22 minutes. Cool the cupcakes in the pan on a wire rack for 10 minutes. Remove the cupcakes from the pan and cool on the wire rack. Frost with your favorite icing.

Calories 230 · Fat 9g · Protein 2g · Carbohydrate 40g · Cholesterol 21mg · Sodium 405mg · Fiber 3g

Gingerbread with Warm Lemon Sauce

This is one of my favorite desserts to serve in autumn, when the spices that make gingerbread unique are most welcome to our palates. And the heavenly aroma of ginger-bread wafting through your kitchen is soul-soothing and entices your guests. You'll make this easy dessert often. Save leftovers, cube them, and layer with pudding or yogurt in a trifle bowl or wine goblets for an impromptu trifle. **SERVES 12**

1¾ cups GF Flour Blend (page 12)

½ cup packed dark brown sugar

1 tablespoon ground ginger

1 tablespoon ground cinnamon

1 teaspoon xanthan gum

½ teaspoon freshly grated nutmeg

½ teaspoon baking soda

½ teaspoon sea salt

¼ teaspoon ground cloves

⅔ cup water, at room temperature

½ cup molasses (not blackstrap)

⅓ cup canola oil

1 teaspoon pure vanilla

½ teaspoon apple cider vinegar

LEMON SAUCE (MAKES ABOUT ⅔ CUP)

½ cup evaporated cane juice

3 tablespoons cornstarch

2 tablespoons water

Juice and zest of 2 lemons

2 tablespoons butter or buttery spread

1. Place a rack in the lower third of the oven. Preheat the oven to 350°F. Grease a 9-inch round nonstick (gray, not black) pan (and line the bottom with parchment paper if you want to serve the gingerbread inverted onto a platter, rather than in the pan).

2. In a small bowl, whisk together the flour blend, brown sugar, ginger, cinnamon, xanthan gum, nutmeg, baking soda, salt, and cloves until well blended.

3. In a large mixing bowl, beat the water, molasses, oil, vanilla, and vinegar with an electric mixer on low speed until well blended, about 10 seconds. Gradually beat in the flour mixture on low speed; increase the speed to medium and beat until the batter thickens slightly, about 30 seconds. Spread the batter evenly in the pan.

4. Bake until a toothpick inserted into the center comes out clean, about 30 to 35 minutes. Place the pan on a wire rack to cool for 10 minutes. To serve on a platter, invert the cake onto a serving platter and remove the parchment paper. Serve slightly warm.

5. Make the Lemon Sauce: In a small saucepan, whisk together the evaporated cane juice and cornstarch until well blended. Whisk in the water and lemon juice, and cook over medium heat, whisking constantly, just until the mixture thickens slightly. Remove from the heat and stir in the butter and lemon zest. Cool slightly, about 10 minutes, before serving. To serve, drizzle about 2 tablespoons of warm sauce over each slice of gingerbread.

Calories 255 · Fat 8g · Protein 1g · Carbohydrates 47g · Cholesterol 5mg · Sodium 160mg · Fiber 1g

Gingerbread Cupcakes: Line a 12-cup nonstick (gray, not black) standard muffin pan with paper liners. Fill each liner with 1/4 cup of batter. Bake until a toothpick inserted into the center of a cupcake comes out clean, about 20 to 25 minutes. Cool the muffin pan on a wire rack for 10 minutes. Remove the cupcakes and finish cooling on the wire rack. Remove the cupcakes from the liners and serve, drizzling each with a scant tablespoon of Lemon Sauce.

For a lighter texture, reduce the water to 1/2 cup and blend one large egg with the liquid ingredients.

No-Bake Cheesecake

This cheesecake is super-simple to assemble yet tastes divine and is perfect for your next party. Vary the flavor by adding citrus zest and alcohol (see page 228). You can top it with any fresh fruit you wish, such as fresh raspberries, blueberries, or blackberries. Freeze it for 2 hours for a firmer, frozen delight, but don't add the fruit on top until just before serving. **SERVES 12**

CRUST

9 whole homemade Golden Vanilla Cookies (page 220) or store-bought GF cookies (enough to make 1½ cups of crumbs)

2 tablespoons butter or buttery spread, melted

1 teaspoon packed light brown sugar

1 teaspoon pure vanilla

FILLING

1½ tub (12 ounces) nonfat cream cheese or vegan cream cheese

1 tub (8 ounces) nonfat sour cream or vegan sour cream

¾ cup powdered sugar

1 tablespoon grated lemon zest

1 teaspoon pure vanilla or almond extract

1. Lightly grease an 8-inch or 9-inch springform pan with removable sides.
2. Make the Crust: Place the cookies in a food processor and process 30 to 45 seconds or until finely ground. Or place the cookies in a plastic bag and crush them with a rolling pin. You should have 1½ cups of cookie crumbs. Add the butter, brown sugar, and vanilla, and process until thoroughly blended, or mix in the plastic bag until the crumbs are thoroughly coated. Press the crumbs firmly and evenly into the pan bottom and ½ inch up the sides.
3. Make the Filling: Wipe out the food processor with a paper towel. Add the cream cheese, sour cream, powdered sugar, lemon zest, and vanilla, and process just until thoroughly blended. Or mix the ingredients together in a mixing bowl with an electric mixer on low speed. Spread the batter in the pan. Refrigerate for 4 hours, or for a firmer cheesecake, freeze for 2 hours. Cut into 8 wedges and serve.

Calories 130 · Fat 4g · Protein 7g · Carbohydrates 16g · Cholesterol 12mg · Sodium 246mg · Fiber 0g

Margarita Cheesecake: Stir 2 tablespoons grated lime zest and 1 tablespoon tequila into the filling.

Everyday to Exceptional

Transform this silky delight into one that looks like it came from a professional bakery with this simple sauce.

2 cups fresh raspberries (or enough frozen, drained, to yield 2 cups)

3 tablespoons evaporated cane juice

2 tablespoons water

2 teaspoons cornstarch

¼ teaspoon almond extract, optional

1. In a blender, puree the raspberries and cane juice until smooth, then strain through a sieve to remove the seeds. Transfer to a small heavy saucepan.
2. Whisk together the water, cornstarch, and almond extract, if using, until smooth, then stir into the raspberries. Cook over medium-high heat, stirring constantly, until the mixture comes to a boil and becomes clear, about 30 seconds. Remove from the heat and cool in the pan 10 minutes. Transfer to a glass jar and refrigerate overnight.
3. To decorate the cake, sprinkle ¼ cup of the sauce in small globs over the cheesecake. Draw a skewer or knife through the sauce, working from the center to the edge, several times to create a radial swirled effect. Refrigerate or freeze until serving time.

Chocolate Mousse

Dense and decadent, this dessert is a divine way to enjoy chocolate—one of the world's best foods. For a large dinner party or buffet table—where individual portions are prettier and easier to handle—serve the mousse in little espresso cups or oversize shot glasses. Even though chocolate is the primary flavor, you can vary this dessert in many ways (see garnishes below). Use milk chocolate chips for milder flavor; dark chocolate chips for heartier flavor. **SERVES 6**

1 package (11.5 to 12 ounces) GF chocolate chips

12 ounces soft silken tofu, at room temperature

16 ounces (2 cups) plain yogurt (coconut, cow, or soy) or Yogurt (page 249)

1 tablespoon coffee liqueur (or almond, chocolate, or orange-flavored liqueur)

1 tablespoon pure vanilla

¼ cup whipped topping, for garnish

1. Place the chocolate chips in a microwave-safe dish. Heat on low until the chips melt, about 1 to 2 minutes. Stir thoroughly and place in a food processor.
2. Add the tofu, yogurt, liqueur, and vanilla, and process until the mixture is very smooth. Scrape down the sides of the bowl and process again until very smooth.
3. Divide evenly among 6 dessert bowls, wine goblets, or coffee cups (or divide evenly in however many shot glasses you have) and refrigerate for 2 to 24 hours. Serve with a dollop of whipped topping and a garnish (see below).

Calories 375 · Fat 19g · Protein 8g · Carbohydrates 51g · Cholesterol 3mg · Sodium 50mg · Fiber 3g

GARNISHES THAT COMPLEMENT THE LIQUEUR YOU USE

Slivered almonds—almond liqueur

Chocolate-covered espresso beans—coffee liqueur

Fresh raspberries—raspberry liqueur

Candied orange rind—orange liqueur

Chocolate shavings—chocolate liqueur

Vanilla Bean Pudding

This is a simple, basic pudding that you can use in many ways. Here, it's chock-full of marvelous vanilla flecks from a whole vanilla bean, but you can also add a tablespoon of vanilla or your favorite liqueur or brandy, or ½ teaspoon flavoring extract such as coconut, lemon, orange, or rum. Use your imagination—the possibilities are endless. The richer the milk, the richer the pudding will be, so make it with almond, coconut, hemp, or soy milk—not rice milk or potato milk, which don't thicken as nicely. **SERVES 4 (MAKES 2 CUPS)**

2 cups milk of choice (the richer the better)

1 vanilla bean, slit lengthwise and seeds scraped

½ cup evaporated cane juice

3 tablespoons cornstarch

⅛ teaspoon sea salt

1 tablespoon butter or buttery spread

1. Place the milk, vanilla bean, and scraped seeds in a small heavy saucepan. Cook over medium heat just until bubbles form around the edge of the pan, taking care not to scorch the milk. Remove from the heat and let stand 20 minutes to infuse the vanilla flavor. Discard the vanilla bean (or rinse with water, pat dry, and store in the evaporated cane juice canister to create vanilla-infused flavor).

2. In a small bowl, whisk together the dried cane juice, cornstarch, and salt, then gradually whisk it into the milk. Bring the mixture to a boil over medium heat, whisking constantly, until it thickens, about 2 to 3 minutes. Remove from the heat and stir in the butter until it melts. Let stand 10 minutes. Pour into four goblets or bowls and press plastic wrap onto the top to prevent a skin from forming. Chill at least two hours before serving. Serve cold.

Calories 190 · Fat 4g · Protein 4g · Carbohydrates 35g · Cholesterol 13mg · Sodium 150mg · Fiber 1g

Everyday to Elegant

Create a stunningly simply dessert by layering fresh berries (blackberries, blue-berries, or raspberries) in an ice cream goblet or a wineglass so the layers are visible from the side. For a dinner party, where you want very small desserts, layer the pudding with crushed cookies in oversized shot glasses (available at kitchen stores or www.kingarthurflour.com). Garnish your creation with whipped topping, fresh mint leaves, and one of the perfect berries and you have a vibrant dessert with very little effort.

Apple Crisp

This apple crisp is best made with tart Granny Smith apples, which contrast nicely with the sweet topping. When I make this for my family, I prefer to leave the skin on the apples for more fiber and nutrients, but you can peel them if you wish. You can also use the topping on other fruit crisps, such as cherry or peach. **SERVES 6**

FILLING

4 large Granny Smith apples

½ cup dried fruit such as candied ginger, cranberries, or raisins

Juice and zest of 1 whole lemon

¼ cup agave nectar or honey

2 tablespoons cornstarch

1 teaspoon pure vanilla

TOPPING FOR FRUIT CRISPS

½ cup packed light brown sugar

½ cup GF Flour Blend (page 12)

¼ cup sliced almonds

¼ cup GF rolled oats*

½ teaspoon ground cinnamon

¼ teaspoon freshly grated nutmeg

⅛ teaspoon ground cloves

⅛ teaspoon sea salt

¼ cup butter or buttery spread, melted

1 cup vanilla ice cream (coconut, cow, or soy)

Check with your physician before eating gluten-free oats.

1. Place a rack in the middle of the oven. Preheat the oven to 350°F. Coat an 8 x 8-inch or 1-quart glass baking dish with cooking spray.
2. Make the Filling: Peel, core, and thinly slice the apples; makes about 4 cups. In a large bowl, toss the apples with the dried fruit, lemon juice and zest, agave nectar, cornstarch, and vanilla until well blended. Spread in the baking dish.
3. Make the Topping: In the same large bowl, toss the brown sugar, flour blend, almonds, oats, cinnamon, nutmeg, cloves, and salt with a spatula until blended. Cut the butter

into the dry ingredients with a fork until the mixture resembles crumbs. Sprinkle this mixture evenly over the fruit.

4. Bake 35 to 45 minutes, or until the topping is crisp and browned. Serve warm, with the ice cream.

Calories 355 · Fat 14g · Protein 4g · Carbohydrates 59g · Cholesterol 30mg · Sodium 145mg · Fiber 3g

Everyday to Exceptional

Drizzle each serving with a tablespoon or two of the decadent Caramel Sauce on page 246 in the "Basics: Homemade Ingredients" chapter.

Ice Cream Pie with Granola and Fresh Fruit Sauce

Ice cream pies are the perfect summer dessert. Whip up these cool, creamy, and comforting pies on a hot summer night when you want to impress, without spending hours in a hot kitchen. You can make your own Granola (page 192), or use your favorite store-bought GF granola. Fresh blueberries or raspberries can be used instead of strawberries.

SERVES 12

3/4 cup toasted almond slices

2 quarts (1/2 gallon) vanilla ice cream
  (cow, coconut, or soy), softened

1 cup GF store-bought granola* or
  homemade Granola (page 192)

2 cups sliced fresh strawberries

2 tablespoons evaporated cane juice

1 teaspoon fresh lemon juice

Check with your physician before eating gluten-free oats.

1. Sprinkle the almonds evenly over the bottom of a 9-inch springform pan. Press the ice cream firmly into the pan. Freeze until slightly firm, about 15 minutes.
2. Sprinkle the ice cream evenly with the granola and lightly press it in with your fingers. Wrap tightly and freeze overnight.
3. To serve, toss the strawberries with the evaporated cane juice and lemon juice, and let them stand 15 minutes. Let the pie stand at room temperature for 10 minutes, then cut into 12 wedges. Serve immediately, topped with the strawberry mixture.

Calories 295 · Fat 17g · Protein 6g · Carbohydrates 32g · Cholesterol 39mg · Sodium 73mg · Fiber 3g

Everyday to Elegant

Turn your ice cream pie into a showpiece by placing 12 Candied Pecans (see below) around the perimeter of the ice cream before pressing the granola into the ice cream.

CANDIED PECANS

2 cups whole pecans

1/3 cup agave nectar

1/2 teaspoon sea salt, or to taste

1/4 teaspoon ground cinnamon (optional)

1. Lay a sheet of waxed paper or parchment paper on a 9 x 13-inch baking sheet.
2. Spread the pecans in a large skillet. Toast them over medium heat, stirring constantly, until they are hot and fragrant, about 3 minutes. Don't let them burn. Add the agave nectar and continue cooking, stirring constantly, until the nuts are lightly caramelized, about 3 minutes. Immediately remove the pan from the heat and sprinkle with the salt and cinnamon, if using. Transfer the nuts to the waxed paper to cool thoroughly. Store leftovers at room temperature, tightly covered.

Tiramisù

Tiramisù (literally "pick-me-up" in Italian) is traditionally a simple layering of ladyfingers, and a mixture of eggs, sugar, and Mascarpone—a formidable combination! I have transformed that concept here with gluten-free cookies instead of ladyfingers (and cream cheese instead of Mascarpone) into a fantastic dessert. This chocolate version was a hit at Easter dinner this year, proving that you can serve Tiramisù anytime. **MAKES 9 SERVINGS**

16 ounces low-fat cream cheese or vegan cream cheese, softened

½ cup low-fat sour cream or vegan sour cream

¾ cup powdered sugar

2 cups GF whipped topping

¾ cup espresso coffee, freshly brewed, or 1 tablespoon espresso powder dissolved in ¾ cup hot water

2 teaspoons pure vanilla

18 homemade Chocolate Cookies (page 214) or your favorite thin GF cookies

2 cups fresh raspberries or strawberries, washed and patted dry, divided, plus more for garnish

4 tablespoons Dutch-process cocoa powder, divided

¼ cup grated bittersweet chocolate, plus more for garnish

½ cup chocolate-covered espresso beans, for garnish (optional)

1. Lightly coat an 8 x 8-inch square glass baking dish with cooking spray. Set aside.
2. In a 2-quart bowl, beat together the cream cheese, sour cream, and powdered sugar until thoroughly combined. With a spatula, gently fold in ⅔ cup of the whipped topping and then gently fold in the remaining whipped topping.
3. Combine the espresso and vanilla in a shallow bowl. Quickly and lightly dip each cookie horizontally in the mixture. (Do not saturate the cookies or they will fall apart.) Place 9 of the cookies on the bottom of the baking dish in a single layer. Spoon half of the cream cheese mixture on top and smooth it with a spatula. Sprinkle evenly with half of the raspberries and then place two tablespoons of the cocoa powder in a sieve or tea ball and dust it evenly over the top.
4. Dip the remaining cookies in the coffee mixture and arrange in a single layer on top of the cream cheese. Top with the remaining cream cheese mixture and smooth it with a spatula. Sprinkle the remaining raspberries on top and gently dust the remaining cocoa powder on top.

5. Cover with foil and refrigerate at least 4 hours. (The flavor will be more fully developed if the Tiramisù is chilled overnight.) To serve, cut into 9 pieces and garnish each slice with grated chocolate and a fresh raspberry. Serve immediately with 3 espresso beans on top for additional garnish.

Calories 455 · Fat 20g · Protein 14g · Carbohydrates 61g · Cholesterol 6mg · Sodium 370mg · Fiber 8g

All-American Cherry Pie

The crust for this all-American favorite will be your basic recipe whenever you want to make a pie or tart. This pie features cherries, but you can also use the same amount of other stone fruits, such as fresh apricots, peaches, or plums. The extremely forgiving dough makes two piecrusts, perfect for a double-crust pie, but I also give directions for a single-crust pie to make it more versatile for your personal recipes. If you make a single-crust pie, freeze the remaining half of the dough for another time. Let the frozen dough thaw overnight in the refrigerator, not in the microwave oven, where it might accidentally "cook" in spots. Gluten-free pies are best eaten the same day they're baked. **MAKES 6 SERVINGS**

SWEET PASTRY PIECRUST

1 cup GF Flour Blend (page 12)

²/₃ cup sweet rice flour

¼ cup almond meal or almond flour
(see Almond Meal Flour, page 240)

3 tablespoons evaporated cane juice,
divided

½ teaspoon xanthan gum

½ teaspoon guar gum

½ teaspoon sea salt

½ cup non-hydrogenated shortening
(palm or soy)

2 tablespoons butter or buttery spread,
at room temperature and cut into
6 pieces

¼ to ⅓ cup milk of choice, plus 2
tablespoons for brushing on the crust

1 teaspoon almond or vanilla extract

1 teaspoon agave nectar or honey, for
brushing on the crust

FILLING

1 cup evaported cane juice

¼ cup instant tapioca granules

Pinch sea salt

4 cups pitted fresh cherries or 3 cans (15
ounces each) drained very thoroughly

1 tablespoon fresh lemon juice

½ teaspoon almond extract

1. To make the Sweet Pastry Piecrust: Place the flour blend, sweet rice flour, almond meal, 2 tablespoons of the evaporated cane juice, and the xanthan gum, guar gum, salt, shortening, and butter in a food processor and process until crumbly. Add ¼ cup of the milk and the almond extract and process until the dough forms a ball. If it doesn't form a ball, use a spatula to break the dough into pieces, add the remaining milk, and process again, scraping down the sides of the bowl as necessary. Remove the dough from the food processor and knead it with your hands until smooth. Halve the dough and shape each half into a 1-inch-thick disk. Wrap tightly with plastic wrap, and refrigerate 1 hour.

2. While the crust chills, make the Filling: In a large bowl, whisk together the evaporated cane juice, tapioca, and salt. Add the thoroughly drained cherries, lemon juice, and almond extract, and toss until completely blended. Set aside.

For a Single-Crust Pie:

3. Massage a disk of dough between your hands until it is as warm as your hands, making the crust easier to handle. With a rolling pin, roll the dough to a 10-inch circle between two pieces of heavy-duty plastic wrap. (Use a damp paper towel between the countertop and the bottom piece of plastic wrap to anchor the plastic and prevent it from slipping.) Move the rolling pin from the center of the dough to the outer edge, moving around the circle in clockwise fashion to assure uniform thickness.

4. Remove the top plastic wrap and invert the crust, centering it over a 9-inch nonstick (gray, not black) pie pan. Remove the remaining plastic wrap and press the crust into place. Trim the edges to an even overhang all around the pan. Shape a decorative edge around the rim of the pie plate and bake in a preheated oven as directed by your recipe.

For a Double-Crust Pie:

5. Follow Steps 1, 2, 3, and 4, leaving the overhang in place without fluting it. Place a rack in the bottom position and another in the middle position of the oven. Preheat the oven to 375°F. Spread the filling evenly in the bottom crust. Massage the remaining disk of dough between your hands until it is as warm as your hands. Roll it to a 10-inch circle, remove the top piece of plastic wrap, invert the bottom crust, and center it on the filled crust. Do not remove the bottom piece of plastic wrap until the dough is centered. Trim

the top crust to the same overhang as the bottom crust. Press the two crusts together and shape a decorative edge around the rim of the pan. Freeze 15 minutes, then remove from the freezer. Stir the agave nectar into the 2 tablespoon of milk, brush the crust with it, and then sprinkle with the remaining tablespoon of evaporated cane juice. Prick the top crust several times with a fork to allow steam to escape. Place the pan on a nonstick baking sheet.

6. Bake 15 minutes on the lower rack to brown the bottom of the crust. Move the baking sheet to the middle rack and bake the pie another 25 to 35 minutes or until the top crust is nicely browned. Cover loosely with foil after 15 minutes if the edges brown too much. Cool completely on a wire rack before cutting.

Calories 595 · Fat 23g · Protein 3g · Carbohydrates 97g · Cholesterol 10mg · Sodium 240mg · Fiber 4g

Almond Meal Flour

Technically, almond meal is ground from the whole almond, while almond flour is ground from (skinned) blanched almonds. In reality, the terms are often used interchangeably, although some experts prefer almond flour in gluten-free baking. Either form works well in the recipes in this book. You can make your own by pulverizing 1/3 cup of blanched slivered almonds in a food processor, or a coffee or spice grinder, to make 1/4 cup almond flour. Or use 1/3 cup whole almonds to make almond meal. Grind the almonds as fine as you can without turning them into almond butter.

Basics: Homemade Ingredients

Sometimes we have to avoid certain ingredients because there are no versions that are gluten- and dairy-free. Other times, these ingredients are simply better when homemade (such as bread crumbs and broth) and are often much less expensive to make yourself. This chapter is designed to fill in those gaps with recipes that will make your food tastier and safer for you and your family.

· BREADS ·

GF Bread Crumbs

· BROTHS ·

Mushroom Broth
Vegetable Broth

INGREDIENTS THAT COMMONLY CONTAIN DAIRY

Caramel Sauce

Cashew Cream

Hazelnut-Chocolate Spread

Yogurt

Sweetened Condensed Milk

Herb-Flavored Cheese

Basil Pesto

GF Bread Crumbs

It is very easy to make your own bread crumbs. This way, they're fresh and you know exactly what's in them. If you want to make flavored versions, add herbs following the guidelines below to suit your own taste. I usually trim the crusts from the slices so the bread is a consistent color, making the crumbs more likely to toast, bake, or brown more evenly. And since I'm not one to throw anything anyway (especially our hard-earned gluten-free bread), I freeze the crusts for later use in bread stuffing (see Stuffing with Pears and Pecans, page 38). **MAKES ABOUT 1 CUP**

4 slices gluten-free bread of choice, torn in small pieces

1. Place the bread in a food processor and pulse until the crumbs reach the consistency you want. Toss the crumbs with seasoning, if using (see variations below). Store tightly covered in the refrigerator for up to two weeks and in the freezer for up to three months.

Italian Bread Crumbs: Add ¼ teaspoon dried oregano and rosemary and ⅛ teaspoon garlic powder.

Mexican Bread Crumbs: Add ½ teaspoon chili powder and ½ teaspoon ground cumin.

French Bread Crumbs: Add ½ teaspoon herbes de Provence and ⅛ teaspoon black pepper.

Per ¼ cup: Calories 66 · Fat 1g · Protein 2g · Carbohydrates 12g · Cholesterol 0mg · Sodium 119mg · Fiber 1g

Mushroom Broth

I am astounded at the full flavor of this easy-to-make broth, so I strongly recommend that you make it and keep it your freezer so it's always ready for you. It lends incredible depth to any dish. **MAKES 7 CUPS**

1 tablespoon olive oil

1 small leek, chopped

1 small onion, chopped

2 celery ribs, chopped

1 pound cremini or button mushrooms, about 5-6 cups, sliced

1 carrot, peeled, sliced in 1-inch coins

½ cup dry white wine

½ cup fresh parsley, coarsely chopped

¼ cup fresh thyme, coarsely chopped

10 whole black peppercorns

1 large bay leaf

2 tablespoons gluten-free tamari soy sauce

1 teaspoon sea salt

8 cups water

1. Heat the oil in a medium stockpot or Dutch oven over medium heat. Swish the chopped leek in water to clean it, then add with the chopped onion and celery to the stockpot; cook, stirring constantly until tender, about 5 minutes. Add the mushrooms and carrot, and cook, stirring constantly, until the mushrooms are tender and begin to shrink, about 10 minutes. Add the wine and cook for 30 seconds or more to reduce it by half. Add the remaining ingredients.

2. Bring to a boil. Reduce the heat, and simmer, covered, for 1 hour.

3. Pour the broth through a fine sieve into a large bowl set in an ice-water bath to cool the broth quickly, and press on the vegetables to extract the juices; discard the solids. Divide the broth into storage containers and refrigerate for up to one week or freeze for up to three months.

Per cup: Calories 70 · Fat 2g · Protein 2g · Carbohydrates 9g · Cholesterol 0mg · Sodium 471mg · Fiber 2g

Vegetable Broth

Making your own vegetable broth is extremely easy; it just takes a little time to simmer the ingredients and develop the flavor. I usually make mine while I'm preparing dinner. I'm in the kitchen anyway, so I might as well make good use of the time. By the time the dishes are done, the broth is ready to be divided into containers and frozen. If you don't have enough time to brown the leeks, the flavor will still be good, just not quite as fully developed.

MAKES 8 CUPS

2 tablespoons canola oil

1 large leek, coarsely chopped

2 large celery ribs, chopped

2 small carrots, chopped

2 garlic cloves, chopped

9 cups water

½ cup dried porcini mushrooms, soaked and drained to remove any dirt

1 tomato

10 sprigs fresh parsley, coarsely chopped

5 sprigs fresh thyme, or 1 teaspoon dried

1 whole bay leaf

1 teaspoon sea salt, or to taste

6 whole black peppercorns

1 pinch cayenne pepper, to taste

1. Heat the oil in a Dutch oven over medium heat. Swish the chopped leek in water to clean it, and cook, stirring often, until lightly caramelized, about 10 minutes. Add the celery, carrots, and garlic, reduce the heat to medium-low, and cook, stirring occasionally, until the vegetables are tender, about 10 minutes.

2. Add the water, mushrooms, tomato, parsley, thyme, bay leaf, salt, peppercorns, and cayenne. Bring to a boil, reduce the heat to low, and simmer 1 hour. Taste and adjust salt, if necessary.

3. Pour the broth through a fine sieve into a large bowl set in an ice-water bath to cool the broth quickly, and press on the vegetables to extract any remaining juices. Discard the vegetables (or save them for soup). Divide the broth into storage containers and refrigerate for up to one week or freeze for up to three months.

Per cup: Calories 90 · Fat 4g · Protein 3g · Carbohydrates 13g · Cholesterol 0mg · Sodium 304mg · Fiber 4g

Caramel Sauce

One of my rudest awakenings came when I learned that my beloved Caramel Sauce—drizzled over cakes, ice cream, and pies, or eaten straight from the jar with an oversize spoon—contained cream. I suspect that many of you have had similar revelations. But not to worry; make this easy version at home and serve it to everyone. They'll never guess it is dairy-free. Just don't leave the boiling sauce unattended; it can burn quickly. The corn syrup makes a silkier sauce, but you can omit it if you wish. **MAKES ¾ CUP**

½ cup evaporated cane juice

3 tablespoons water

1 teaspoon corn syrup (optional)

¼ teaspoon freshly squeezed lemon juice

½ cup fat-free half-and-half or coconut milk or Cashew Cream, thinned with water to the consistency of canned coconut milk (page 247)

1 tablespoon butter or buttery spread

2 teaspoons pure vanilla

Pinch salt (optional)

1. In a small heavy saucepan whisk together the evaporated cane juice, water, corn syrup (if using), and lemon juice. Continuing to whisk, cook over medium heat until the cane juice dissolves. Increase the heat to medium-high and bring to a boil, but do not stir. Continue to boil until the sauce turns a deep golden brown, about 4 to 6 minutes. The deeper the color, the more intense the flavor—but watch carefully to avoid burning.

2. Remove the pan from the heat. Whisk in the half-and-half, butter, and vanilla until the butter melts. Be careful—the mixture will bubble up. Cool slightly, then taste, and add salt, if desired. Serve warm. Refrigerate leftover Caramel Sauce in a glass jar. It will thicken when cool; warm on low power in the microwave before serving, if desired.

Per tablespoon: Calories 50 · Fat 1g · Protein 1g · Carbohydrates 10g · Cholesterol 3mg · Sodium 40mg · Fiber 0g

Cashew Cream

I have been making this wonderfully creamy concoction for nearly ten years. Use it to make Yogurt (see page 249), ice cream, or puddings. It can also be used in baking, but you should add a tablespoon of sugar for each cup of cashew cream used. **MAKES 4 CUPS**

2 cups raw cashews or blanched almonds

4 cups water

⅛ teaspoon sea salt

1. Soak the nuts overnight in enough water to cover. Drain thoroughly.
2. In a blender, combine the nuts, water, and salt; blend until completely smooth, about 5 minutes, scraping down the sides of the blender a couple of times. You may strain the mixture through a sieve to remove any stray particles of nuts if you wish. Refrigerate for up to one week.

Per ½ cup: Calories 335 · Fat 28g · Protein 11g · Carbohydrates 40g · Cholesterol 0mg · Sodium 40mg · Fiber 2g

Hazelnut-Chocolate Spread

Popular in Europe, this spread is used much as Americans use peanut butter. My daughter-in-law grew up eating it on toast for breakfast or snacks, and now my grandchildren also eat it. However, the commercial version contains dairy, so use this easy recipe to make your own dairy-free, natural version. Kids love it, but it is addictive for adults, too. You've been forewarned. . . . (Hazelnut meal can be purchased at natural food stores or online.)

MAKES 1½ CUPS

2 cups hazelnut meal

1½ cups powdered sugar

¾ cup unsweetened cocoa powder

⅓ cup boiling water

4 tablespoons hazelnut oil (or walnut oil)

1 teaspoon pure vanilla

¼ teaspoon sea salt

1. Preheat the oven to 375°F. Line a 9 x 13-inch baking sheet with parchment paper. Spread the hazelnut meal evenly on the baking sheet and toast until it becomes aromatic and slightly golden, about 5 to 7 minutes. Cool 5 minutes.

2. In a food processor, blend the hazelnut meal, powdered sugar, cocoa powder, boiling water, oil, vanilla, and salt to a very smooth butter, scraping the sides often, about 5 minutes. The finished spread should have the consistency of creamy peanut butter. If it is too dry and stiff, add more hot water, a tablespoon at a time, to reach the desired consistency. Refrigerate, tightly covered, for up to one week. The spread will firm up during refrigeration. Serve at room temperature.

Per tablespoon: Calories 130 · Fat 10g · Protein 2g · Carbohydrates 11g · Cholesterol 0mg · Sodium 21mg · Fiber 2g

Yogurt

There are wonderful yogurts on the market, but you can also make your own quite easily and for a fraction of the cost. Plus, you know exactly what ingredients are in it. Soaking the nuts makes a creamier yogurt and also makes them easier to digest than raw nuts. But if you forget to soak them don't let that stop you from making this recipe. If you prefer to use a commercial yogurt starter, choose one that is both gluten-free and dairy-free, such as Custom Probiotics (www.customprobiotics.com). **SERVES 8 (MAKES 4 CUPS)**

4 cups Cashew Cream (page 247)

2 to 4 tablespoons plain store-bought yogurt or your homemade yogurt, or ½ scoop yogurt starter

1. Place the cashew cream in a saucepan and cook over medium heat, stirring constantly, until it reaches 180°F but doesn't boil, about 3 to 5 minutes; be careful not to scorch it. This kills any harmful organisms. Remove from the heat and cool to 100°F.

2. Transfer the mixture to a yogurt maker and stir in the yogurt or yogurt starter. Process the yogurt according to the manufacturer's directions. Refrigerate, covered, for up to 1 week.

Note: If you want to make kefir, a fermented yogurt-type drink made from milk, the Body Ecology kefir starter is gluten-free and dairy-free, and the one I use to make my own kefir at home. You may use any type of milk you prefer, but I like to use hemp milk because of its good nutrients, mild flavor, neutral color, and rich texture. Follow the instructions on the package.

Per ½ cup: Calories 335 · Fat 28g · Protein 11g · Carbohydrates 16g · Cholesterol 0mg · Sodium 42mg · Fiber 2g

Sweetened Condensed Milk

This is one of those ingredients that we don't use very often. But there are times when a recipe depends on it, and there is not a commercial, dairy-free version on the market. For those dishes, this recipe comes in very handy. **MAKES 1¼ CUPS**

½ cup evaporated cane juice

3 tablespoons sweet rice flour

⅛ teaspoon sea salt

1 cup milk of choice, preferably coconut,
    hemp, or soy

2 tablespoons unsalted butter or buttery spread

1 teaspoon pure vanilla extract

1. In a small heavy saucepan whisk together the evaporated cane juice, sweet rice flour, and salt until thoroughly blended. Whisk in the milk until smooth, then add the butter and heat the mixture on medium heat, whisking constantly, until it thickens slightly, about 3 to 4 minutes.

2. Remove from the heat and stir in the vanilla. Cool to room temperature to thicken a bit more. It is best used at room temperature but can be refrigerated for up to two weeks. Bring to room temperature again before using.

Per 2 tablespoons: Calories 85 · Fat 3g · Protein 1g · Carbohydrates 14g · Cholesterol 7mg · Sodium 36mg · Fiber 1g

Herb-Flavored Cheese

Use this flavorful cheese as a spread for bagels, toast, or crackers or whenever a recipe calls for the commercial variety of herbed cheese known as Boursin. Dried herbs work better than fresh herbs in this recipe because they're more intense and don't make the cheese turn green. **SERVES 16 (MAKES 2 CUPS)**

16 ounces low-fat cream cheese or vegan cream cheese

¼ cup low-fat sour cream or vegan sour cream

¼ cup grated Parmesan cheese or soy Parmesan

2 garlic cloves, minced

1 tablespoon dried parsley

1 tablespoon dried chives, crumbled

1 tablespoon dried dill weed, crumbled, or 1 tablespoon chopped fresh

½ teaspoon dried marjoram

½ teaspoon dried basil

½ teaspoon black pepper or lemon pepper

¼ teaspoon dried thyme

1 teaspoon lemon juice

Salt and pepper, to taste

Beat the cream cheese and sour cream in a small bowl with an electric mixer on low speed until well blended. Add the remaining ingredients, except for the salt and pepper, and mix until thoroughly blended. Taste, and add salt and pepper to taste. Refrigerate, tightly covered, for up to one week.

Per tablespoon: Calories 35 · Fat 1g · Protein 5g · Carbohydrates 2g · Cholesterol 4mg · Sodium 181mg · Fiber 1g

Basil Pesto

Many people who eat a dairy-free diet don't realize that store-bought pesto contains Parmesan cheese. But you can easily make your own at home using soy Parmesan and at a fraction of the cost . . . especially if you grow your own basil. You can also make pesto with many other herbs such as parsley, mint, cilantro, oregano, and so on, or any mixture of these herbs. Always include a little parsley, and its chlorophyll will help keep your pesto looking green longer. **MAKES 1 CUP**

¼ cup pine nuts, almonds, or walnuts

3 large garlic cloves, mashed

2 cups fresh basil leaves, washed, patted dry, and tightly packed

¼ cup fresh parsley sprigs

¼ cup extra-virgin olive oil

¼ cup grated Parmesan cheese or soy Parmesan

¼ teaspoon sea salt, or to taste

⅛ teaspoon freshly ground black pepper, or to taste

In a food processor, process all the ingredients until smooth, then season with salt and pepper. If it is too thick, add hot water a tablespoon at a time to reach the desired consistency. Pesto may be made two days ahead and chilled, covered with plastic wrap.

Per tablespoon: Calories 50 · Fat 5g · Protein 1g · Carbohydrates 1g · Cholesterol 1mg · Sodium 53mg · Fiber 1g

Appendix

Brand-Name Ingredients Used in This Book

These are the brands I used in developing the recipes for this book. You may have other gluten-free brands in your area, but always read the label to verify a food's gluten-free status. These products were gluten-free at the time I used them; however, manufacturers may choose to discontinue or change a product, so always check the label each time you make a purchase.

Whole Grains, Flour, and Nut Meals

ALMOND MEAL OR FLOUR: Bob's Red Mill, Honeyville

AMARANTH: Bob's Red Mill, Nu-World Amaranth

BEAN FLOURS: Bob's Red Mill

CHESTNUT FLOUR: Dowd and Dowd

HAZELNUT MEAL: Bob's Red Mill

MILLET: Bob's Red Mill

MODIFIED TAPIOCA STARCH (EXPANDEX): Celiac Specialties, Gifts of Nature, and more sources at www.expandexglutenfree.com

MONTINA PURE BAKING SUPPLEMENT: Montina by Amazing Grains

OAT BRAN: Legacy Valley

OAT FLOUR: Bob's Red Mill, Cream Hill Estates, Gluten-Free Oats, Only Oats

POLENTA/CORN GRITS: Bob's Red Mill

POLENTA TUBE: Food Merchants

POTATO STARCH: Bob's Red Mill

RICE BRAN: Bob's Red Mill, Ener-G Foods

SORGHUM FLOUR: Bob's Red Mill

SORGHUM WHOLE GRAIN: Shiloh Farms

TAPIOCA FLOUR: Bob's Red Mill

TEFF: Bob's Red Mill, the Teff Company

YELLOW CORNMEAL: Bob's Red Mill

• Cereals •

BUCKWHEAT CEREAL: Birkett Mills, Bob's Red Mill

CORN CHEX: General Mills

GRANOLA: Udi's

ROLLED OATS: Bob's Red Mill; Cream Hill Estates, Lara's Rolled Oats; Gifts of Nature; Gluten Free Oats; Only Oats

QUICK-COOKING OATS: Bob's Red Mill

STEEL-CUT OATS: Bob's Red Mill, Cream Hill Estates

• Cookies, Crackers, and Pretzels •

CRACKERS: Crunchmasters, Mary's Gone Crackers

GINGERSNAPS: Pamela's Ginger with Sliced Almonds

PRETZELS: Ener-G, Glutino

• Dairy and Cheese •

BUTTERY SHORTENING STICKS: Earth Balance

BUTTERY SPREAD: Earth Balance (soy and soy-free versions)

CHEESE ALTERNATIVE: Follow Your Heart Vegan Gourmet, Daiya

CREAM CHEESE: Follow Your Heart Vegan Gourmet, Tofutti

COFFEE CREAMER: Silk (soy), So Delicious (coconut)

ICE CREAM: Edy's, Dreyer's, Häagen-Dazs, So Delicious

MAYONNAISE: Vegenaise

MILK: So Delicious (coconut), Living Harvest (hemp), Silk (soy and almond), Rice Dream (rice)

PARMESAN: Galaxy (soy)

SHORTENING (NON-HYDROGENATED): Spectrum (palm oil), Earth Balance (soy)

SOUR CREAM: Follow Your Heart Vegan Gourmet, Tofutti

WHIPPED TOPPING: Lucerne (soy), Soyatoo (rice and soy)

YOGURT: So Delicious (coconut), WholeSoy (soy), Wildwood (soy—the only dairy-free unsweetened plain yogurt; good for savory items), or homemade Yogurt (page 249)

• Sweeteners •

AGAVE NECTAR: Madhava

BROWN RICE SYRUP: Lundberg

CHOCOLATE CHIPS: Enjoy Life, Ghirardelli (check the label)

CHOCOLATE SYRUP: Dagoba, Smucker's Sundae Syrup

EVAPORATED (DRIED) CANE JUICE: Bob's Red Mill

• Mixes •

BROWNIE: Bob's Red Mill

CORN BREAD: Bob's Red Mill

• Bread •

CORN TORTILLAS (YELLOW AND WHITE): Mission Foods

ENGLISH MUFFINS: Food for Life

FLOUR TORTILLAS: Food for Life, La Tortilla Factory

SANDWICH BREAD: Rudi's, Udi's, Whole Foods

• Pasta •

CELLOPHANE NOODLES: Annie Chun's
FETTUCINE: Tinkyada
JUMBO SHELLS: Tinkyada
LASAGNA: Ener-G Foods, Orgran, Tinkyada
MACARONI: Ener-G Foods, Orgran, Tinkyada
PENNE, OR FUSILLI OR OTHER SPIRAL: Tinkyada
SPAGHETTI: De Boles, Mrs. Leepers, Tinkyada

• Broth •

VEGETARIAN BROTH: Imagine No-Chicken

• Meat Substitutes •

SOY FRANKS: Lightlife Tofu Pups
TOFU (EXTRA-FIRM): Nasoya
TOFU (SOFT-SILKEN): Mori-Nu

• Spices, Condiments, Sauces, and Baking Ingredients •

ANCHO CHILE POWDER: McCormick
CHIPOTLE CHILE POWDER: McCormick
LIQUID SMOKE FLAVOR: Wrights
MAYONNAISE: Vegenaise
MARINARA SAUCE: Classico, Prego
MISO: Eden Foods' Gen Mi Brown Rice Miso, Shiro Miso (avoid any brands with barley)
PICANTE SAUCE: Pace
PICO DE GALLO: Goya
SALSA (TOMATO): Tostito

SOY SAUCE: San J's gluten-free tamari soy sauce

SWEET RED CHILI SAUCE: Taste of Thai, Thai Kitchen

TOMATILLO SAUCE: Goya, La Victoria (called Salsa Verde)

UNSWEETENED COCOA POWDER: Hershey's, Nestlé

WASABI POWDER: McCormick

WORCESTERSHIRE SAUCE: French's, Lea & Perrins (GF in the U.S. only)

YEAST: Fleischmann's, Red Star, SAF

Special thanks to Bob's Red Mill for supplying the flours, grains, and evaporated (dried) cane juice used in developing these recipes.

Tools of the Trade

This may seem like a long list, but having the right appliances and utensils makes food preparation so much easier. And since those of us with special dietary needs prepare more of our own food than other people, I think these tools are perfectly justifiable investments in our health.

Here are the tools I wouldn't be without in my kitchen:

- Metal baking sheets (9 x 13-inch and 13 x 18-inch, sometimes called half sheets), cupcake/muffin pans (6- and 12-cup sizes), pizza pans (12-inch), loaf pans (8 x 4, 5 x 9, and 4 x 6 inches)
- I prefer nonstick metal (gray, not black) baking sheets and pans for breads, muffins, and cakes because they reflect heat, and brown gluten-free dough nicely. This browning is necessary to avoid sogginess and to provide a structure for the dough to cling to as it rises. Black nonstick metal pans reflect too much heat and can burn baked goods. Some manufacturers suggest reducing the oven temperature by 25 degrees. Shiny metal baking sheets are best for cookies and other items that should not brown too much on the bottom. Glass baking dishes don't provide enough browning action; they are more likely to produce soggy baked goods so I only use them for foods that don't require browning such as casseroles or certain fruit dishes such as apple crisp.
- Coffee or spice grinder: These little powerhouses grind nuts and spices quickly and thoroughly. Reserve one for this job and another for grinding coffee so you don't mix the flavors.

- Cutting board: I prefer plastic over wood because it can be washed in the dishwasher. Do not use boards with deep cuts, which can harbor germs.
- Dry measure cups: In sizes ¼, ⅓, ½, ¾, 1, 1 ½, and 2 cup(s).
- Food processor: Perhaps my most valued appliance. It blends dough quickly and thoroughly, and cleans up nicely in the dishwasher.
- Ice cream scoops: I prefer metal, spring-action versions, and have one in every size available. Use them to shape equal-size balls of cookie dough so the cookies bake uniformly and to divide bread dough evenly in baking pans for equal-size loaves. They assure equal portions when serving whipped cream or ice cream.
- Liquid measure cups: In sizes 1, 2, and 4 cup(s), for measuring liquids, not dry ingredients. I also use an 8-cup glass Pyrex mixing bowl because unmixed ingredients are clearly visible on the bottom, and I can measure the volume of the dough or batter.
- Measuring spoons: In sizes ⅛, ¼, ½, 1, and 2 tablespoon(s). The miniature spoons in dash, pinch, and smidgen sizes are convenient as well.
- Parchment paper: Perfect for lining baking sheets; prevents sticking and aids cleanup.
- Pastry (silicone) brush: For brushing glazes or oil on pastries or pizza. Silicone brushes clean up easily.
- Stand mixer and portable mixer: Stand mixers are handy for big batches, especially when you are beating something for an extended period. Portable mixers are suitable for smaller recipes or beating items while they're on the stove (such as cooked frostings).
- Spatula: Rubber and heat-resistant versions for folding, scraping dough, and stirring, plus an offset spatula for frosting cakes.
- Thermometer: Instant-read thermometers are available in the kitchen section of grocery stores. Use them to judge the internal temperature of bread or the temperature of heated milk for the yeast in bread-baking or for yogurt. An oven thermometer indicates whether your oven bakes at the stated temperature.
- Whisks: I have a variety of shapes and sizes, so I always have the right tool for the job.
- Wire racks: For cooling just-baked items, preventing sogginess on the bottom.

Adding Animal Protein
to Recipes

If you or someone in your family prefers a little animal protein with meals, here are suggestions for how to add it to appropriate recipes in this book. These are guidelines; add the amount or type of protein that pleases you.

• Main Dishes •

LASAGNA—Add ¼ pound browned Jimmy Dean Italian sausage between layers of noodles.

SPAGHETTI WITH SPAGHETTI SAUCE: Add ½ pound cooked meatballs made from ground beef.

SOBA NOODLES WITH PEANUT-GINGER SAUCE: Add ½ pound cooked, deveined medium shrimp.

THAI NOODLE BOWL: Add ¼ pound cooked, cubed pork.

STUFFING WITH PEARS AND PECANS: Add ¼ pound browned Jimmy Dean Italian sausage.

SAVORY LEEK-ONION BREAD PUDDING: Add 3 cooked bacon strips, crumbled into the bread cubes.

STUFFED BELL PEPPERS WITH PICADILLO RICE: Add ¼ cup browned ground beef to the picadillo.

STUFFED CABBAGE ROLLS: Add ¼ pound browned ground beef or turkey to the filling.

STUFFED POBLANO PEPPERS: Add ¼ pound browned ground pork or turkey to the filling.

CREOLE VEGETABLES ON BASMATI RICE: Add ¼ pound cooked shrimp.

RED BEANS AND BROWN RICE: Add ¼ pound browned Andouille sausage links, sliced.

SWEET-AND-SOUR TOFU CASSEROLE: Add ¼ pound browned pork cubes.

VEGETABLE TIKKA MASALA: Add ¼ pound cooked, cubed chicken.

VEGGIE PIZZA: Add ¼ pound pepperoni or browned Jimmy Dean Italian sausage, sliced.

TOFU STROGANOFF: Add ¼ pound browned beef cubes.

TOFU AU VIN: Add ¼ pound cooked, cubed chicken.

VEGETABLE PAELLA: Add ¼ pound cooked, deveined medium shrimp and 2 links browned Andouille sausage, sliced.

CHILI CORN BREAD CASSEROLE: Add ¼ pound browned ground beef to the chili.

EGGPLANT ROLL-UPS: Add ⅛ pound browned ground beef or turkey to the filling.

EGGPLANT PARMESAN STACKS: Add ⅛ pound browned ground beef or turkey to the sauce.

SOUTHWESTERN BEAN AND GRAIN CASSEROLE: Add ¼ pound browned ground beef or turkey.

MOUSSAKA: Add ¼ pound browned ground lamb.

OLD-FASHIONED VEGETABLE POT PIE WITH SAVORY PASTRY CRUST: Add ¼ pound cooked, cubed chicken or turkey to the filling.

ENCHILADAS: Add ¼ pound browned ground beef or turkey to the filling.

MOROCCAN MILLET-STUFFED ACORN SQUASH: Add ⅛ pound browned turkey to the millet stuffing.

ONION-LEEK TART: Add 2 cooked bacon slices, crumbled.

SOFT CORN TACOS WITH BLACK BEAN BURGERS: Add ¼ pound browned ground beef or turkey.

PINTO BEAN-POLENTA FAJITAS WITH TOMATILLO SAUCE: Add ¼ pound browned sirloin strips or chicken breasts to the filling.

SMOTHERED BEAN BURRITOS WITH GREEN CHILE SAUCE: Add ¼ pound browned pork or turkey to the filling.

Soups and Stews

CINCINNATI CHILI: Add ½ pound browned ground beef.

LENTIL SOUP: Add ¼ pound browned Andouille sausage, sliced.

MINESTRONE: Add ¼ pound browned Italian sausage.

THAI CORN CHOWDER: Add ½ pound cooked, deveined shrimp.

POSOLE WITH CRISPY TORTILLA STRIPS: Add ¼ pound cooked, cubed chicken.

VEGETABLE SOUP WITH DUMPLINGS: Add ¼ pound cooked, cubed chicken or turkey.

• Little Bites (Appetizers, Small Meals, and Snacks) •

MINI CORN DOGS: Use Thumann's Cocktail Franks.

GREEK SALAD SKEWERS WITH GREEK SALAD DRESSING: Add a cooked whole medium shrimp to each skewer.

STUFFED MUSHROOMS: Brown ¼ pound Jimmy Dean sausage and add to stuffing.

GAZPACHO SHOOTERS: Add 2 tiny shrimps to each shooter.

ROASTED RED PEPPER PANINI WITH WHITE TRUFFLE AIOLI: Add a thin slice of deli ham to each panino.

• Breakfast •

ASPARAGUS (OR EGGS) BENEDICT WITH HOLLANDAISE SAUCE: Add a thin slice of deli ham to each serving.

BREAKFAST EGG STRATA: Add 1 layer of thinly sliced deli ham between the bread layers.

MEDITERRANEAN FRITTATA: Add ¼ pound browned Jimmy Dean Italian sausage.

QUICHE: Add 3 browned bacon slices, crumbled.

How to Use Modified Tapioca Starch in These Recipes

Modified tapioca starch, or Expandex, is an excellent addition to improve the texture of gluten-free baked goods—especially items that are egg-free. This white powdery starch, made from tapioca, lends a higher rise, better texture, and longer shelf life to baked goods, especially quick breads and yeast breads, without imparting any color or flavor. Plain tapioca flour does not lend the same result as Expandex, so the two are not interchangeable. For more information, go to www.ExpandexGlutenFree.com.

RECIPE	REPLACE	WITH EXPANDEX
Banana Oatmeal Muffins with Streusel Topping	¼ cup of GF Flour Blend	¼ cup
Basic Muffins with Fruit and Nut Variation	¼ cup of GF Flour Blend	¼ cup
Angel Pan Biscuits	¼ cup of cornstarch	¼ cup
Hearty Bran Muffins	¼ cup of GF Flour Blend	¼ cup
Breadsticks	¼ cup of tapioca flour	¼ cup

(continued)

RECIPE	REPLACE	WITH EXPANDEX
Chili Corn Bread Casserole	⅓ cup of GF Flour Blend	⅓ cup
Corn Bread and Corn Bread Muffins	¼ cup of GF Flour Blend	¼ cup
French Baguettes	⅓ cup of cornstarch	⅓ cup
Hearty Flax Bread	¼ cup of GF Flour Blend	¼ cup
Old-Fashioned Vegetable Pot Pie with Savory Pastry Crust	2 tablespoons of tapioca flour	2 tablespoons
Onion-Leek Tart	2 tablespoons of tapioca flour	2 tablespoons
Rosemary Focaccia with Onion Marmalade	¼ cup of GF Flour Blend	¼ cup
Basic Scones with Drizzle	¼ cup of GF Flour Blend	¼ cup

Resources

Allergy-Free Passport
27 N. Wacker Drive, Suite 258
Chicago, IL 60606-2800
312.952.4900; 312.276.8001
http://www.allergyfreepassport.com

American Academy of Allergy,
    Asthma & Immunology
611 E. Wells Street
Milwaukee, WI 53202
800.822.2762 (help line); 414.272.6071
http://www.aaaai.org

American Celiac Disease Alliance
2504 Duxbury Place
Alexandria, VA 22308
703.622.3331
http://www.americanceliac.org

American Dietetic Association
120 S. Riverside Plaza, Suite 2000
Chicago, IL 60606
312.899.0040
http://www.eatright.org

Asthma/Allergy Foundation of America
1125 15th Street, N.W., Suite 502
Washington, D.C. 20005
800.7ASTHMA (help line); 202.466.7643
    (fax)
http://www.aafa.org

Autism Society of America
7910 Woodmont Avenue, Suite 300
Bethesda, MD 20814-3015
800.3Autism, ext. 150 (main); 301.657.0881;
    303.657.0869 (fax)
http://www.autism-society.org

Autism Speaks
2 Park Avenue, 11th Floor
New York, NY 10016
212.252.8584; 212.252.8676 (fax)
http://www.autismspeaks.org

Celiac.com (Scott-Free Newsletter)
4927 Sonoma Highway, Suite C1
Santa Rosa, CA 95409
866.575.3720; 707.324.6060
http://www.celiac.com

Celiac Center (Harvard-Beth Israel)
330 Brookline Avenue
Boston, MA 02215
617.667.7000
http://www.bidmc.harvard.edu/celiaccenter

Celiac Disease Center, Columbia University
New York Presbyterian Hospital
161 Fort Washington Avenue
New York, NY 10032
212.305.5590
http://www.celiacdiseasecenter.columbia
    .edu

Celiac Disease Center
University of Chicago
5839 S. Maryland Avenue MC 4065
Chicago, IL 60637-1470
773.702.7593; 773.702.0666 (fax)
http://www.celiacdisease.net

Celiac Disease Clinic, Mayo Clinic
Celiac Disease Research Program
200 First Street S.W.
Rochester, MN 55905
507.284.2511
http://www.mayoclinic.org

Celiac Disease Foundation
13251 Ventura Boulevard, Suite 1
Studio City, CA 91604-1838
818.990.2354; 818.990.2379 (fax)
http://www.celiac.org

Celiac Sprue Association/USA
P.O. Box 31700
Omaha, NE 68131-0700
402.558.0600; 402.558.1347 (fax)
http://www.csaceliacs.org

Center for Celiac Research
University of Maryland
20 Penn Street, Room S303B
Baltimore, MD 21201
http://www.celiaccenter.org

Food Allergy and Anaphylaxis Network
  (FAAN)
11781 Lee Jackson Highway, Suite 160
Fairfax, VA 22030
800.929.4040 or 703.691.3179
http://www.foodallergy.org
http://www.fankids.org (for kids)

Gluten-Free Living Magazine
560 Warburton Avenue, 2nd floor
Hastings-on-Hudson, NY 10706
914.231.6361
http://www.glutenfreeliving.com

Gluten Intolerance Group of North
    America
Gluten-Free Restaurant Awareness Program
Gluten-Free Certification Organization
    (GFCO)
31214-124 Avenue SE
Auburn, WA 98092
253.833.6655; 253.833.6675 (fax)
http://www.gluten.net
http://www.glutenfreerestaurants.org
http://www.gfco.org

Journal of Gluten Sensitivity
4927 Sonoma Highway, Suite C1
Santa Rosa, CA 95409
707.509. 4528
http://www.celiac.com

Living Without Magazine
800 Connecticut Avenue
Norwalk, CT 06854
800.424.7887
http://www.livingwithout.com

National Foundation for Celiac Awareness
P.O. Box 544
Ambler, PA 19002-0544
215.325.1306
http://www.celiaccentral.org

Triumph Dining
124 East Broad Street, 2nd Floor
Falls Church, VA 22046
800.558.2906
http://www.triumphdining.com

William K. Warren Medical Research
    Center for Celiac Disease
University of California at San Diego
9500 Gilman Drive, #0623D
La Jolla, CA 92093-0623
858.822.1022
http://celiaccenter.ucsd.edu

Index

Also available from Carol Fenster, Ph.D.